DELHI & AGRA

A Travellers' Companion

SELECTED AND INTRODUCED BY

Michael Alexander

Constable London

First published in Great Britain 1987
by Constable and Company Limited
10 Orange Street London WC2H 7EG
Copyright © by Michael Alexander 1987
Set in Monophoto Baskerville 11pt
by Servis Filmsetting Ltd, Manchester
Printed in Great Britain by
St Edmundsbury Press Ltd
Bury St Edmunds, Suffolk

British Library CIP data
Delhi & Agra : a traveller's companion –
(The Travellers' companion series)
1. Agra (India) – History – Sources
2. Delhi (India) – History – Sources
I. Alexander, Michael, *1920–*   II. Series
954'.2   DS486.A3

ISBN 0 09 466550 8
ISBN 0 09 467740 9 Pbk

Delhi and Agra

for Roger and Olga

from Krishna & Madhu Jain

wishing them 'bon voyage' and
a happy stay in India.

Oxford 1987.

The Travellers' Companion series

General editor: Laurence Kelly

St Petersburg: a travellers' companion
Selected and introduced by Laurence Kelly (1981)

Moscow: a travellers' companion
Selected and introduced by Laurence Kelly (1983)

Naples: a travellers' companion
Selected and introduced by Desmond Seward (1984)

Edinburgh: a travellers' companion
Selected and introduced by David Daiches (1986)

Florence: a travellers' companion   .
Selected and introduced by Harold Acton and Edward Chaney
(1986)

Istanbul: a travellers' companion
Selected and introduced by Laurence Kelly (1987)

Contents

8   *Contents*

Contents   9

Contents   11

Illustrations

Acknowledgements

Most of the works quoted in this anthology have been perused in the libraries at the Victoria & Albert Museum, the India Office, and the Royal Geographical Society, as well as (a home from home) the London Library; and I have assembled enough interesting material to fill at least another volume. I am grateful to the staffs of all these libraries.

As is the case in other books in the series, spelling, punctuation and accents appear in the extracts quoted as they were published originally. However, strategic excisions have not been notified by the use of ellipsis dots, which could be disconcerting. I have used the old spelling 'Mogul', which I prefer to the more modern 'Mughal'.

I wish to make acknowledgement to the following for extracts used from their writings, editions or translations, or where copyright permission was needed:

Webb & Bower for *The Golden Calm*, edited by M.M. Kaye; Mark Bence-Jones for *Palaces of the Raj*; the University of Bombay for *Delhi: a study in urban sociology* by A. Bopegamage; Macmillan and Gordon Brooke-Shepherd for *Where the Lion Trod*; Grafton Books and Larry Collins for *Freedom at Midnight* by Larry Collins and Dominique Lapierre; W.H. Allen and Rupert Croft-Cooke for *The Gorgeous East*; Hamish Hamilton and Michael Edwardes for *Red Year*; Edward Arnold and Harcourt Brace Jovanovich for E.M. Forster's *The Hill of Devi*; Yale University and Robert Grant Irving for *Indian Summer*; Heinemann and Dom Moraes for *Gone Away*; Jonathan Cape, London Management and Salman Rushdie for *Shame*; Mrs Laura Huxley, Chatto & Windus and Harper and Row for Aldous Huxley's *Jesting Pilate*; Macmillan for Victor Jacquemont's *Letters from India, 1829–32*, translated by C.A. Phillips; Sir Jadunath Sarkar for *Fall of the Mughal Empire*; Hutchinson for Eleanor Roosevelt's *India and the Awakening East*; Robert Byron for his article in the *Architectural Review*; and the National Archives of India in Delhi for *The Indian Travels of Thévenot and Careri*, edited by Surendranath Sen.

I am particularly grateful to Neil Hobhouse of Hobhouse Ltd in London who lent us a photograph of the Daniells' aquatint of the Taj Mahal for use on the jacket, and also the picture that appears on pages 192–3. My thanks are also due to Patrick Leeson, who drew the map; to Imogen Olsen and Prudence Fay for minding my p's and q's; to Ayesha Kapoor for scissors and paste and to Air India and the Indian Tourist Board for travel facilities.

M.A.
1987

Introduction

Visitors to Delhi, especially those arriving by air, may not easily orientate themselves with the sub-continent as a whole and, since Delhi's location has affected its history, readers may care to be reminded that we are in the centre of the rump or continental part before the country tapers into the plateau of the Deccan and down into the sub-tropical south. Globally speaking we are on the same latitude as Cairo and Cape Canaveral; we are in the middle of a central plain and can thus expect hot seasons; the Thar desert of Rajasthan flanks us to the west; the fertile Punjab plain is an available granary; we are on the river Jumna which passes through Agra to the south to join the Ganges at Allahabad; it may not always be appreciated that we are only a few hours' drive from the Himalayas as they curve south-eastwards. A map of the time of Sir Thomas Roe, James I's ambassador to the Mogul emperor Jahangir, (reproduced on p. oo), is better than Mercator's version which Roe presented to that monarch. The doughty knight arrived at Surat, entrepôt port of the British and the Portuguese, in 1615: Bombay is not marked because it did not exist. Note a lack of emphasis on the mountains to the north which are generally thought to have been such an inhibiting bastion – indeed, the Hindu Kush did not form much more than a base camp for those invaders from Alexander the Great onwards who from time to time descended the Khyber Pass to despoil the cities of the plain. It might also be noted that the five branches of the Indus spreading across the Punjab, which our map indicates with over-thickened lines, were no great discouragement to advance: invaders, with bridges of boats, seemed to take these obstacles in their stride and were rarely challenged on the banks – Akbar claimed to have swum across every river between Kabul and Agra. It was not until Panipat was reached, about fifty miles north of Delhi, that elephantine armies would stand to defend the city, invariably without success.

The map emphasises a diagonal line from Lahore to Agra with 'Delli' in the middle. On closer inspection this diagonal will be seen to be a line of trees such as the great French traveller François Bernier described in a letter dated 1663: 'a double row

of trees planted by order of Jehan-Guyre, and continued for one
hundred and fifty leagues, with small pyramids, or turrets, every
two miles or so. Wells are frequently met with, affording drink to
travellers.' Bernier also mentions caravanserais, enclosed courtyards with rooms and stabling, hardly Hiltons, a day's journey
apart (see extract 13). Thus Lahore-Delhi-Agra might be
termed the Mogul power-base in attempts to dominate the non-
Mogul sub-continent. Roe's map cuts off the southern part but
shows the rugged plateau where Hindu rajahs ruled. To the west
'The Persians', a paramount Moslem power, are indicated; to
the north are the Afghans and beyond lie Uzbeks and Tartars,
barbarian offspring of the Horde.

It was on the tree-lined highway that Roe met the eccentric
tourist Tom Coryat, walking the world on twopence a day, 'that
most unwearied walker, who on foote has passed most of Europe
and Asya and is now in India, being the beginning of his travels.'
Coryat continued through Delhi to Agra, a hundred and fifty
miles on. Today, aeroplane and train will carry you there if you
wish to avoid the rigours of that ugly road. Agra is usually part of
the Delhi 'package', with the Taj Mahal, Fattephur Sikri and
Sikandra as additional viewing, and can thus appropriately be
packaged between these covers. As required of this series of
Travellers' Companions, it is to buildings that our text is mainly
linked and it is the aim of this introduction to place them in a
narrow historical frame. There follows a superficial – since
entertainment rather than exposition is our editorial brief –
survey of local history linked specifically to our chosen cities. Too
wide a sweep would steal space from the anthology.

Agra was still a village, with no past worthy of print, until
Akbar, greatest of the Mogul dynasty, came to glorify it in the
sixteenth century. Delhi claims a nobler history as the site of at
least seven capital cities, dating from before the days of Alexander
the Great, who invaded India in 326 BC. But the great Buddhist
civilisation that had developed in India since the days of Ashoka
seems to have passed it by. Thus there was little to interest the
fanatical Muhammed of Ghazni, scourge of the Hindus in the
name of the Prophet, who in the eleventh century invaded the
plains an estimated seventeen times from his capital in the Hindu
Kush. Known as 'the idol-breaker', he looted, destroyed and
enslaved; he did not build, except his own capital at Ghazni. So
let us start our summary with the death of the Rajput leader

Sir Thomas Roe's map of 'East' India, 1619

Prithiviraja in 1192 while opposing the advance of another invader from the Afghan hills, Muhammed of Ghor, who, before returning to his lair, left as viceroy one Qutb-ud-din-Aibek. This former Turki slave or janissary carried on his master's destructive mission into Bihar and Bengal. When Muhammed of Ghor was assassinated in 1206, the former slave-general styled himself Sultan of Delhi and founder of a dynasty. Before he died of an accident while playing polo four years later, he had started to build the Quwaat-ul-Islam mosque from the remains of twenty-seven Hindu temples and beside it began to raise the mighty tower of victory, the Kutb-Minar, to be completed by his successors to a height of over two hundred and forty feet.

This line of Sultans had continual trouble with the Mongol Tartars (they were not unrelated to them) who, if despised, were dangerous and would make tip-and-run incursions into the plains. Said to have 'rough skin fit only for shoe leather' and to be 'covered in lice like sesame seed', their heathen herdsmen brethren were, in 1220, to overrun Persia under the dreaded Genghis Khan.

Qutb-ud-din-Aibek was succeeded by his son-in-law Iltumish (1211–36), who trebled the size of the Quwaat-ul-Islam mosque next to the Kutb-Minar by adding arches. Iltumish nominated his daughter to succeed him, but she offended her council of advisers by unduly favouring an African Negro and was deposed. The line of so-called Slave Kings was extinguished by murder in 1296. Ala-ud-din of the Afghan Khiljis (1296–1316) is the next name of note in the annals of Delhi. Scourge of the Mongol raiders and mass-murderer of their Delhi colony, he extended his power southwards and captured the fortress of Chitor, suicidally defended by the Rajputs. Delhi, for the first time, became the capital city of India. There he built a great 'tank' or reservoir, added another six arches to the Quwaat-ul-Islam mosque and began work on a second minaret to be twice as high as the adjoining Kutb. No more than its ambitious base commemorates the 'second Alexander'.

In 1321 Ghiyas-ud-din-Tughlak, of Turki-Mongol blood, led a military revolt and founded a new dynasty: a stern soldier of Allah who planned to cut out an empire from the Unbelieving Hindu states, he had been made governor of the Punjab for his defeat of the restless Mongol converts settled in north India whose forces had even dared reach Delhi. He was succeeded by his son Muhammad II, and it was at his court that Ibn Battuta, most celebrated of early Arab travellers, arrived in 1334: he gives an account of a 'vast and magnificent capital' and its 'impetuous and inexorable ruler' (see extract 1). The fort and tombs of the Tughlaks, with massive sloping walls, still squat in the scrubland haunted, perhaps, by the ghost of the saint who vengefully pronounced, because the king had taken workmen away from his reservoir project to build a palace, that none but Gujars should inhabit the place. Gujars, dispossessed gypsies, are there today. The metal pillar with its ancient Gupta text (extract 1), described by Ibn Battuta as 'awe-inspiring', still stands near the Minar. This king twice moved his reluctant subjects from Delhi to Dalautabad and back, seven hundred miles south.

Muhammad Tughlak died fighting Hindus in Gujerat. He was succeeded by his nephew, Firoz Shah, remembered for his canal and the re-erection by a cunning piece of engineering of two ancient pillars inscribed with the edicts of Ashoka. One of these pillars is to be seen standing on the site of his own city named Firozabad just to the south of the Red Fort. Firoz Shah died in 1388; ten years later, Timur the Lame, the dreaded Tamerlane, swept down from Kabul and, collecting his force at Panipat, took Delhi. The account of his sack of the city (see extract 2), as told by himself, is somewhat milder than contemporary historians would have it. Timur stayed two weeks in Delhi before returning to his capital, Samarkand, with the spoils, which included a hundred and twenty elephants and most of Delhi's masons and craftsmen to embellish his own city.

The last of the Tughlaks died in 1414. Their successors were the Sayyids, descendants of the Prophet, who made little impact on history. Then came three generations of Lodhi kings of Pathan blood who made their first headquarters round the Kutb-Minar. The second in line, Sikander, moved his capital to the neighbourhood of Agra and built a new city for himself called Sikanderabad. The devious behaviour of his son Ibrahim, and the intrigues that followed, had unexpected results: a dispossessed adventurer, overlord of Ferghana, a miniature kingdom not far from Samarkand, was looking for an empire he could call his own. His name was Babur. With only the most romantic claim to legitimacy as a descendant of Timur on the one hand and Genghis Khan on the other, Babur decided that India should be his – there was nowhere else just then available. So it was that his rag-tag army moved to invade Hindustan. 'Great and small, good and bad, servants and no servants,' he wrote in his readable memoirs, 'the force numbered twelve thousand persons.' He estimated the Lodhi army opposing him at Panipat at a hundred thousand men and nearly a thousand elephants. From behind barricades of carts joined with rawhide, Babur's matchlockmen mowed down the enemy's charging cavalry. Ibrahim Lodhi was killed and the field was Babur's.

Babur made a quick tour of the sights of Delhi and then marched on to Agra and the treasure, which included the Koh-i-noor diamond. This was no incursion, no Mongol or Pathan raid on accumulated treasure, but an occupation and the founding of the 'Mogul' dynasty. Babur by no means liked Agra; his generals liked it even less (see extract 60): such a fly-blown, baking, desiccated place was not to be compared with the temperate valleys of their mountainous homeland. Some of them quit, but Babur had come to stay, and one of the first things he did was to set about making a garden (see extract 61). He died four years later at Agra, but his final resting place would have been more to his liking: a garden near Kabul of which he had written wistfully in his memoirs, his greatest gift to posterity: 'when the argwhan flowers are in bloom, the yellow mingling with the red, I know of no placc in the world to compare with it.'

Babur, first of the Great Moguls, was succeeded by his son Humayun, who had accompanied him on his campaign. Humayun, too, rejected the insalubrious air of Agra and moved north to Delhi. He built his new fort-capital, known as the Purana-Qila, on the banks of the Jumna where his tomb stands today. He called his capital Din-Panah, 'Asylum of the Faith', a sort of southern Samarkand, as a refuge for learned men of all Islamic sects in contrast to the bigoted wrangling then being conducted in Persia and Turkey by the descendants of the Prophet. Problems with his brothers and antagonism from the Afghans led to Humayun's flight to Persia where he paid his way with, among other things, the Koh-i-noor diamond. An Afghan adventurer Sher Shah took Humayun's place on the Delhi throne until, with the help of the Safavid Shah, his host, Humayun was able to reclaim it. Though he left his diamond he brought back something of greater value – the two best painters at the Persian court, who effectively founded the Mogul school. It was at this time that the Turkish admiral, Sidi Ali Reis, paid his visit and argued the extent of relative empire (see extract 104). It will be noted that he claimed Vienna as the possession of his Padishah. A short time later, in 1556, Humayun fell down the stairs of the library built by Sher Shah, known today as the Sher Mandal, supposedly on his way to prayers (see extract 104). His mausoleum inspired the Taj; if not so perfect in its architecture, it is indeed a noble tomb.

Humayun was succeeded by his thirteen-year-old son Akbar, destined to be the greatest Mogul of them all. He first showed his mettle by defeating the dwarfish Hindu Hemu, a former seller of saltpetre, who set himself up as an independent ruler with the title of Raja Vikramaditya. Panipat was the scene of yet another defeat for the defenders when Hemu, high up in his howdah, was shot by an arrow in the eye. A massacre of his men followed and Akbar regained Delhi. Then he marched south and, having re-taken the Rajput stronghold at Chitor in a campaign to initiate his dominion of the Deccan, he repaired to Agra. Here he began to build the great sandstone wall that was to enclose the mosques and pavilions, throne rooms and harems of his new court – today's Red Fort. But he was first to devote his creative energies to the construction of Fattephur Sikri, amazing complex of finely cut pink sandstone (described by Bishop Heber as being the same colour as potted meat) which can be sawn like planks of wood; men can still be seen working it in the old manner. Overlooking a broad, now waterless, plain is a vast sandstone platform upon which fanciful edifices are constructed like houses of cards. Despite the presence of the local saint who enhanced Akbar's fertility, the site proved unpropitious owing to water problems (extract 92) and was abandoned after ten years. What with polo and *pachese* (human chess) (extracts 94 and 95), it must have been a joyous place. The deserted courts are as intact today as if just built.

It was at Fattephur Sikri that Akbar, who had an open mind about religion and tried to synthesise one of his own, built his 'House of Argument', where Mullahs and Jesuit priests tested their casuistry before the Emperor who sat on top of a pillar with walkways to him from various sides of the argument (extract 89). If the Jesuits scored more points they never actually converted him, though he held Christianity in the greatest respect, had a Christian wife, and allowed his grandsons to be christened if only to exclude them from the succession. It seemed that all *they* wanted was to acquire Christian ladies for their harems following which, as a Jesuit expressed it, the princes 'rejected the light and returned to their vomit.' Akbar's rich life was chronicled by his friend and counsellor, Abu-l Fazl, who gives fascinating details on every aspect of social and administrative matters. Abu-l Fazl was assassinated by order of Akbar's rebel son Salim who was necessarily reconciled with his father, his two brothers having died of drink. Akbar died in 1605. He was buried in the mighty mausoleum at Sikandra (extracts 97 and 98) which he had designed but which was to be completed by Salim who now designated himself Jahangir, 'seizer of the world'. Jahangir, too, expressed an interest in Christianity: Finch, the English traveller, tells us that he 'affirmed before all his nobles that Christianity was the soundest faith, and that of Mahomet lies and fables.'

In 1605, Jahangir's son Khusrau left Agra on the pretext of visiting his grandfather's tomb at Sikandra but in fact to gather together an army to invade Lahore. The father soon put a stop to his pretensions by sending the imperial army after him. His punishment was to ride an elephant along a line of stakes upon which his followers had been impaled alive. Like many of his line, Jahangir was something of a sadist. There are gory tales by early travellers of his cruelty: William Hawkins tells us that 'he delighteth to see men executed himselfe and torne in peeces by elephants.' But he was also a naturalist and employed artists to delineate the birds and animals he loved and studied. Opium and alcohol seem to have induced Mogul monstrosity: his memoirs – *Tuzuk-i-Jahangir* – tell us that he would drink twenty cups of wine a day laced with arak before working up to a double-distilled liquor so strong that it made Sir Thomas Roe, then at the court at Ajmere, sneeze. Roe spent most of his time at Ajmere and thus his very interesting account does not qualify for inclusion in this book; Jahangir was for most of the time at Lahore and contributed little to the architecture of our cities. He did, however, supervise the construction of his father's tomb at Sikandra which he is said to have visited for the first time three years after building began and, 'since it did not come up to my idea of what it ought to be', ordered a fresh start.

Jahangir died at Lahore in 1627 after a visit to Kashmir. His son, Shah Jahan, then expanding the empire in the Deccan, returned to Agra to mount the throne. It was Shah Jahan who made Delhi once more a capital, despite the fact that he spent the first twenty years of his reign in Agra building the Taj Mahal (see extract 77). He called his Delhi Shahjahanabad: it measured four miles around and contained the citadel-palace we call the Red Fort, the splendid mosque or Jami-Masjid and the broad avenue of shops and houses known as the Chandni Chowk for state processions to pass along. The mosque was completed in 1658 and Delhi was now the regal centre of the Mogul empire in all its pride and glory. This was the Delhi we read about in the account of the Frenchman Bernier, whose book is essential reading for anyone interested in the background of the period. From his work, and that of the Italian Manucci, we learn intimate details of Mogul public and private lives – dramas of drunkenness and drug-taking, amiability and cruelty, piety and poisonings, intellectual enquiry and liberal ordinances, of great armies on the move and great buildings under construction. The Moguls were tolerant of foreigners, especially those bearing gifts or information about the great world; the British wanted trade: indigo (for making dye), cloths and precious stones were their most favoured goods. The tales they brought home to their bemused compatriots inspired Dryden to write his drama *Aurungzeb*.

Aurungzeb, the next emperor, was one of the three sons of Shah Jahan who fought bitterly among themselves for the succession. Aurungzeb, who played the champion of Moslem orthodoxy, was the winner. Having captured his brother Murad and imprisoned him on an island in the Jumna, he confined his old father to the Fort at Agra (extracts 67 and 72). His other brother, the tragic Dara, who had been strangely influenced by a naked Dervish of homosexual and heretical tendencies, fled to Sind where Bernier met him and subsequently witnessed his humiliating parade through the streets of Delhi (see extract 109). Dara's head was presented (some say) to Aurungzeb; his remains are in Humayun's tomb. Murad was taken to the fortress of Gwalior and murdered; his son was given the sinister '*pouste*', a daily infusion of poppy heads that produced a lingering death. Shah Jahan survived eight years after his deposition; harassed by Aurungzeb, he would sit on the walls of Agra Fort staring over the Jumna at the Taj Mahal where his beloved wife was entombed; denied watching elephant fights by his son's order, he had to make do with the sparring of tame antelopes in the palace yard. He died in 1666 and was buried beside his wife in the Taj. Tavernier, the jeweller at his court, tells us that he had planned to build a replica in black marble on the other side of the river but the illiberal Aurungzeb would not countenance the expense. The Taj, after all, had taken seventeen years to build even with twenty thousand workmen on the job and had cost a fortune. But Aurungzeb did not stint on his own coronation at Delhi when he took his place on the Peacock Throne, another of his father's little extravagances (see extract 12).

We are now in the eighteenth century. Aurungzeb, last of the so-called Great Moguls, died in 1707 at the age of eighty-nine. His son, Bahadur Shah, succeeded him; already sixty-three, he was glad merely to have survived in such murderous times. He spent his five remaining years trying to keep the empire intact; if he occasionally passed through Delhi on his marches he never once set foot in the Red Fort nor added to its buildings. He died in Lahore in 1712.

The dynasty was now in its decadence and a tempting target. In 1738 Nadir Shah, a Turk from Khurasan, displacer of the equally decadent Safavid Shah of Persia, came down from the north and defeated the Mogul ruler Mohammed Shah, dubbed 'the pleasure-loving', at Karnal. Already weakened by Maratha incursions into Delhi itself, Mohammed Shah tried to accommodate the invader but his 'friendly' reception was soon compromised by provocations from the crowd that led Nadir Shah to order an indiscriminate massacre which he observed from the mosque at the end of the Chandni Chowk. The killing went on for five hours before he was prevailed upon to call a halt. Like Timur before him, Nadir Shah did not stay; he returned to Persia bearing the Peacock Throne among his booty. It was broken up for the jewels with which it was encrusted.

Before the stricken city had time to return to prosperity disaster struck again in civil war between two rival ministers, Safdar Jung and Imad-ul-Mulk. For six months their supporters skirmished in the no-man's-land between Humayun's tomb and the Red Fort. Safdar Jung, Nawab of Oudh and Wazir of the empire, had been dismissed by the Mogul Ahmad Shah, who supported Imad-ul-Mulk from the Red Fort. Safdar Jung was defeated and retired to Oudh. On the outskirts of Delhi is his magnificent tomb, the last great Mogul architectural achievement (extract 7). Then came the visitation of the Afghan Ahmad

Shah Abdali, who carried away most of what Nadir Shah had overlooked, including the silver ceiling in the audience room in the Fort. The Empire of Hindustan had been reduced to the kingdom of Delhi: Shah Alam, the next Mogul incumbent, was little more than a cipher by the end of his reign: 'From Delhi to Palam, Is the realm of Shah Alam' was a current quip – Palam is now Delhi's domestic airport. Shah Alam had sought protection from the British at Allahabad and left Delhi under the protection of a stern Rohilla chief who kept at bay Marathas, Jats, Sikhs and other would-be predators until it was safe for him to return ten years later.

Following the defeat of the French in the Carnatic by Eyre Coote, the British were now in the ascendant on the sub-continent. Still under the control of the East India Company, which had been in business since before the days of its servant Sir Thomas Roe, British-led forces under Clive had been victorious at Arcot (1751) and Plassey (1757). Warren Hastings, on the political front, held the destiny of India in his hands. But nothing was done to prevent the occupation of Delhi by a demented Rohilla called Ghulam Kadir who, in a rage at not finding Shah Alam's treasure, seized the old man by the throat and personally gouged out his eyes (see extract 19). When the Rohilla mockingly asked him what he could now see, the King is said to have replied: 'Nought but the holy Koran between thee and me.' Shah Alam was something of a poet and he encouraged poets at his court: his ode to his blindness is said to be one of the most moving compositions in Urdu, a tongue that was replacing Persian as the court vernacular. The Maratha prince Scindia, who captured Ghulam Kadir and had him torn limb from limb, now ruled the city in the King's name.

In 1803 the Marathas went to war against the forces of the East India Company. Lord Lake defeated Scindia on the Jumna opposite Humayun's tomb and occupied the town (extract 116). The blinded king received the British general in the *diwan-i-khas* in the Fort and accepted British authority in return for his position, protection and a pension. A Maratha counter-attack was frustrated by Sir David Ochterlony, who hastily repaired the walls: after a fortnight of battering at them the Marathas left. Shah Alam died in 1806 at the age of eighty-three, under the control of the British 'Resident' but a monarch to the last. When the nineteen-year-old Thomas Twining, emissary of a British general in Bengal, was presented to him he described the blind king as 'an extraordinary and most distressing spectacle' (see extract 20).

The ensuing period was the beginning of a British presence in Delhi where an autumnal renaissance under their protection seemed to be taking place. In St James's Church they sang praises to the Lord and left their bones in the cemetery. If the city life still seemed to be centred round the seedy court, with two thousand royal princelings and their parents cluttering up the corridors, substantial bungalows were springing up on the approaches to the Ridge; buggies and chaises, men in British uniform and women in unsuitable clothes can be seen in the prints of the period. The British seemed to think it was their city and as good landlords proceeded to further its amenities and organise its administration. In 1857 this illusion of acceptance was to be shattered.

Whatever the cause – pig fat on Moslem cartridges, the prognostications of astrologers, a fever of accumulated aggravations, a general threat to religion – the Sepoys, native soldiers of the East India Company, stationed at Meerut, mutinied almost to a man and joined forces at Delhi some fifty miles away. Crossing the Jumna by the Bridge of Boats they marched on the Red Fort as the seat of their symbolic emperor. The story of their reception and subsequent behaviour is told in our text (see extract 47). Lucknow and Cawnpore were to undergo even worse experiences; at Agra the British prepared to defend the Fort but were never seriously challenged. At Delhi, following the brave breach of the Kashmir Gate, where marks of shot and shell are still to be seen, the British regained the city and another period of pillage and reprisal began. The emperor's sons paid a premature penalty when the dashing Major Hodson seized them from Humayun's tomb and shot them on the way back to the Fort (see extract 51). Condign punishment was applied elsewhere: executions took place daily in front of the police station in the Chandni Chowk; three thousand were tried and executed by the military courts. Bahadur Shah, the two-way king, was found guilty of assisting the mutineers but not of organising the mutiny. His punishment was comfortable exile to Rangoon.

The Fort was occupied by relieving troops; barracks and canteens burgeoned in the courts and pavilions of the Moguls. There was talk of demolishing the Jami-Masjid and raising a Christian cathedral in its place; buildings were blown up in front of the Fort to make a proper field of fire; royal princesses drifted dirty and barefooted through the bazaars. One disgruntled Englishman, Hugh Chichester, wrote home: 'There are several mosques in the city most beautiful to look at. But I should like to see them all destroyed. The rascally brutes desecrated our churches and graveyards, and I do not think we ought to have any regard for their stinking religion. One was always supposed to take off one's shoes on going to visit one of these mosques, or to have an interview with the king. But these little affairs we drop now. I have seen the old Pig of a king. He is a very old man and just like an old *Khitmugar* (waiter).' Delhi was indeed defiled. 'What can I write?' the poet Ghalib moaned. 'The life of Delhi depends on the Fort, Chandni Chowk, the daily gatherings on the Jamuna Bridge and the annual *Gulfaroshan*. When all these things are no longer there, how can Delhi live?'

But Delhi came to life again. In 1858 rule was removed from the East India Company, and Canning, now dubbed 'Clemency' for his alleged liberality with the mutineers, was promoted from Governor-General to Viceroy. In 1867 the first train steamed into Delhi station and established the city's importance as a centre of communications. Delhi was now on the tourist track, though there were dire warnings about 'Delhi-belly' and disease. A visitor in 1874 was Edward Lear: he stayed ten days, 'making Dehlineations of the Dehlicate architecture, as is all impressed on my mind as inDehlibly as the Dehliterious quality of the water of that city.' Lear also visited Agra, where the Taj Mahal so filled him with enthusiasm that he wrote: 'Henceforth, let the inhabitants of the world be divided into 2 classes, – them as has seen the Taj, – and them as hasn't.'

Victoria was proclaimed Queen-Empress on New Year's Day, 1877, and the Viceroy, Lord Lytton, arranged a magnificent assemblage to hear the proclamation read. All the great chiefs of India attended with their retinues and were given banners, gold medals and two extra guns in their salute. Curzon, a later Viceroy, vied to outdo his predecessor with his Durbar of 1903 which was followed by a ball in the Red Fort. The *diwan-i-khas* was lit by electric light and the beautiful Lady Curzon dazzled in a ball-gown decorated with peacock feathers. Delhi had got back its spirit – a dour Scot, John Matheson, noted that in the Chandni Chowk 'the array of tinsel and ornaments far outshone the products of sober usefulness'.

In 1911, after considerable argument, it was decided that

Self-portrait of Edward Lear on an elephant,
inspired by his visit to India

Delhi, rather than viceregal and commercial Calcutta, should be
the seat of government. The new King George V announced the
fact in person. The following year Curzon's successor, Hardinge,
came down from Simla, hot season headquarters of government,
to occupy his new residence, an extended bungalow dubbed
Viceregal Lodge. As his procession moved slowly along the
Chandni Chowk Lord Hardinge, up on an elephant with his
wife, said to her: 'I am sure something dreadful is going to
happen.' Seconds later his helmet was blown off and his elephant
lurched to a halt. 'I am afraid it's a bomb,' he said to his wife.
And indeed it was, and quite an efficient one: Hardinge's
umbrella bearer was killed and the Viceroy received a nasty
wound in his shoulder in which were embedded nails, screws and
gramophone needles.

There was to be no further serious act of terrorism until 1929
when two bombs were thrown into the Government benches of
the Legislative Assembly, although in fact they did no harm.
Following the 1914–18 war, in which Indian troops had
staunchly participated, Indian politicians in the Congress Party

were harassing the Government in other ways and keeping a long and covetous eye on power. Gandhi started his first Civil Disobedience campaign in 1919. 'Dear me, what a damned nuisance these saintly fanatics are!' the then Viceroy, Lord Chelmsford, observed. 'Gandhi is incapable of hurting a fly and is as honest as the day, but he enters quite light-heartedly on a course of action which is the negation of all government and may lead to much hardship to people who are ignorant and easily led astray.' Three weeks of rioting in Delhi and the Punjab were to follow and there was even an invasion, just like in the old days, by the Amir of Afghanistan, Amanullah.

When Hardinge arrived in Delhi on the day of the bomb he had come with plans to implement the building of a great Imperial city. 'He is mad on Delhi at present,' said Harcourt Butler, a member of his Council, still operating from Calcutta. 'I am afraid we shall not get much policy out of him, as he can think of little else but Delhi.' On the commission to select a site was Edwin Lutyens: an ebullient personality well-considered in England as an inventive architect of country houses and business headquarters, he was also something of a genius with ideas bigger than the public purse. But had not George V in his Durbar speech declared that it was his desire that 'the planning and designing of the public buildings to be erected be considered with the greatest deliberation and care so that the new creation may in every way be worthy of this ancient and beautiful city'? Lutyens did not always see eye to eye with Hardinge, who had ideas of his own especially when it came to economy. The Viceroy had less trouble with Herbert Baker, Lutyens' collaborator, who knew more about the requirements of officialdom than about art. It was official parsimony that lost the full effect of the main approach, originally called 'Kingsway': Lutyens' noble dome was allowed to disappear from view beneath the eyeline for want of funds to cut back the inhibiting mound (see illustration overleaf).

The newest of New Delhis was formally opened in 1930 by the Viceroy, Lord Irwin, later known as Lord Halifax. Sited at an appropriately patrician distance from the bazaars and milling mobs of the old city, and with its own Georgian-style shopping centre, Connaught Place (extract 57), its main attributes are the great administrative buildings, the viceregal residence, individual palaces for attendant princes and a massive, almost Tughlak,

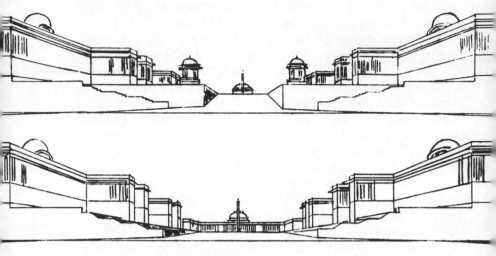

Top sketch shows actual view from the centre of the Great Court;
bottom sketch shows Lutyens's proposal to cut back the slope and
reveal Government House

hulk of a church. Most of it is built in that ruddy sandstone that
Robert Byron (extracts 55 and 56) likened to the colour of
rhubarb. Though there were meaningful references on all sides
to the decline and fall of earlier rulers, Indian politicians read in
all this imperial aggrandisement a message that the British
intended to stay. When Lord Irwin was on his way to take up
residence, a bomb almost derailed his train. There were riots and
near-revolution in that year and Gandhi and Nehru had to be
locked up, as well as thirty-four thousand political prisoners.
Gandhi was released a year later and an unexpected dialogue
was opened up between an accommodating Viceroy and 'that
strange little man', as Irwin described him, or, as Winston
Churchill phrased it: 'the nauseating and humiliating spectacle
of this one-time Inner Temple lawyer, now seditious fakir,
striding half-naked up the steps of the Viceroy's palace to
negotiate and parley on equal terms with the representative of
the King-Emperor'. But the outcome of the meeting was a
success for Irwin, described by an Indian politician as 'the most
Christian and the most gentlemanly representative of Great
Britain among them all'; Gandhi agreed to call off Civil
Disobedience and attend a conference.

This is no place for a discussion on Indian politics. In brief, Delhi saw a succession of Viceroys come and go without any real concession to Indian nationhood. Indian divisions fought bravely against Germans and Japanese, despite the machinations of Chandra Bose, in league with the Axis powers. With the war came a promise of Dominion status. The troublesome Mahatma was released from another term of imprisonment but could not gain much influence over General Wavell, Lord Linlithgow's successor, who thought him 'malignant, malevolent, fifteen per cent charlatan, fifteen per cent saint and seventy per cent extremely astute politician.' Wavell, man of feeling and former army commander, may have known his man better than some. Nor was there much love for Mohomad Ali Jinnah, leader of the Moslems; Jawaharlal Nehru, for the Hindus, was thought to be more of a gentleman, despite his Harrow education.

And so to Mountbatten, last of the Viceroys, with his brief to disgorge India with or without tears. With Hindu and Moslem at each other's throat, Partition – Pakistan to the Moslems – was the fateful decision. Gandhi's efforts to defuse the confrontation in Delhi by going on a protracted hunger strike ended in his murder by hotheads of his own side. An echo of the awful events that were to follow, in the streets as opposed to the council chamber, is given in extract 59.

The former imperial seat of government serves its bureaucratic purpose still, even if the great avenues leading to it, once named after Viceroys and Mogul emperors, now do honour to Indian politicians. The big hotels in Delhi and Agra seem just as palatial and considerably more comfortable that the dwellings of the Moguls. At the Red Fort *son et lumière* reveal even the sanctums of their palace. There is a cafeteria at the Kutb-Minar and elephantine buses will carry the tourist to Fattephur Sikri and Sikandra. The Taj Mahal, still sublimely aloof, does not belie earlier superlatives. Delhi has over a hundred buildings of historical interest, albeit many of them lesser mosques and minor mausoleums. It is hoped that the edifices selected will be sufficient to give the reader, relaxing in air-conditioned comfort, with a genie marked Room Service at his command, a certain sense of time and space not otherwise so painlessly acquired.

The Mogul Dynasty

Timur(Tamerlane) 1398

Ruled

Babur	1526–1530
Humayun	1530–1556*
Akbar	1556–1605
Jahangir	1605–1627
Shah Jahan	1627–1658
Aurungzeb	1658–1707
Bahadur Shah	1707–1712
Jahandar Shah	1712–1713
Farukhsiyar	1713–1719
Mohammad Shah	1719–1748
Ahmad Shah	1748–1754
Alamgir	1754–1759
Shah Alam	1759–1806
Akbar II	1806–1837
Bahadur Shah II	1837–1857

* (Sher Shah 1540–1555)

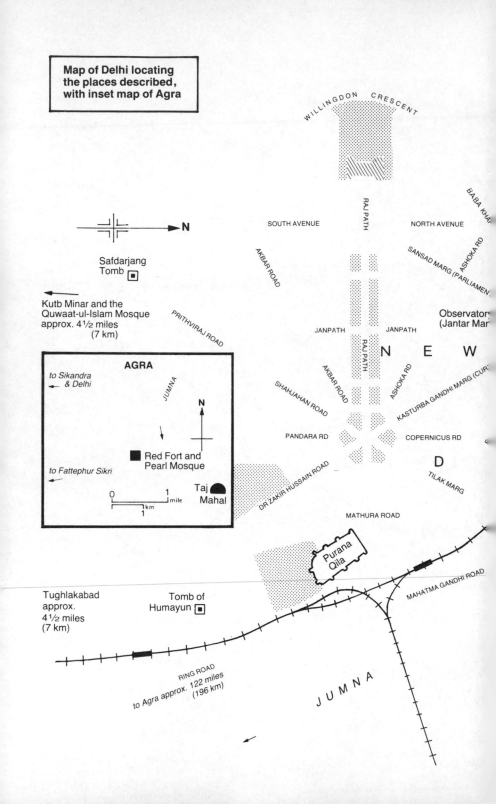

Map of Delhi locating the places described, with inset map of Agra

WILLINGDON CRESCENT

N

Safdarjang Tomb

Kutb Minar and the Quwaat-ul-Islam Mosque approx. 4½ miles (7 km)

SOUTH AVENUE

RAJ PATH

NORTH AVENUE

BABA KHA

AKBAR ROAD

SANSAD MARG (PARLIAMEN

ASHOKA RD

PRITHVIRAJ ROAD

JANPATH

JANPATH

Observator (Jantar Mar

RAJ PATH

N   E   W

AKBAR ROAD

ASHOKA RD

KASTURBA GANDHI MARG (CUR

SHAHJAHAN ROAD

PANDARA RD

COPERNICUS RD

D

TILAK MARG

AGRA

to Sikandra & Delhi

JUMNA

N

Red Fort and Pearl Mosque

to Fattephur Sikri

0   1 mile
1 km
1

Taj Mahal

DR ZAKIR HUSSAIN ROAD

MATHURA ROAD

Purana Qila

MAHATMA GANDHI ROAD

Tughlakabad approx. 4½ miles (7 km)

Tomb of Humayun

RING ROAD
to Agra approx. 122 miles (196 km)

JUMNA

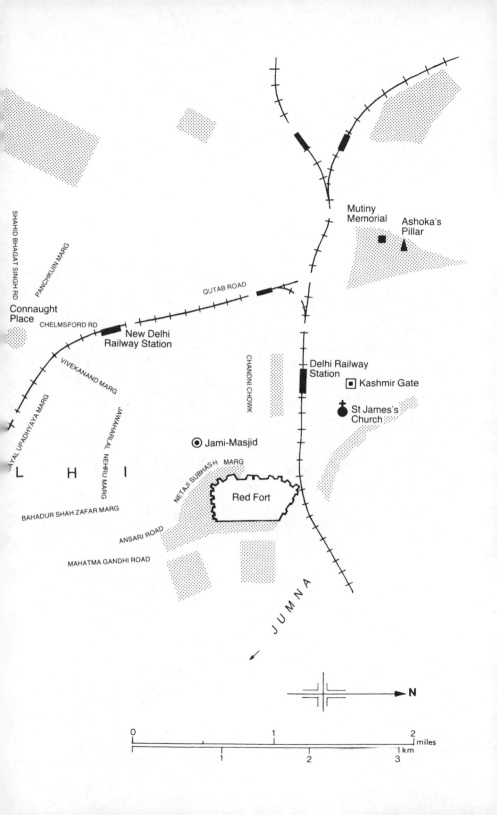

SHAHID BHAGAT SINGH RD

PANCHKUIN MARG

Connaught
Place

CHELMSFORD RD

New Delhi
Railway Station

VIVEKANAND MARG

AYAL UPADHYAYA MARG

JAWAHARLAL NEHRU MARG

L   H   I

BAHADUR SHAH ZAFAR MARG

ANSARI ROAD

MAHATMA GANDHI ROAD

QUTAB ROAD

CHANDNI CHOWK

Mutiny
Memorial

Ashoka's
Pillar

Delhi Railway
Station

■ Kashmir Gate

St James's
Church

◉ Jami-Masjid

NETAJI SUBHASH   MARG

Red Fort

J U M N A

N

0   1   2 miles

1 km
1   2   3

 Delhi

Cities of the Plain and the Kutb-Minar

[1] Cities of the plain of Delhi, 1334; from *Selections of the Travels of Ibn Batuta* translated and edited by H.A.R. Gibb

On the next day we arrived at the city of Dihli, the metropolis of India, a vast and magnificent city, uniting beauty with strength. It is surrounded by a wall that has no equal in the world, and is the largest city in the Muslim Orient.

The city of Dihli is made up now of four neighbouring and contiguous towns. One of them is Dihli proper, the old city built by the infidels and captured in the year 1188. The second is called Siri, known also as the Abode of the Caliphate; this was the town given by the Sultan to Ghiyath ad-Din when he came to his court. The third is called Tughlaq Abad, after its founder the Sultan Tughlaq, father of the Sultan of India to whose court we came. The fourth is called Jahan Panah, and is set apart for the residence of the reigning Sultan, Muhammed Shah. He was the founder of it, and it was his intention to unite these four towns within a single wall, but after building part of it he gave up the rest because of the expense required for its construction.

The cathedral mosque occupies a large area; its walls, roof, and paving are all constructed of white stones, admirably squared and firmly cemented with lead. There is no wood in it at all. It has thirteen domes of stone, and it has four courts. In the centre of the mosque is an awe-inspiring column, and nobody knows of what metal it is constructed. One of their learned men told me that it is called *Haft Jush*, which means 'seven metals', and that it is constructed from these seven. A part of this column, of a finger's breadth, has been polished, and gives out a brilliant gleam. Iron makes no impression on it. It is thirty cubits high, and he rolled a turban round it, and the portion which encircled it measured eight cubits. At the eastern gate there are two enormous idols of brass prostrate on the ground and held by stones, and everyone entering or leaving the mosque treads on them. The site was formerly occupied by an idol temple, and was converted into a mosque on the conversion of the city. In the northern court is the Kutub Minar, which has no parallel in the lands of Islam. It is built of red stone, unlike the rest of the edifice, ornamented with sculptures and of great height. The ball on the top is of glistening white marble and its apples are of pure gold. The passage is so wide that elephants could go up by it. A person in whom I have confidence told me that when it was built he saw an elephant climbing with stones to the top. The Sultan Qutb ad-Din wished to build one in the western court even larger, but was cut off by death when only a third of it had been completed. This minaret is one of the wonders of the world for size and the width of its passage is such that three elephants could mount it abreast. The third of it built equals in height the whole of the other minaret we have mentioned in the northern court, though to one looking at it from below it does not seem so high because of its bulk.

Outside Dihli is a large reservoir from which the inhabitants draw their drinking water. It is supplied by rain water and is about two miles in length by half that in breadth. In the centre there is a great pavilion built of squared stones two stories high. When the reservoir is filled with water it can be reached only in boats, but when the water is low the people go into it. Inside it is a mosque, and at most times it is occupied by mendicants devoted to the service of God. When the water dries up at the sides of this reservoir, they sow sugar canes, cucumbers, green melons and pumpkins there. The melons and pumpkins are very sweet but of small size. Between Dihli and the Abode of the Caliphate is the private reservoir which is larger than the other. Along its sides there are about forty pavilions, and round about it live the musicians.

[2] Tamerlane's version of the Sack of Delhi in 1398; from the *Malfuzat-i-Timuri* in *The History of India as told by its own Historians* edited by Sir H.M. Elliot and J. Dowson.

On the 16th of the month some incidents occurred which led to the sack of the city of Dehlí, and to the slaughter of many of the infidel inhabitants. One was this. A party of fierce Turk soldiers had assembled at one of the gates of the city to look about them and enjoy themselves, and some of them laid violent hands upon the goods of the inhabitants. When I heard of this violence, I sent some *amírs*, who were present in the city, to restrain the Turks. A party of soldiers accompanied these *amírs* into the city. Another reason was that some of the ladies of my harem expressed a wish to go into the city and see the palace of *Hazár-sutún* (thousand columns) which Malik Jauná built in the fort called Jahán-panáh. I granted this request, and I sent a party of soldiers to escort the litters of the ladies. Another reason was that Jalál Islám and other *díwáns* had gone into the city with a party of soldiers to collect the contribution laid upon the city. Another reason was that some thousand troopers with orders for grain, oil, sugar, and flour, had gone into the city to collect these supplies. Another reason was that it had come to my knowledge that great numbers of Hindus and *gabrs*, with their wives and children, and goods, and valuables, had come into the city from all the country round, and consequently I had sent some *amírs* with their regiments (*kushún*) into the city and directed them to pay no attention to the remonstrances of the inhabitants, but to seize and bring out these fugitives. For these several reasons a great number of fierce Turkí soldiers were in the city. When the soldiers proceeded to apprehend the Hindus and *gabrs* who had fled to the city, many of them drew their swords and offered resistance. The flames of strife were thus lighted and spread through the whole city from Jahán-panáh and Sírí to Old Dehlí, burning up all it reached. The savage Turks fell to killing and plundering. The Hindus set fire to their houses with their own hands, burned their wives and children in them, and rushed into the fight and were killed. The Hindus and *gabrs* of the city showed much alacrity and boldness in fighting. The *amírs* who were in charge of the gates prevented any more soldiers from going into the place, but the flames of war had risen too high for this precaution to be of any avail in extinguishing them. On that day, Thursday, and all the night of Friday, nearly 15,000 Turks were engaged in slaying, plundering, and destroying. When morning broke on the Friday, all my army, no longer under control, went off to the city and thought of nothing but killing, plundering, and making prisoners. All that day the sack was general. The following day, Saturday, the 17th, all passed in the same way, and the spoil was so great that each man secured from fifty to a hundred prisoners, men, women, and children. There was no man who took less than twenty. The other booty was immense in rubies, diamonds, garnets, pearls, and other gems; jewels of gold and silver; *ashrafís, tankas* of gold and silver of the celebrated 'Aláí coinage; vessels of gold and silver; and brocades and silks of great value. Gold and silver ornaments of the Hindu women were obtained in such quantities as to exceed all account. Excepting the quarter of the *saiyids*, the *'ulamá*, and the other Musulmáns, the whole city was sacked. The pen of fate had written down this destiny for the people of this city. Although I was desirous of sparing them I could not succeed, for it was the will of God that this calamity should fall upon the city.

I sent a party of men into the city to bring out the elephants which Sultan Mahmud had abandoned when he fled. They found 120 enormous elephants and several rhinoceroses, which they brought out to my Court. As the elephants passed by me I was greatly amused to see the tricks which their drivers had taught them. Every elephant, at the sign of the driver, bowed his head to the ground, made his obeisance, and uttered a cry. At the direction of their drivers they picked up any object from the ground with their trunks and placed it in their driver's hands, or put in into their mouths and kept it. When I saw these mighty animals, so well trained and so obedient to weak man, I was greatly astonished, and I ordered that they should be sent to Túrán and Írán, to Fárs, and Ázur, and Rúm, so that the princes and nobles throughout my dominions might see these animals. Accordingly I sent five to Samarkand, two to Tabríz, one to Shíráz, five to Hirát, one to Sharwán, and one to Ázurbaiján.

When Friday came, I sent Mauláná Násiru-d dín 'Umar, with some other holy and learned men that accompanied my camp to the *Masjid-i jámi'*, with directions to say the prayers for the Sabbath, and to repeat the *khutba* of my reign in the metropolis of Dehlí. Accordingly, the *khutba* with my name, was repeated in the pulpits of the mosques in the city of Dehlí, and I rewarded the preachers with costly robes and presents.

When the preparations for holding a court in Dehlí were complete I gave orders for the princes, the *amírs*, the *núyáns*, and other of my officers, and the *saiyids*, the *'ulamá*, the *shaikhs*, and all the principal men of the city to attend my Court. When they had all arrived I entered and took my seat upon the throne. The Turk and Tájik musicians and singers began to play and sing. Wine (*sharáb*) and sharbat, and sweetmeats, and all kinds of bread and meat were served.

[3] 'Stupendous fortifications' and the Kutb-Minar; from *Rambles and Recollections of an Indian Official* by Major-General W.H. Sleeman.

(As Colonel Sleeman (1788–1856) he was well known in India as a pundit of esoteric Indian matters. He introduced sugar cane into the country and is given credit for suppressing the *thugs* – religious killers – and forbidding *suttee* or widow-burning.)

On the 21st we went on eight miles to the Kutb Mīnār, across the range of sandstone hills, which rise to the height of about two hundred feet, and run north and south. The rocks are for the most part naked, but here and there the soil between them is covered with *famished* grass, and a few stunted shrubs; anything more unprepossessing can hardly be conceived than the aspect of these hills, which seem to serve no other purpose than to store up heat for the people of the great city of Delhi. We passed through a cut in this range of hills, made apparently by the stream of the river Jumna at some remote period, and about one hundred yards wide at the entrance. This cut is crossed by an enormous stone wall running north and south, and intended to shut in the waters, and form a lake in the opening beyond it. Along the brow of the precipice, overlooking the northern end of the wall, is the stupendous fort of Tughlakābād, built by the Emperor Tughlak the First of the sandstones of the range of hills on which it stands, cut into enormous square blocks. On the brow of the opposite side of the precipice, overlooking the southern end of the wall, stands the fort of Muhammadābād, built by this Emperor's son and successor, Muhammad, and resembling in all things that built by his father. These fortresses overlooked the lake, with the old city of Delhi spread out on the opposite side of it to the west. There is a third fortress upon an isolated hill, east of the great barrier wall, said to have been built in honour of his master by the Emperor Tughlak's *barber*. The Emperor's tomb stands upon an isolated rock in the middle of the once lake, now plain, about a mile to the west of the barrier wall. The rock is connected with the western extremity of the northern fortress by a causeway of twenty-five arches, and about one hundred and fifty yards long. This is a fine tomb, and contains in a square centre room the remains of the Emperor Tughlak, his wife, and his son. The tomb is built of red sandstone, and surmounted by a dome of white

marble. The three graves inside are built of brick covered with
stucco work. The outer sides of the tomb slope slightly inwards
from the base, in the form of a pyramid; but the inner walls are, of
course, perpendicular.

The impression left on the mind after going over these
stupendous fortifications is that the arts which contribute to the
comforts and elegancies of life must have been in a very rude state
when they were raised. Domestic architecture must have been
wretched in the extreme. The buildings are all of stone, and
almost all without cement, and seem to have been raised by
giants, and for giants, whose arms were against everybody, and
everybody's arm against them. This was indeed the state of the
Pathān sovereigns in India – they were the creatures of their
armies; and their armies were also employed against the people,
who feared and detested them all.

The Emperor Tughlak, on his return at the head of the army,
which he had led into Bengal to chastise some rebellious subjects,
was met at Afghānpur by his eldest son, Jūnā, whom he had left
in the government of the capital. The prince had in three days
raised here a palace of wood for a grand entertainment to do
honour to his father's return; and when the Emperor signified his
wish to retire, all the courtiers rushed out before him to be in
attendance, among the rest, Jūnā himself. Five attendants only
remained when the Emperor rose from his seat, and at that
moment the building fell in and crushed them and their master.
Jūnā had been sent at the head of an army into the Deccan,
where he collected immense wealth from the plunder of the
palaces of princes and the temples of their priests, the only places
in which much wealth was to be found in those days. This wealth
he tried to conceal from his father, whose death he probably thus
contrived, that he might the sooner have the free enjoyment of it
with unlimited power.

Only thirty years before, Alā-ud-dīn, returning in the same
manner at the head of an army from the Deccan loaded with
wealth, murdered the Emperor Fīrōz the Second, the father of
his wife, and ascended the throne. Jūnā ascended the throne
under the name of Muhammad the Third; and, after the remains
of his father had been deposited in the tomb I have described, he
passed in great pomp and splendour from the fortress of
Tughlakābād, which his father had just then completed, to the
city in which the Mīnār stands, with elephants before and

behind loaded with gold and silver coins, which were scattered among the crowd, who everywhere hailed him with shouts of joy. The roads were covered with flowers, the houses adorned with the richest stuffs, and the streets resounded with music.

He was a man of great learning, and a great patron of learned men; he was a great founder of churches, had prayers read in them at the prescribed times, and always went to prayers five times a day himself. He was rigidly temperate himself in his habits, and discouraged all intemperance in others. These things secured him panegyrists throughout the empire during the twenty-seven years that he reigned over it, though perhaps he was the most detestable tyrant that ever filled a throne. He would take his armies out over the most populous and peaceful districts, and hunt down the innocent and unoffending people like wild beasts, and bring home their heads by thousands to hang them on the city gates for his mere amusement. He twice made the whole people of the city of Delhi emigrate with him to Daulatābād in Southern India, which he wished to make the capital, from some foolish fancy; and during the whole of his reign gave evident signs of being in an unsound state of mind.

The Kutb Mīnār was, I think, more beyond my expectations than the Tāj; first, because I had heard less of it, and secondly, because it stands as it were alone in India – there is absolutely no other tower in this Indian empire of ours.

[4] A jump from the Kutb in 1831; from *Rambles and Recollections of an Indian Official* by Major-General W.H. Sleeman.

About five years ago, while the emperor [*Akbar II*] was on a visit to the tomb of Kutb-ud-dīn, a madman got into his private apartments. The servants were ordered to turn him out. On passing the Mīnār he ran in, ascended to the top, stood a few moments on the verge, laughing at those who were running after him, and made a spring that enabled him to reach the bottom, without touching the sides. An eye-witness told me that he kept his erect position till about half-way down, when he turned over, and continued to turn till he got to the bottom, when his fall made a report like a gun. He was of course dashed to pieces.

The Kutb-Minar, showing the top as it was before an earthquake
shattered it in 1803; aquatint by Thomas and William Daniell,
1789. (Note the base of larger, uncompleted minar at left)

[5] A visit to the Kutb in the 1830s; from *Tours in Upper India* by Major Archer.

From Togluckabad we went to the Cootub Minar, or Pillar; this enormous column rises out of a large plain, and is at its base fifty-two feet in diameter; its extreme height is two hundred and sixty-two feet. It is divided into stories of different characters and appearance; the first story of ninety feet, having alternately semicircular and angular divisions one above the other; the next division is wholly angular, all the others are of mixed ornaments and designs. Balustrades have been thrown out by the engineer who has had the charge of repairing it, and the masterly manner in which he has executed the work, would alone stamp his character for talent and ingenuity. There is a platform at each stage, upon which the visitor can go round the pillar outside, by no means a pleasant piece of curiosity; a pavilion sort of building is at the top, and a flag-staff displaying the British colours crowned the whole; this last addition was little dreamed of, when the first stone was laid.

An iron pillar stands in a sort of court-yard, having the remains of cloisters on the four sides. Its history is veiled in darkest night. There is an inscription on it which nobody can decipher; nor is there any account, historical or traditional, except we may refer to the latter class, a prevalent idea of all people, that the pillar is on the most sacred spot of the old city, which spot was also its centre. It is also said, that as long as the pillar stood, so long would Hindoostan flourish. This was the united dictum of the Bramins and astrologers of the day. The pillar is fifteen or sixteen inches in diameter. It has the marks of two cannon-shot, fired by the Jauts when they had possession of Delhi: the attempt to destroy it was unavailing. The colonnades or cloisters, above-mentioned, were all of stone: the roofs were of flat pieces laid across. It does not appear whether the people of those times had any knowledge of the arch save the one already mentioned. The carvings on the pillars which support these precious remains of past ages are strikingly rich and elaborate; there are different compartments with a variety of figures, but no two precisely alike. The human figures of both sexes were correct as to proportion, but it was in the countenances that the artist was faithful to anatomical precision. The attitude of the figures was very graceful; the general position of them was standing upon one leg, with the other crossed over. Wherever these figures were introduced, the fanatic Moslem had hammered to pieces all those within his reach; and when this process was too slow for the work of demolition, another mode of obliteration was requisite. Whole compartments of sculpture were plastered over to hide the profane imagery.

In clearing away the rubbish to bring these beautiful remains to light, the engineer stumbled on a long frieze, part of which had had the destroying mallet passed over it; but this method of despatch was not active enough; and that portion which had escaped violence had been plastered over with a composition of the colour of the stone. There was one stone which formed the architrave of a door-way; it was a battle piece, and, but for the sacrilege, was fitting to be conveyed to Europe. Those lines of peculiar beauty and expression of Lord Byron's, started to the mind's eye. 'Cold is thy heart, fair Greece.'

The commencement of another cootub, which would have been of larger dimensions than the present, may here be seen: it has lost its coating of stone, which has been taken away for other purposes. The enormous piles of ruins lying in mountains all around the pillar, have been organized into various forms, shaped into pyramids, or worn into some design more agreeable to the eye. Broad roads have been opened, having the cootub for their centre-piece. The Moslems had formerly designed a large mosque close to the pillar; all that now remains are some lofty arches, which give the ruins a cathedral or abbey-like appearance. The party breakfasted in a tomb of some former noble of the state, a huge single room, square, and domed; nautch singers entertained us during our meal. If the dead had perception, the spirit of the defunct must have been rather 'up' to witness such unhallowed use of a last lodging.

The task of repairing this pillar was allotted to Major Smith, and it is but justice to say, he has put it into as good a state as when it was new, perhaps better. Lightning had struck and injured it severely; a large gap had fallen out at its base, so as to excite fears for the whole coming down at once; the staircase inside had fallen into a confused mass of stone rubbish; added to this, many thought they perceived an inclination from its perpendicular; yet the talented architect did not shrink from the charge of its restoration, and if the approval of the scientific, and the admiration of all who have witnessed the perfect state in which the building is now, can speak to the thanks he deserves for his exertions, he has fully acquired them.

The Cootub Minar is supposed to have been built by a monarch of that name, who sat on the throne about the year 1206, and was one of the early Moslem sovereigns of the Goor dynasty; 'Cootub' signifies an axle or axis. It is placed in the centre of the olden city of Delhi, which old city existed previously to the Mahomedan invasion, and was called Indraput in the first ages of the Hindoos. Colonnades and cloisters of old Hindoo temples of stone surround the pillar, and the few fragments which remain, point out most unequivocally the great perfection to which the art of sculpture was carried; these fragments are in the shape of friezes, cornices, pillars, and the inner part of domes of a peculiar construction. They are formed by stones projecting over each other, all fixed by the key-stone at the top. The Cootub was the effect of bigotry and fanaticism, the invariable associates of Moslem invasion and power. The Hindoo temples were destroyed, for many of their relics are perceptible in parts of the Cootub. This fact alone decides the controversy as to the people by whom the pillar was raised. The Hindoos, with perhaps pardonable assumption, claim it to their honour, not being aware of the circumstance above-mentioned, even if it were not known that they were a people who never thought of building for the mere honour of the arts, or to commemorate any act of national importance. The Moslems, on the contrary, were celebrated for such works.

[6] Emily Eden is impressed in 1838; from *Up the Country* . . . by Emily Eden.

(The Hon. Emily Eden (1797–1869) accompanied her brother George, Lord Auckland, to India and stayed with him during his term of office as Governor-General (1835–42). She was an accomplished artist and a lively letter-writer.)

Well, of all the things I ever saw, I think this is the finest. Did we know about it in England? I mean, did you and I, in our old ancient Briton state, know? Do you know now without my telling you, what the Kootûb is? Don't be ashamed, there is no harm in not knowing, only I do say it is rather a pity we were so ill taught.

I have had so many odd names dinned into me during the countless years I seem to have passed in this country, that I cannot remember the exact degree of purity of mind (which enemies may term ignorance) with which I left home; but after all that had been said, I expected the Kootûb would have been rather inferior to the Monument. One has those little prejudices. It happens to be the Monument put at the top of the column in the Place Vendôme, and that again placed on a still grander base. It is built of beautiful red granite, is 240 feet high and 50 feet in diameter, and carved all over with sentences from the Koran, each letter a yard high, and the letter again interlaced and ornamented with carved flowers and garlands; it is between six and seven hundred years old, and looks as if it were finished yesterday, and it stands in a wilderness of ruins, carved gateways, and marble tombs, one more beautiful than the other.

They say that the man who built it meant it for one minaret of a mosque – a mosque, you are to understand, always possessing two minarets and three domes. But as some say Kootûb himself built this, and others say that a particular emperor called Alexander II has the merit of it, and as nobody knows whether there ever were a Kootûb or an Alexander II, I think it is just possible that we do not know what a man who never was born meant to make of a building that never was built. As it stands it is perfect.

[7] Via Safdar Jung's tomb to 'the loftiest and most remarkable column in the world'; from *From New York to Delhi* by Robert B. Minturn.

(Robert B. Minturn visited Delhi in the 1850s. His family shared with the Welds of Boston the reputation of being the greatest shipowners in America in the days of the clippers.)

About half-way between the walls of Delhi and the Kootub is the manificent mausoleum of Sufdur Jung, who was a wuzeer of the Mogul empire, and usurped the independent government of Oude, of which country he had been viceroy. This event occurred about a hundred years ago. The Honourable Company recognized his family in the government of Oude, and even conferred upon them the royal title, both of which they retained until within three years. The Delhi Moosulmans, however, never acknowledged the superior title conferred on the ruler of Oude by the Company, but always considered and spoke of him as a wuzeer, or minister of the Padshah.

The mausoleum is about a hundred feet square, having at each corner a round minár surmounted by a kiosk. It is elevated upon a marble terrace or chubootra, and is surmounted by a white marble dome of great beauty. The walls are constructed of red sandstone relieved by layers and arches of marble. The windows, of which there are two tiers, are not glazed, but closed by marble slabs most delicately cut into open fretwork. The interior contains one large apartment and four smaller ones. In the centre of the large apartment, under the dome, is the cenotaph, a plain white marble tomb; immediately under it, but beneath the terrace, is the real tomb, which protects the body.

The garden in which the mausoleum is situated is three hundred and fifty yards square. It has been at one time beautifully laid out, and is still filled with trees. The red stone wall which surrounds it is formed into a cloister on the inner side, and is used as a serai by native travellers. The gateways are very large and fine.

Outside the gateway we found several hundred natives encamped. They were the followers of a young relation of the Rajah of Jaipoor. He had come to Delhi to get married. There were in the camp about thirty of his soldiers in a green uniform, on the English model, but very shabby. None of them wore shoes.

After driving about six miles from Sufdur Jung's tomb we came to the Kootub – the loftiest and most remarkable column in the world – now in perfect order, having been thoroughly repaired by the Company in 1826, at the cost of several thousand pounds sterling.

We ascended to the top of the minár, from which we obtained a most extensive view of the country, which was everywhere covered with ruins as far as the eye could reach.

After descending from the minár, we walked through the courts of a very old and now ruinous mosque, built by Kootub-ood-Deen, the deputy of Sooltan Mohummud, one of the early Pathán conquerors, in the year 592 of the Hijra, answering to 1195 of our era. The Moosulmans contend that the Kootub was intended as one of the minárs of this mosque, the Hindoos, on the other hand, assert, that it existed before the advent of the

Moosulmans. Each view has earnest supporters, who find very strong arguments for their respective opinions. Whichever party is right, the Kootub is certainly perfectly unique. If it was built by the Mahommedans, it is unlike every other minár in India or the world, both in form and decoration; if, on the contrary, it was constructed by the Hindoos, it is the only edifice of considerable dimensions erected by them which has come down to the present day. I suppose the question will never be decided, for no nation would willingly give up for its race the honour of having devised and completed a monument which so far surpasses in sublimity every other creation of oriental art, and which, whether we consider the grandeur and originality of the conception, or the workmanlike knowledge of art displayed in its construction – whether we look at the boldness, grace, and exquisite execution of the ornaments with which it is covered, or their perfect harmony and entire subordination to the grand features of the design, – must, I think, be allowed a rank by the side of the most renowned triumphs of western architecture.

[8] Getting away from Father; from the *Journal* of Lady (Emily) Bayley in *The Golden Calm* edited by M.M. Kaye.

(Emily Metcalfe, born in India in 1831 and educated in England, returned to Delhi in 1848 to stay with her father, Sir Thomas Metcalfe. In 1850 she married Sir Clive (Edward) Bayley, under-secretary to the Foreign Department, at St James's Church. She returned to England just before the Mutiny in 1857.)

As soon as all the first visits had been paid, my Father took me out to spend a few days at the Kutub, where he had built another house, and it was always a refreshment to him to go there when he could spare a few days from his regular attendance at office.

It was a delightful residence, and a very quaint one, for it was originally a Mohammedan tomb, surrounded by a big stone dome. The family to whom it belonged had become impoverished, and had handed over this tomb as the only available asset to the banker to whom they owed a large sum of money. He wished to sell it, and so my Father bought it, but, making no use of the ground floor below which the tomb lay, built a suite of rooms in the verandah surrounding the central hall above, which he used as a dining-room. The building was octagonal in shape and consisted of my Father's bedroom and library, a drawing-room and my bedroom, a spare bedroom and dressing-room, a tiny room called an oratory, and two entrance halls, east and west, which were reached by flights of steps from the outside.

He was an excessively fastidious man, and very particular as to the habits of ladies. He could not bear to see them eat cheese, and as for eating mangoes and oranges he thought ladies ought to indulge in them only in the privacy of the bath-room. Many a time have I, with Colonel Richard Lawrence, taken a basket of oranges to the top of the Kutub Minar, two hundred and eighty-three feet high, to indulge in a feast in that seclusion, taking care to bring down all the peel, etc., with us, as nothing disorderly was allowed within the precincts of those beautiful ruins and buildings.

The Red Fort

[9] Shah Jahan builds a new city; from *Storia do Mogor* by Niccalao Manucci.

(Niccalao Manucci (1659?–1717?) was a Venetian who shipped to India aged fourteen in the service of 'an English gentleman in disguise called Lord Bellomont' – a refugee from Cromwell. As a 'doctor' (he claims to have invented the enema), he was close to several Mogul rulers.)

After the death of his beloved queen Tāj Mahal [*in 1629*], Shahjahan selected in Hindūstān the city of Dihlī in order to build there a new city as his capital, and thereby perpetuate his memory, the climate at that spot being healthy. He used the ruins of ancient Dihlī and Toquilabad (Tughlaqābād) for building this new Dihlī, to which he gave the name of Shāhjahānābād – that is to say, 'Built by Shāhjahān.'

He expended large sums in the construction of this city, and in the foundations he ordered several decapitated criminals to be placed as a sign of sacrifice. The said city is on the bank of the river Jamnah, in a large plain of great circumference, and it is in the shape of an imperfect half-moon. It has twelve gates, and ancient Dihlī forms a suburb, as also do several other villages.

The walls of the city are built one half of brick and the rest of stone. At every hundred paces is a strengthening bastion, but on these there is no artillery. The chief gates are the one leading to Āgrah and the one leading to Lāhor. Within the city are large and well-built *bāzārs*, where are sold things of every kind. The chief *bāzārs* are those that correspond with the streets leading to the fortress, and end with the two above-named gates. There are also in Dihlī fine palaces for the nobles; a great number of the other houses have thatched roofs, but are highly decorated and commodious inside. The city on the eastern side, along which the river Jamnah flows, has no wall. In one corner of the city, on the northern side, is the royal fortress, facing to the east. In front of it, between it and the river, is left a sufficient space for the elephant fights. The king sits at a window to look on, as likewise the women, but they are behind gratings. Thence also the king beholds the parades held on the same space, of the grandees, rajahs, and nobles. Beneath the royal balconies there is, night and day, a mad elephant kept, out of ostentation.

[10] 'Account of the founding of the splendid fort' (1639); from the *Shah Jahan-nama* of Inayat Khan in *The History of India as told by its own Historians* edited by Sir H.M. Elliot and J. Dowson.

The following is an exact account of the founding of the splendid fort in the above-named metropolis, with its edifices resembling Paradise, which was constructed in the environs of the city of Dehlí, on the banks of the river Jumna. It first occurred to the omniscient mind that he should select on the banks of the aforesaid river some pleasant site, distinguished by its genial climate, where he might found a splendid fort and delightful edifices, agreeably to the promptings of his generous heart, through which streams of water should be made to flow, and the terraces of which should overlook the river. When, after a long search, a piece of ground outside of the city of Dehlí, lying between the most distant suburbs and Núrgarh, commonly called Salímgarh, was fixed upon for this purpose, by the royal command, on the night of Friday, the 25th of Zí-l hijja, in the twelfth year of his auspicious reign, corresponding to 1048 AH, being the time appointed by the astrologers, the foundations were marked out with the usual ceremonies, according to the plan devised, in the august presence. Active labourers were then employed in digging the foundations, and on the night of Friday, the 9th of Muharram, of the year coinciding with 1049 AH (1639 AD), the foundation-stone of that noble structure was laid. Throughout the Imperial dominions, wherever artificers could be found, whether plain stone-cutters, ornamental sculptors, masons, or carpenters, by the mandate worthy of implicit obedience, they were all collected together, and multitudes of common labourers were employed in the work. It was ultimately completed on the 24th of Rabí'u-l awwal, in the twenty-first year of his reign, corresponding to 1058 AH, at an outlay of 60 *lacs* of rupees, after taking nine years three months and some days in building.

[11] 'The Court of the Great Mogul' in the seventeenth century; from *Indian Travels of Thévenot and Careri* edited by Surendranath Sen.

(Jean de Thévenot (1633–86) travelled widely in the Orient and spoke Turkish, Arabic and Persian.)

Here I should give a description of the inside of the Fort and Palace, and having begun with the two Elephants at the entry which carry two Warriours, speak of the Canal that enters into it; of the Streets that lead to the several Appartments; of the Officers and others who are upon the Parapets of these Streets of Duty; of the Portico's and stately Courts of Guard, where the *Mansepdars* and *Emirs* or *Omras* keep Guard; of the Halls where all sorts of Artisans, who have the Kings Pay work; of that great Court of the *Amcas* with its Arches, and the Consort that's made there; of the *Amcas* it self, that stately Hall adorn'd with thirty two Marble-Pillars, where the King (having all his Officers great and small standing before him, with their Hands a-cross their Breasts) gives every Day at noon Audience to all who have recourse to his Justice.

I should also describe that other Court, and Inner-hall where the Prince gives Audience to his Ministers, concerning the Affairs of his State, and Household, and where the *Omras* and other great Men repair every Evening to entertain the King in the Persian Language though they be of different Nations. In fine, all the particulars of the Palace ought to be described, without forgetting that stately Throne of Massive Gold with its Peacock, so much talked of in the *Indies*, which the Moguls say was begun by *Tamerlan*, though that be very unlikely: For to whom could King *Humayon* and his Father have entrusted it in the time of their disasters?

The two chief Streets of *Dehly* may be reckoned amongst the rarities of it, for they are wide, streight, and very long: They have Arches all along on both sides, which serve for Shops for those who have their Ware-house backwards. Over these Arches there is a Terras-walk to take the Air on when they come out of their Lodgings; and these Streets ending at the great Square and Castle, make the loveliest Prospect that can be seen in a Town. There is nothing else considerable in *Dehly*. The ordinary Houses are but of Earth and Canes; and the other Streets are so narrow, that they are altogether incommodious.

But that inconvenience seems to contribute somewhat to the Reputation of that Capital City of the Empire of the Mogul, for seeing there is an extraordinary croud in the Streets while the Court is there, the Indians are perswaded that it is the most populous City in the World; and nevertheless I have been told, that it appears to be a Desart when the King is absent. This will not seem strange if we consider, that the Court of the *Great Mogul* is very numerous, because the great Men of the Empire are almost all there, who have vast retinues, because their Servants cost them but little in Diet and Cloaths; that that Court is attended by above thirty five thousand Horse, and ten or twelve thousand Foot, which may be called an Army; and that every Souldier hath his Wife, Children and Servants, who for the most part are married also, and have a great many Children as well as their Masters. If to those we add all the drudges and rascally People which Courts and Armies commonly draw after them, and then the great number of Merchants and other Trading People, who are obliged to stick to them, because in that Countrey there is no Trade nor Money to be got but at Court. When I say, we consider *Dehly* void of all those I have mentioned, and of many more still, it will easily be believed, that that Town is no great matter when the King is not there; and if there have been four hundred thousand Men in it when he was there, there hardly remains the sixth part in his absence.

[12] The plan for the Peacock Throne; from the *Tabakat-i Akbari* of Nizam ud din Ahmad Bakshi in *The History of India as told by its own Historians* edited by Sir H.M. Elliot and J. Dowson.

In the course of years many valuable gems had come into the Imperial jewel-house, each one of which might serve as an ear-drop for Venus, or would adorn the girdle of the Sun. Upon the accession of the Emperor [*Shah Jahan*], it occurred to his mind that, in the opinion of far-seeing men, the acquisition of such rare jewels and the keeping of such wonderful brilliants can only render one service, that of adorning the throne of empire. They ought therefore, to be put to such a use, that beholders might share in and benefit by their splendour, and that Majesty might shine with increased brilliancy. It was accordingly ordered that, in addition to the jewels in the Imperial jewel-house, rubies, garnets, diamonds, rich pearls and emeralds, to the value of 200 *lacs* of rupees, should be brought for the inspection of the Emperor, and that they, with some exquisite jewels of great weight, exceeding 50,000 *miskáls*, and worth eighty-six *lacs* of rupees, having been carefully selected, should be handed over to Be-badal Khán, the superintendent of the goldsmith's department. There was also to be given to him one *lac* of *tolas* of pure gold, equal to 250,000 *miskáls* in weight and fourteen *lacs* of rupees in value. The throne was to be three *gaz* in length, two and a half in breadth, and five in height, and was to be set with the above-mentioned jewels. The outside of the canopy was to be of enamel work with occasional gems, the inside was to be thickly set with rubies, garnets, and other jewels, and it was to be supported by twelve emerald columns. On the top of each pillar there were to be two peacocks thick set with gems, and between each two peacocks a tree set with rubies and diamonds, emeralds and pearls. The ascent was to consist of three steps set with jewels of fine water. This throne was completed in the course of seven years at a cost of 100 *lacs* of rupees. Of the eleven jewelled recesses formed around it for cushions, the middle one, intended for the seat of the Emperor, cost ten *lacs* of rupees. Among the jewels set in this recess was a ruby worth a *lac* of rupees, which Sháh 'Abbás, the King of Írán, had presented to the late Emperor Jahángír, who sent it to his present Majesty, the Sáhib Kirán-i sání, when he accomplished the conquest of the Dakhin. On it were engraved the names of Sáhib-kirán (Tímúr), Mír Sháh Rukh, and Mirzá Ulugh Beg. When in course of time it came into the possession of Sháh 'Abbás, his name was added; and when Jahángir obtained it, he added the name of himself and of his father. Now it received the addition of the name of his most gracious Majesty Sháh Jahán. By command of the emperor, the following *masnawí*, by Hájí Muhammad Ján, the final verse of which contains the date, was placed upon the inside of the canopy in letters of green enamel.

[13] Daily life within the walls; from *Travels in the Mogul Empire (1659–67)* by François Bernier.

(Born in Anjou, François Bernier (1620–88) attached himself to the Mogul court as a doctor. This gave him useful insight into the

The Peacock Throne of Shah Jahan, carried off to Persia in 1739; from the Gentil Album, Faizabad, 1774

politics and mores of the time of Aurungzeb and Dara. He died of an apoplectic fit caused by 'some rude bantering'.)

After passing into the citadel . . . there is seen a long and spacious street, divided in the midst by a canal of running water. The street has a long divan, or raised way, on both sides, in the manner of the *Pont-neuf*, five or six feet high and four broad. Bordering the divan are closed arcades, which run up the whole way in the form of gates. It is upon this long divan that all the collectors of market-dues and other petty officers exercise their functions without being incommoded by the horses and people that pass in the street below. The *Mansebdars* or inferior *Omrahs* mount guard on this raised way during the night. The water of the canal runs into the *Seraglio*, divides and intersects every part, and then falls into the ditches of the fortification. This water is brought from the river *Gemna* by means of a canal opened at a distance of five or six leagues above *Dehly*, and cut with great labour through fields and rocky ground.

The other principal gate of the fortress also conducts to a long and tolerably wide street, which has a divan on both sides bordered by shops instead of arcades. Properly speaking, this street is a *bazar*, rendered very convenient in the summer and the rainy season by the long and high arched roof with which it is covered. Air and light are admitted by several large round apertures in the roof.

The citadel, which contains the *Mehalle* or *Seraglio*, and the other royal apartments of which I shall have occasion to speak hereafter, is round, or rather semicircular. It commands a prospect of the river, from which it is separated by a sandy space of considerable length and width. On these sands are exhibited the combats of elephants, and there the corps belonging to the *Omrahs* or lords, and those of the Rajas or *gentile* princes, pass in review before the Sovereign, who witnesses the spectacle from the windows of the palace. The walls of the citadel, as to their antique and round towers, resemble those of the city, but being partly of brick, and partly of a red stone which resembles marble, they have a better appearance. The walls of the fortress likewise excel those of the town in height, strength, and thickness, being capable of admitting small field-pieces, which are pointed toward the city. Except on the side of the river, the citadel is defended by a deep ditch faced with hewn stone, filled with water, and stocked with fish. Considerable as these works may appear, their real strength is by no means great, and in my opinion a battery of moderate force would soon level them with the ground.

Adjoining the ditch is a large garden, filled at all times with flowers and green shrubs, which, contrasted with the stupendous red walls, produce a beautiful effect.

Next to the garden is the great royal square, faced on one side by the gates of the fortress, and on the opposite side of which terminate the two most considerable streets of the city.

The tents of such *Rajas* as are in the King's pay, and whose weekly turn it is to mount guard, are pitched in this square; those petty sovereigns having an insuperable objection to be enclosed within walls. The guard within the fortress is mounted by the *Omrahs* and *Mansebdars.*

In this place also at break of day they exercise the royal horses, which are kept in a spacious stable not far distant; and here the *Kobat-kan,* or grand Muster-master of the cavalry, examines carefully the horses of those who have been received into the service. If they are found to be *Turki* horses, that is, from *Turkistan* or *Tartary,* and of a proper size and adequate strength, they are branded on the thigh with the King's mark and with the mark of the *Omrah* under whom the horseman is enlisted. This is well contrived, to prevent the loan of the same horses for different review days.

Here too is held a *bazar* or market for an endless variety of things; which like the *Pont-neuf* at *Paris,* is the rendezvous for all sorts of mountebanks and jugglers. Hither, likewise, the astrologers resort, both *Mahometan* and *Gentile.* These wise doctors remain seated in the sun, on a dusty piece of carpet, handling some old mathematical instruments, and having open before them a large book which represents the signs of the zodiac. In this way they attract the attention of the passengers, and impose upon the people, by whom they are considered as so many infallible oracles. They tell a poor person his fortune for a *payssa* (which is worth about one sol); and after examining the hand and face of the applicant, turning over the leaves of the large book, and pretending to make certain calculations, these impostors decide upon the *Sahet* or propitious moment of commencing the business he may have in hand. Silly women, wrapping themselves in a white cloth from head to foot, flock to the astrologers, whisper to them all the transactions of their lives, and disclose every secret with no more reserve than is practised by a scrupulous penitent in the presence of her confessor. The ignorant and infatuated people really believe that the stars have an influence which the astrologers can control.

There are, besides, many divans and tents in different parts of the fortress, which serve as offices for public business.

Large halls are seen in many places, called *Kar-kanays* or workshops for the artisans. In one hall embroiderers are busily employed, superintended by a master. In another you see the goldsmiths; in a third, painters; in a fourth, varnishers in lacquer-work; in a fifth, joiners, turners, tailors, and shoemakers; in a sixth, manufacturers of silk, brocade, and those fine muslins of which are made turbans, girdles with golden flowers, and drawers worn by females, so delicately fine as frequently to wear out in one night. This article of dress, which lasts only a few hours, may cost ten or twelve crowns, and even more, when beautifully embroidered with needlework.

The artisans repair every morning to their respective *Kar-kanays*, where they remain employed the whole day; and in the evening return to their homes. In this quiet and regular manner their time glides away; no one aspiring after any improvement in the condition of life wherein he happens to be born. The embroiderer brings up his son as an embroiderer, the son of a goldsmith becomes a goldsmith, and a physician of the city educates his son for a physician. No one marries but in his own trade or profession; and this custom is observed almost as rigidly by *Mahometans* as by the *Gentiles*, to whom it is expressly enjoined by their law. Many are the beautiful girls thus doomed to live singly, girls who might marry advantageously if their parents would connect them with a family less noble than their own.

I must not forget the *Am-Kas*, to which you at length arrive, after passing the places just mentioned. This is really a noble edifice: it consists of a large square court of arcades, not unlike our *Place Royale*, with this difference, however, that the arcades of the *Am-Kas* have no buildings over them. Each arcade is separated by a wall, yet in such a manner that there is a small door to pass from one to the other. Over the grand gate, situated in the middle of one side of this court, is a capacious divan, quite open on the side of the court, called the *Nagar-Kanay*. In this place, which thence derives its name, are kept the trumpets, or

Shah Jahan riding with one of his sons and an escort;
water-colour, Mogul, c. 1615

rather the hautboys and cymbals, which play in concert at certain hours of the day and night. To the ears of an *European* recently arrived, this music sounds very strangely, for there are ten or twelve hautboys, and as many cymbals, which play together. One of the hautboys, called *Karna*, is a fathom and a half in length, and its lower aperture cannot be less than a foot. The cymbals of brass or iron are some of them at least a fathom in diameter. You may judge, therefore, of the roaring sound which issues from the *Nagar-Kanay*. On my first arrival it stunned me so as to be insupportable: but such is the power of habit that this same noise is now heard by me with pleasure; in the night, particularly, when in bed and afar, on my terrace this music sounds in my ears as solemn, grand, and melodious. This is not altogether to be wondered at, since it is played by persons instructed from infancy in the rules of melody, and possessing the skill of modulating and turning the harsh sounds of the hautboy and cymbal so as to produce a symphony far from disagreeable when heard at a certain distance. The *Nagar-Kanay* is placed in an elevated situation, and remote from the royal apartments, that the King may not be annoyed by the proximity of this music.

Opposite to the grand gate, which supports the *Nagar-Kanay*, as you cross the court, is a large and magnificent hall, decorated with several rows of pillars, which, as well as the ceiling, are all painted and overlaid with gold. The hall is raised considerably from the ground, and very airy, being open on the three sides that look into the court. In the centre of the wall that separates the hall from the *Seraglio*, and higher from the floor than a man can reach, is a wide and lofty opening, or large window, where the Monarch every day, about noon, sits upon his throne, with some of his sons at his right and left; while eunuchs standing about the royal person flap away the flies with peacocks' tails, agitate the air with large fans, or wait with undivided attention and profound humility to perform the different services allotted to each. Immediately under the throne is an enclosure, surrounded by silver rails, in which are assembled the whole body of *Omrahs*, the *Rajas*, and the *Ambassadors*, all standing, their eyes bent downward, and their hands crossed. At a greater distance from the throne are the *Mansebdars* or inferior *Omrahs*, also standing in the same posture of profound reverence. The remainder of the spacious room, and indeed the whole courtyard, is filled with persons of all ranks, high and low, rich and poor; because it is in this extensive hall that the King gives audience indiscriminately to all his subjects: hence it is called *Am-Kas*, or audience-chamber of high and low.

During the hour and a half, or two hours, that this ceremony continues, a certain number of the royal horses pass before the throne, that the King may see whether they are well used and in a proper condition. The elephants come next, their filthy hides having been well washed and painted as black as ink, with two large red streaks from the top of the head down to the trunk, where they meet. The elephants are covered with embroidered cloth; a couple of silver bells are suspended to the two ends of a massive silver chain placed over their back, and white cow-tails from *Great Tibet*, of large value, hang from the ears like immense whiskers. Two small elephants, superbly caparisoned, walk close to these colossal creatures, like slaves appointed to their service. As if proud of his gorgeous attire and of the magnificence that surrounds him, every elephant moves with a solemn and dignified step; and when in front of the throne, the driver, who is seated on his shoulder, pricks him with a pointed iron, animates and speaks to him, until the animal bends one knee, lifts his trunk on high and roars aloud, which the people consider as the elephant's mode of performing the *taslim* or usual reverence.

Other animals are next introduced; – tame antelopes kept for the purpose of fighting with each other; *Nilgaux*, or grey oxen, that appear to me to be a species of elk; rhinoceroses; large *Bengale* buffaloes with prodigious horns which enable them to contend against lions and tigers; tame leopards, or panthers, employed in hunting antelopes; some of the fine sporting dogs from *Usbec*, of every kind, and each dog with a small red covering; lastly, every species of the birds of prey used in field sports for catching partridges, cranes, hares, and even, it is said, for hunting antelopes, on which they pounce with violence, beating their heads and blinding them with their wings and claws.

Besides this procession of animals, the cavalry of one or two *Omrahs* frequently pass in review before the King; the horsemen being better dressed than usual, the horses furnished with iron armour, and decorated with an endless variety of fantastic trappings.

The King takes pleasure also in having the blades of cutlasses tried on dead sheep, brought before him without the entrails and neatly bound up. Young *Omrahs*, *Mansebdars*, and *Gourze-berdars*, or mace-bearers, exercise their skill, and put forth all their strength to cut through the four feet, which are fastened together, and the body of the sheep at one blow.

But all these things are so many interludes to more serious matters. The King not only reviews his cavalry with peculiar attention, but there is not, since the war has been ended, a single trooper or other soldier whom he has not inspected, and made himself personally acquainted with, increasing or reducing the pay of some, and dismissing others from the service. All the petitions held up in the crowd assembled in the *Am-Kas* are brought to the King and read in his hearing; and the persons concerned being ordered to approach are examined by the Monarch himself, who often redresses on the spot the wrongs of the aggrieved party. On another day of the week he devotes two hours to hear in private the petitions of ten persons selected from the lower orders, and presented to the King by a good and rich old man. Nor does he fail to attend the justice-chamber, called *Adalet-Kanay*, on another day of the week, attended by the two principal *Kadis*, or chief justices. It is evident, therefore, that barbarous as we are apt to consider the sovereigns of *Asia*, they are not always unmindful of the justice that is due to their subjects.

What I have stated in the proceedings of the assembly of the *Am-Kas* appears sufficiently rational and even noble; but I must not conceal from you the base and disgusting adulation which is invariably witnessed there. Whenever a word escapes the lips of the King, if at all to the purpose, how trifling soever may be its import, it is immediately caught by the surrounding throng; and the chief *Omrahs*, extending their arms towards heaven, as if to receive some benediction, exclaim *Karamat! Karamat!* wonderful! wonderful! he has spoken wonders! Indeed there is no Mogol who does not know and does not glory in repeating this proverb in Persian verse:

Aguer chah ronzra Goyed cheb est in
Bubayed Gouft inck mah ou peruin.
[Should the King say that it is night at noon,
Be sure to cry, Behold, I see the moon!]

[14] Elephant fights below the Fort; from *Travels in the Mogul Empire (1659–67)* by François Bernier.

The festivals generally conclude with an amusement unknown in *Europe* – a combat between two elephants; which takes place in the presence of all the people on the sandy space near the river: the King, the principal ladies of the court, and the *Omrahs* viewing the spectacle from different apartments in the fortress.

A wall of earth is raised three or four feet wide and five or six high. The two ponderous beasts meet one another face to face, on opposite sides of the wall, each having a couple of riders, that the place of the man who sits on the shoulders, for the purpose of guiding the elephant with a large iron hook, may immediately be supplied if he should be thrown down. The riders animate the elephants either by soothing words, or by chiding them as cowards, and urge them on with their heels, until the poor creatures approach the wall and are brought to the attack. The shock is tremendous, and it appears surprising that they ever survive the dreadful wounds and blows inflicted with their teeth, their heads, and their trunks. There are frequent pauses during the fight; it is suspended and renewed; and the mud wall being at length thrown down, the stronger or more courageous elephant passes on and attacks his opponent, and, putting him to flight, pursues and fastens upon him with so much obstinacy, that the animals can be separated only by means of fireworks, which are made to explode between them; for they are naturally timid, and have a particular dread of fire, which is the reason why elephants have been used with so very little advantage in armies since the use of fire-arms. The boldest come from *Ceylon*, but none are employed in war which have not been regularly trained, and accustomed for years to the discharge of muskets close to their heads, and the bursting of crackers between their legs.

[15] Various ambassadors bearing gifts; from *Travels in the Mogul Empire (1659–67)* by François Bernier.

The Uzbeks
The war being ended, the *Tartars* of *Usbec* eagerly despatched ambassadors to *Aureng-Zebe*. Whether they dreaded his just resentment, or hoped, in their inbred avarice and sordidness, to

obtain some considerable present, the two *Kans* sent ambassadors, with a proffer of their services, and with injunctions to
perform the ceremony of the *Mobarek*: that is, to express in a
solemn manner their wishes that his reign might be long and
auspicious. *Aureng-Zebe* knew how to value an offer of service
made at the conclusion of a war: he knew the fear of punishment,
or the expectation of advantage, had induced the *Kans* to send
their ambassadors. They were received, however, with due form
and politeness, and as I happened to be present at the audience, I
can relate the particulars with accuracy.

The ambassadors, when at a distance, made the *Salam*, or
Indian act of obeisance, placing the hand thrice upon the head,
and as often dropping it down to the ground. They then
approached so near that *Aureng-Zebe* might easily have taken the
letters from their own hands; but this ceremony was performed
by an *Omrah*: the letters were received and opened by him, and
then presented to the King, who, after having perused the
contents with a grave countenance, commanded that there
should be given to each of the ambassadors a *Ser-apah* or vesture
from head to foot; namely, a vest of brocade, a turban, and sash
or girdle, of embroidered silk. This done, the presents from the
Kans were brought before the King, consisting of some boxes of
Lapis-lazuli or the choicest *Azure*; a few long-haired camels;
several horses of great beauty, although the *Tartar* horses are
generally something better than merely beautiful: some camel-
loads of fresh fruit, such as apples, pears, grapes, and melons;
Usbec being the country which principally supplies *Dehli* with
these fruits, which are there eaten all the winter, and many loads
of dry fruit, as *Bokara* prunes, apricots, *kichmiches*, or raisins,
apparently without stones, and two other kinds of raisins, black
and white, extremely large and delicious.

Aureng-Zebe expressed himself well pleased with the liberality
of the *Kans*; extolling in exaggerated strains the beauty and
rareness of the fruits, horses, and camels; and when he had
spoken a few words on the fertility of their country, and asked
two or three questions concerning the College at *Samarcande*, he
desired the ambassadors to go and repose themselves, intimating
that he should be happy to see them often.

These people remained more than four months at *Dehli*,
notwithstanding all their endeavours to obtain their *congé*. This
long detention proved extremely injurious to their health; they

and their suite sickened, and many of them died. It is doubtful whether they suffered more from the heat of *Hindoustan*, to which they are unaccustomed, or from the filthiness of their persons, and the insufficiency of their diet. There are probably no people more narrowminded, sordid, or uncleanly, than the *Usbec Tartars*.

During their stay I paid them three visits, having been introduced as a physician by one of my friends, the son of an *Usbec*, who has amassed a fortune at this court. It was my design to collect such useful particulars concerning their country as they might be able to supply, but I found them ignorant beyond all conception. They were unacquainted even with the boundaries of *Usbec*, and could give no information respecting the *Tartars* who a few years ago subjugated *China*. In short, I could elicit by my conversation with the ambassadors scarcely one new fact. Once I was desirous of dining with them, and as they were persons of very little ceremony, I did not find it difficult to be admitted at their table. The meal appeared to me very strange; it consisted only of horseflesh. I contrived, however, to dine. There was a *ragoût* which I thought eatable, and I should have considered myself guilty of a breach of good manners if I had not praised a dish so pleasing to their palate. Not a word was uttered during dinner; my elegant hosts were fully employed in cramming their mouths with as much *pelau* as they could contain; for with the use of spoons these people are unacquainted. But when their stomachs were sated with the dainty repast, they recovered their speech, and would fain have persuaded me that the *Usbecs* surpass all other men in bodily strength, and that no nation equals them in the dexterous management of the bow. This observation was no sooner made than they called for bows and arrows, which were of a much larger size than those of *Hindoustan*, and offered to lay a wager that they would pierce an ox or a horse through and through. They proceeded to extol the strength and valour of their country-women, in comparison with whom the *Amazons* were soft and timorous.

The Persians

On his entry into the capital, the ambassador was received with every demonstration of respect. The *Bazars* through which he passed were all newly decorated, and the cavalry lining both sides of the way extended beyond a league. Many *Omrahs*, accompanied with instruments of music, attended the procession, and a salute of artillery was fired upon his entering the gate of the fortress, or royal palace. *Aureng-Zebe* welcomed him with the greatest politeness; manifested no displeasure at his making the *salam* in the *Persian* manner, and unhesitatingly received from his hands the letters of which he was the bearer; raising them, in token of peculiar respect, nearly to the crown of his head. An eunuch having assisted him to unseal the letters, the King perused the contents with a serious and solemn countenance, and then commanded that the ambassador should be clad, in his presence, with a vest of brocade, a turban, and a silken sash, embroidered with gold and silver, called a *serapah*, as I have before explained. This part of the ceremony over, the *Persian* was informed that the moment was come for the display of his presents; which consisted of five-and-twenty horses, as beautiful as I ever beheld, with housings of embroidered brocade; twenty highly bred camels, that might have been mistaken for small elephants, such was their size and strength; a considerable number of cases containing excellent rosewater, and another sort of distilled water called *Beidmichk*, a cordial held in the highest estimation and very scarce; five or six carpets of extraordinary size and beauty; a few pieces of brocade extremely rich, wrought in small flowers, in so fine and delicate a style that I doubt if anything so elegant was ever seen in *Europe*; four *Damascus* cutlasses, and the same number of poniards, the whole covered with precious stones; and lastly, five or six sets of horse-furniture, which were particularly admired. The last were indeed very handsome and of superior richness; ornamented with superb embroidery and with small pearls, and very beautiful turquoises, of the old rock.

It was remarked that *Aureng-Zebe* seemed unusually pleased with this splendid present; he examined every item minutely, noticed its elegance and rarity, and frequently extolled the munificence of the King of *Persia*. He assigned the ambassador a place among the principal *Omrahs*; and after speaking about his long and fatiguing journey, and several times expressing his desire to see him every day, he dismissed him.

The Dutch

About the time when Aurangzeb recovered his health [1662] there arrived at Delhi an ambassador from the Dutch called

Adrian to offer congratulations on the king's accession. This man was of sound judgment and thoroughly acquainted with the Mogul customs, having been for a long time at the head of the Dutch factory at Surat. Since he knew that those who bring the largest present and the heaviest purse are the most acceptable, the best received, and the soonest attended to, he brought a present for the king. It consisted in a large quantity of very fine scarlet broadcloth, much fine green cloth, some large mirrors, many earthenware dishes, bric-à-brac from China and Japan, and a small throne in appearance like a litter, a piece of Japanese work with many pleasing paintings. For the ministers there was a large sum in gold and silver, with different kinds of cloth and other bric-à-brac. As soon as he arrived he began to set forth to the ministers what he desired. Thus in a few days leave was granted to him to be presented to the king, on condition of making obeisance first in the European, and then in the Indian manner.

Next Aurangzeb ordered the present to be brought, and above everything else he prized the throne, and, as it was ornamented, he had it covered with glass to preserve the pictures from the great dust, and until this day he makes use of it. Then he sent to say to the ambassador that he might withdraw, and he would soon receive his leave to depart. But the ambassador knew the vaingloriousness of the Moguls, who hold it a point of honour to keep ambassadors dancing attendance upon them. They like to have a foreign ambassador always attending at the court audiences. For this reason he sent more gifts to the ministers, and succeeded in obtaining leave to go after four months.

[16] Sir Thomas Roe, the English ambassador, complains to the East India Company in 1616; from *The Embassy of Sir Thomas Roe to India* edited by William Foster.

(Sir Thomas Roe (1580–1644) went to the court of Jahangir as representative of the East India Company and as ambassador for James I to impress upon the Mogul the greatness of his master and the might of his fleet. Jahangir seems to have appreciated his company but was unimpressed by his credentials.)

The Presentes (for the Mogull) you have this yeare sent are extreamly despised by those who have seene them; the lyining of

the Coach and Cover of the Virginalls scorned, beeing velvett of
these parts and faded to a base Tawny; the knives little and
meane, soe that I am enforced to furnish the Case of my own
store; the burning glasses and prospectives (telescopes) such as
no man hath face to offer to give, much less to sell, such as I can
buy for sixe peence a piece; your pictures are not woorth one
Penny, and finally such error in the chooyce of all things, as I
think no man ever heard of the Place that was of Councell.

[17] The *seraglio* from under a shawl; from *Travels in the
Mogul Empire (1659–67)* by François Bernier.

It would afford me pleasure to conduct you to the *Seraglio*, as I
have introduced you into other parts of the fortress. But who is
the traveller that can describe from ocular observation the
interior of that building? I have sometimes gone into it when the
King was absent from *Dehli*, and once pretty far I thought, for
the purpose of giving my professional advice in the case of a great
lady so extremely ill that she could not be moved to the outward
gate, according to the customs observed upon similar occasions;
but a *Kachemire* shawl covered my head, hanging like a large scarf
down to my feet, and an eunuch led me by the hand, as if I had
been a blind man. You must be content, therefore, with such a
general description as I have received from some of the eunuchs.
They inform me that the *Seraglio* contains beautiful apartments,
separated, and more or less spacious and splendid, according to
the rank and income of the females. Nearly every chamber has its
reservoir of running water at the door; on every side are gardens,
delightful alleys, shady retreats, streams, fountains, grottoes,
deep excavations that afford shelter from the sun by day, lofty
divans and terraces, on which to sleep coolly at night. Within the
walls of this enchanting place, in fine, no oppressive or
inconvenient heat is felt. The eunuchs speak with extravagant
praise of a small tower, facing the river, which is covered with
plates of gold, in the same manner as the two towers of *Agra*; and
its apartments are decorated with gold and azure exquisite
paintings and magnificent mirrors.

[18] Lascivious ladies in the seventeenth century; from *Storia do Mogor* by Niccalao Manucci.

There are also at the doors women, ordinarily natives of Kashmīr, who are employed to carry away and to bring back anything that may be necessary; these women do not veil themselves to anybody. The chief doors of the *mahal* are closed at sunset, and the principal door of all is guarded by good sentinels posted for the purpose, and a seal is attached. Torches are kept burning all night. Each of the ladies has a clock, and a scribe who is obliged to report to the *názir* all that comes in or goes out, and everything that happens.

When a physician enters, he is conducted by the eunuchs with his head and body covered as far down as the waist, and he is taken out again in the same way. All the nobles exercise the same exact supervision of their women that the king does. The reason is that Mahomedans are most extraordinarily distrustful upon this chapter; and what deserves mention is that some do not even trust their own brothers, and do not permit their women to appear before them, being jealous of them. Thus the women, being shut up with this closeness and constantly watched, and having neither liberty nor occupation, think of nothing but adorning themselves, and their minds dwell on nothing but malice and lewdness. Confession of this was made to me once by one of these ladies herself.

It was the wife of Asad Khān, the *wāzīr*; her name was Naval Bāe, and she told me that her only thoughts were to imagine something by which she could please her husband and hinder his going near other women. From this I can assert that they are all the same. If they have any other thought, it is to regale themselves with quantities of delicious stews; to adorn themselves magnificently, either with clothes or jewellery, pearls, *et cetera*; to perfume their bodies with odours and essences of every kind. To this must be added that they have permission to enjoy the pleasure of the comedy and the dance, to listen to tales and stories of love, to recline upon beds of flowers, to walk about in gardens, to listen to the murmur of the running waters, to hear singing, and other similar pastimes.

There are some who from time to time affect the invalid, simply that they may have the chance of some conversation with, and have their pulse felt by, the physician who comes to see them.

The latter stretches out his hand inside the curtain; they lay hold of it, kiss it, and softly bite it. Some, out of curiosity, apply it to their breast, which has happened to me several times; but I pretended not to notice, in order to conceal what was passing from the matrons and eunuchs then present, and not arouse their suspicions.

[19] The blinding of Shah Alam, 1788; from *Fall of the Mughal Empire* by Sir Jadunath Sarkar.

(Sir Jadunath Sarkar (1870–1958) was founder member of the Indian Historical Records Association and Vice-Chancellor of Calcutta University (1926–8).)

The deposed monarch was pressed to divulge his treasure hoards. When he replied that [*he*] had nothing more beyond what had been already found in the treasury and stores, he was threatened and insulted. Ghulām Qādir sat down by his side, passed his arm familiarly round his neck and blew his tobacco smoke into his sovereign's face! Then the unhappy king was kept seated in the sun, without food or drink.

On being urged again and again to disclose the hiding place of his wealth, Shah Alam at last replied in bitterness, 'What I possessed, you have already found in the store-rooms. Have I kept anything hidden in my belly?' The Ruhela's retort was, 'May be your belly will have to be ripped open'. On 10th October, in a frenzy of vindictiveness and avarice, Ghulām Qādir had needles driven through the eyes of Shah Alam. Next day, in unimaginable brutality, he called for the Court-painter and bade him draw a picture of himself as he knelt on his half-dead master's bosom and carved out one eye-ball with his dagger, while the other eye was extracted by Qandahārī Khan. The wounded old man was left for days together without a drop of water; three valets were killed and two water-carriers were wounded by Ghulām Qādir with his sword, in order to deter others from relieving the royal distress in secret.

The maid-servants of the palace were subjected to inhuman and disgusting tortures, and the eunuchs were beaten to death to make them confess where the fort treasure lay buried. The screw was next put on the princes and princesses; all members of the royal family were kept without food or drink for three or four days, till many of the children and old ladies sank into death and one wife of the new Emperor died from utter terror. Two ex-Empresses died of privation, and one of them was by the Ruhela's order left unburied for three days until the stench became unbearable. Maniyār Singh reported that in two days 21 princes and princesses had died and others were in a dying condition.

[20] Nineteen-year-old Thomas Twining visits Shah Alam; from *Travels in India a Hundred Years Ago* by Thomas Twining.

(Thomas Twining, a member of the East India company's civil service, was entrusted with the delivery of a friendly message from the British Commander-in-Chief, Bengal, to Shah Alam in 1794.)

A few steps farther brought me to the edge of the carpet, and near the extremity of the first line of persons sitting. Here, looking over the line towards the persons standing in the colonnade, I had a glimpse of the Padshah – at least of the upper part of his person. His Majesty seemed to be sitting before the persons standing. As this was a stolen glance, I did not bow, nor take any particular notice of him. At the edge of the carpet I took off my sandals, and leaving Sind Razy Khan and the moonshy, advanced alone a little beyond the first line of persons sitting, and turning to my right, when half way between the two lines I saw the Emperor immediately before me at the farther extremity of the lines. He was sitting, with his face towards the terrace, upon a low tukkt or throne, covered with crimson velvet or silk, and was surrounded by numerous persons standing, some behind him in the divan, others along the corridor on each side.

In conformity with the lesson I had received, I now made three low salaams, bending slowly forwards and almost touching the carpet each time with my right hand, and then raising it to my forehead. I here cast a deliberate look around me, when I perceived that curiosity was not on my side alone, for all eyes were fixed upon me. I observed also that the extremities of the lines near me were composed of very young men, and that the rows *mounted* gradually towards the other end near the throne, being there formed of persons considerably older. All were princes of the imperial family, sons and grandsons of Shah Allum, the reigning emperor. Their numbers, I understood, exceeded forty. I now advanced very slowly forward five or six paces between the lines, and then stopped and made three more profound salaams, after which I retreated backwards to where I had stood at first. Here I made three low bows as before, and then advanced slowly, followed by Sind Razy Khan and the moonshy, till I came close to the aged monarch, who sat erect in the oriental fashion. Large cushions of silk lay on each side of him and behind him, but he did not seem to rest upon them.

Though seventy-one years of age, he looked the tallest and stoutest of all present. Though prepared to see him blind, as he was, the appearance of the Great Mogol upon his throne in such a situation was an extraordinary and most distressing spectacle, especially as his affliction did not proceed from accident, nor arise in the course of nature, but resulted from an act of most inhuman barbarity committed by one of his subjects. There was, however, nothing repulsive in the Emperor's appearance, nothing being perceptible but a depression of the eyelids.

[21] King (Akbar II) takes Bishop (Heber); from *Narrative of a Journey through the Upper Provinces of India* . . . by Bishop Reginald Heber.

(Reginald Heber (1783–1826) was Bishop of Calcutta. He wrote a popular account of a tour of his extensive see, which covered all of British India. Southey commemorated his death at Trichnopoly in mournful verse.)

The 31st *December* was fixed for my presentation to the Emperor, which was appointed for half-past eight in the morning. Lushington and a Captain Wade also chose to take the same opportunity. At eight I went, accompanied by Mr. Elliott, with nearly the same formalities as at Lucknow, except that we were on elephants instead of in palanquins, and that the procession was, perhaps, less splendid, and the beggars both less numerous and far less vociferous and importunate. We were received with presented arms by the troops of the palace drawn up within the barbican, and proceeded, still on our elephants, through the noblest gateway and vestibule which I ever saw. It consists, not merely of a splendid gothic arch in the centre of the great gate-tower, – but, after that, of a long vaulted aisle, like that of a gothic cathedral, with a small, open, octagonal court in its centre, all of granite, and all finely carved with inscriptions from the Koran, and with flowers. This ended in a ruinous and exceedingly dirty stable-yard! where we were received by Captain Grant, as the Mogul's officer on guard, and by a number of elderly men with large gold-headed canes, the usual ensign of office here, and one of which Mr. Elliott also carried. We were now told to dismount and proceed on foot, a task which the late rain made inconvenient to my gown and cassock, and thin shoes, and during which we were pestered by a fresh swarm of miserable beggars, the wives and children of the stable servants. After this we passed another richly-carved, but ruinous and dirty gateway, where our guides, withdrawing a canvas screen, called out, in a sort of harsh chaunt, 'Lo, the ornament of the world! Lo, the asylum of the nations! King of Kings! The Emperor Acbar Shah! Just, fortunate, victorious!' We saw, in fact, a very handsome and striking court, about as big as that at All Souls, with low, but richly-ornamented buildings. Opposite to us was a beautiful open pavilion of white marble, richly carved, flanked by rose-bushes and fountains, and some tapestry and striped curtains hanging in festoons about it, within which was a crowd of people, and the poor old descendant of Tamerlane seated in the midst of them. Mr. Elliott here bowed three times very low, in which we followed his example. This ceremony was repeated twice as we advanced up the steps of the pavilion, the heralds each time repeating the same expressions about their master's greatness. We then stood in a row on the right-hand side of the throne, which is a sort of marble bedstead richly ornamented with gilding, and raised on two or three steps. Mr. Elliott then stepped forwards, and, with joined hands, in the usual eastern way, announced, in a low voice, to the Emperor, who I was. I then advanced, bowed three times again, and offered a nuzzur of fifty-one gold mohurs in an embroidered purse, laid on my handkerchief, in the way practised by the Baboos in Calcutta. This was received and laid on one side, and I remained standing for a few minutes, while the usual court questions about my health, my travels, when I left Calcutta, &c.

were asked. I had thus an opportunity of seeing the old gentleman more plainly. He has a pale, thin, but handsome face, with an aquiline nose, and a long white beard. His complexion is little if at all darker than that of an European. His hands are very fair and delicate, and he had some valueable-looking rings on them. His hands and face were all I saw of him, for the morning being cold, he was so wrapped up in shawls, that he reminded me extremely of the Druid's head on a Welch halfpenny. I then stepped back to my former place, and returned again with five more mohurs to make my offering to the heir apparent, who stood at his father's left hand, the right being occupied by the Resident. Next, my two companions were introduced with nearly the same forms, except that their offerings were less, and that the Emperor did not speak to them. [*See picture on p 105*].

The Emperor then beckoned to me to come forwards, and Mr. Elliott told me to take off my hat, which had till now remained on my head, on which the Emperor tied a flimsy turban of brocade round my head with his own hands, for which, however, I paid four gold mohurs more. We were then directed to retire to receive the 'Khelâts' (honorary dresses) which the bounty of 'the Asylum of the World' had provided for us. I was accordingly taken into a small private room, adjoining the Zennanah, where I found a handsome flowered caftan edged with fur, and a pair of common-looking shawls, which my servants, who had the delight of witnessing all this fine show, put on instead of my gown, my cassock remaining as before. In this strange dress I had to walk back again, having my name announced by the criers (something in the same way that Lord Marmion's was) as 'Bahadur, Boozoony, Dowlut-mund,' &c. to the presence, where I found my two companions who had not been honoured by a private dressing-room, but had their Khelâts put on them in the gateway of the court. They were, I apprehend, still queerer figures than I was, having their hats wrapped with scarfs of flowered gauze, and a strange garment of gauze, tinsel, and faded ribbands flung over their shoulders above their coats. I now again came forward and offered my third present to the Emperor, being a copy of the Arabic Bible and the Hindoostanee Common Prayer, handsomely bound in blue velvet laced with gold, and wrapped up in a piece of brocade. He then motioned to me to stoop, and put a string of pearls round my neck, and two glittering but not costly ornaments in the front of my turban, for which I again offered five gold mohurs. It was, lastly, announced that a horse was waiting for my acceptance, at which fresh instance of imperial munificence the heralds again made a proclamation of largesse, and I again paid five gold mohurs. It ended by my taking my leave with three times three salams, making up, I think, the sum of about threescore, and I retired with Mr. Elliott to my dressing-room, whence I sent to her Majesty the *Queen*, as she is generally called, though Empress would be the ancient and more proper title, a present of five mohurs more, and the Emperor's chobdars came eagerly up to know when they should attend to receive their bukshish. It must not, however, be supposed that this interchange of civilities was very expensive either to his Majesty or to me. All the presents which he gave, the horse included, though really the handsomest which had been seen at the court of Delhi for many years, and though the old gentleman evidently intended to be extremely civil, were not worth much more than 300 s. rupees, so that he and his family gained at least 800 s. rupees by the morning's work, besides what he received from my two companions, which was all clear gain, since the Khelâts which they got in return were only fit for May-day, and made up, I fancy, from the cast-off of the Begum.

[22] The palace – 'a melancholy sight' – in the 1830s; from *Up the Country . . .* by Emily Eden.

It is a melancholy sight – so magnificent originally, and so poverty-stricken now. The marble hall where the king sits is still very beautiful, all inlaid with garlands and birds of precious stones, and the inscription on the cornice is what Moore would like to see in the original: 'If there be an Elysium on earth, it is this, it is this!'

The lattices look out on a garden which leads down to the Jumna, and the old king was sitting in the garden with a chowrybadar waving the flies from him; but the garden is all gone to decay too, and 'the Light of the World' had a forlorn and darkened look. All our servants were in a state of profound veneration; the natives all look upon the King of Delhi as their rightful lord, and so he is, I suppose. In some of the pavilions belonging to the princes there were such beautiful inlaid floors, any square of which would have made an enviable table for a palace in London, but the stones are constantly stolen; and in some of the finest baths there were dirty charpoys spread, with dirtier guards sleeping on them. In short, Delhi is a very suggestive and moralising place – such stupendous remains of power and wealth passed and passing away – and somehow I feel that we horrid English have just 'gone and done it,' merchandised it, revenued it, and spoiled it all.

[23] A king in his own palace; from *A Visit to India, China and Japan in the year 1853* by Bayard Taylor.

(Born in Pennsylvania, Bayard Taylor (1825–78) was told at the age of fourteen by an itinerant phrenologist that he would be 'a traveller and a poet'. He lived up to this forecast by translating Goethe's *Faust* in the original metre and travelling widely in India, China and Japan. It was said that 'the brilliance of his life for many years deluded men as to the mediocrity of his actual achievement'.)

Akbar II has reigned in this little dominion since 1805 and is now upward of eighty years of age. He was the last of the line, but having four sons, the succession will be continued. He devotes his time to literature, amusements and sensuality. The Mussulmen speak highly of his literary acquirements, and his poems in the Persian language are said by those who have read them to possess considerable merit. There is a Court newspaper, entitled *The Lamp of News*, published within the palace, but its columns are entirely devoted to the gossip of the city, and private scandal. Until recently the law administered within the palace bore a resemblance to the bloody rule of former days. Persons who had incurred the royal displeasure had their hands, ears or noses cut off, and were then thrust out of the gates. Finally the English Resident at the Court hinted to his Majesty that these things were very disagreeable and ought to cease. 'What!' said the descendant of Tamerlane; 'am I not King in my own palace?' 'Undoubtedly,' blandly replied the Resident; 'your Highness is the Conqueror of the World and the Protector of Princes; but such a course is not pleasing to the Governor-General, and it would be a great evil to the world if the friendship of two such

The Red Fort at Delhi – the Lahore Gate;
from the *Illustrated London News* in 1857

mighty and illustrious Sovereigns were to be interrupted!' The
forms of respect to the phantom of the old authority being thus
preserved, the Emperor instituted a milder regimen.

[24] 'A den of iniquity'; from the *Journal* of Lady (Emily)
Bayley in *The Golden Calm* edited by M.M. Kaye.

A fine broad road led to the King's Palace, which was
surrounded by another magnificent wall of cut red sandstone,
with a battlemented top, and approached by a superb gateway
at which always stood a guard of native soldiers. High above this
gateway and approached by a long flight of steps were the rooms
assigned to the Assistant Resident, my Father's immediate
subordinate, who was supposed to keep a kind of surveillance
over the Palace and to be at hand if the King wished to make any
urgent communication to him. But alas! the proximity to the
Palace was the cause of the murder of all the inhabitants of those
rooms on May 11th 1857. On that day Captain Douglas, and my
friend the Rev Mr Jennings and his daughter Margaret, who
had been brought up with me at Belstead, and Miss Clifford,
another visitor, were all murdered while sitting at breakfast in

those rooms; and when I went there early in 1859 the splashes of blood were still on the walls.

The Palace itself covered an enormous space of ground; in fact it was quite a town in itself, thronged with thousands of natives, hangers-on of an oriental court.

Separated from the city by this great wall, it was open to the river all along one side of it, where sublimely beautiful buildings were erected, intermixed with gardens. Here were all the apartments devoted to the King of Delhi's harem, exquisite buildings of white marble, many of them inlaid with beautiful mosaics of different coloured stones, in the style of the Taj. Here also was the wonderful 'Hall of Audience', the Dewan-i-Khas, than which a more beautiful building does not exist in the world. No picture can give an adequate idea of it, for in design, proportion, material and finish, it was faultless.

Floored and built entirely, inside and out, of polished white marble, it stood on a white marble terrace overlooking the river, and was a noble building, open on three sides and formed of exquisite arches, all inlaid with mosaics of cornelians and precious stones, with tracery in pure gold marking out the panels in different designs. It was erected for a Hall of Audience, where the great Moghuls of Delhi used to receive their subjects on state occasions. There was a great block of crystal at one end of the hall on which the famous Peacock Throne once stood – the golden chair of state from which rose a magnificent ornament representing the feathers of an outspread peacock's tail, every feather being encrusted with precious stones of enormous value, the Koh-i-noor being one of them.

Of course I never saw this Peacock Throne, as it had been looted by Nadir Shah in 1739. But the block of crystal remained, on the top of which luxurious cushions of cloth of gold used to be spread for the King to sit on when receiving his subjects. In four of the panels above the arches and just below the ceiling, which was of white marble inlaid with gold, were beautifully engraved Persian words inlaid in gold, the translation of which was: *If there be a Paradise upon Earth, It is this, it is this, it is this*. This inscription suggested to Thomas Moore the lines in 'Lalla Rookh'.

There was another Hall of Audience in the centre of the Palace, which was used for ordinary occasions, when the King sat to give judgement or hear petitions. This was not nearly so beautiful in the materials used, although the architecture was in the same style, and on these occasions the King sat in a kind of opera box, large enough to hold him and a few of his attendants. In the walls of this opera box were some beautiful Italian mosaics in the Florentine style, executed by Italians in the seventeenth century. They consisted principally of different kinds of birds and flowers, but one larger one about a foot high represented Orpheus with his lute playing to animals at his feet. These mosaics of course belonged strictly to the Government, but this large one was taken out of the wall as loot by an officer commanding one of the English regiments, and afterwards *sold* as his private property to the India Office in London, who deposited it in the South Kensington Museum.

One of the most beautiful buildings in the Palace, indeed in all India, was the Pearl Mosque, a small white marble mosque erected for and used by the ladies of the King's household. The entire mosque and courtyard and surrounding walls were all of beautiful white marble, highly polished, and the mosque itself had all its arches and interior inlaid with gold tracery, and was crowned with three beautifully shaped domes covered with plates of pure gold. It was a perfect gem of art and beauty. But these plates of gold were removed after the siege and sold for prize money for the benefit of the army.

Up to the time of the Mutiny, the King had entire control of and jurisdiction within the walls of the Palace; and any criminal or ruffian could secure an asylum there and could never be found if wanted. Hence it was really a den of thieves and murderers and criminals of all classes, a source of never-ending difficulty and annoyance to the British Government, and arrangements had been made to completely alter this state of things at the death of the King of Delhi. But the Mutiny did this for us, in that it cleared out this den of iniquity, as everyone fled from the Palace when our soldiers entered it, and thousands were killed.

The bathing establishments for both the King and the ladies of his family were all of white marble, the walls being inlaid with the same beautiful mosaics.

The Dewan-i-Khas, or Hall of Audience which I have just described, was screened from the King's private apartments by means of white marble so elaborately pierced that its traceries appeared just like lacework. Behind this hung curtains of richest silks to ensure privacy, but which allowed the old Queen to hear everything that was going on in the public audiences.

Outside the arches there were curtains of brilliant red cloth, which could be either raised or lowered according to the weather.

This superb building still exists, as fortunately it was not materially injured in the siege, but many of the mosaics were thoughtlessly spoilt by the soldiers with their bayonets, when it was taken possession of after the siege, and used as a church by the regiments occupying the Palace.

[25] Romance in the Red Fort; from *Shame* by Salman Rushdie.

In Delhi, in the days before partition, the authorities rounded up any Muslims, for their own safety, it was said, and locked them up in the red fortress, away from the wrath of the stone-washers. Whole families were sealed up there, grandmothers, young children, wicked uncles . . . including members of my own family. It's easy to imagine that as my relatives moved through the Red Fort in the parallel universe of history, they might have felt some hint of the fictional presence of Bilquìs Kemal, rushing cut and naked past them like a ghost . . . or vice versa. Yes. Or vice versa.

The tide of human beings carried Bilquìs along as far as the large, low, ornately rectangular pavilion that had once been an emperor's hall of public audience; and in that echoing *diwan*, overwhelmed by the humiliation of her undress, she passed out. In that generation many women, ordinary decent respectable ladies of the type to whom nothing ever happens, to whom nothing is supposed to happen except marriage children death, had this sort of strange story to tell. It was a rich time for stories, if you lived to tell your tale.

Shortly before the scandalous marriage of her younger daughter, Good News Hyder, Bilquìs told the girl the story of her meeting with her husband. 'When I woke up,' she said, 'it was daytime and I was wrapped in an officer's coat. But whose do you think, goof, of course his, your own father Raza's; what to tell you, he saw me lying there, with all my goods on display in the window, you know, and I suppose the bold fellow just liked what there was to see.' Good News went *haa!* and *tch tch!*, feigning shock at her mother's sauciness, and Bilquìs said shyly: 'Such encounters were not uncommon then.' Good News dutifully replied, 'Well, Amma, as for his being impressed, I'm not one bit surprised.'

One last detail. It was said of Captain Hyder that he did not sleep for four hundred and twenty hours after the Muslims were gathered in the red fortress, which would explain the black pouches under his eyes. These pouches would grow blacker and baggier as his power increased, until he no longer needed to wear sunglasses the way the other top brass did, because he looked like he had a pair on anyway, all the time, even in bed. The future General Hyder: Razzoo, Raz-Matazz, Old Razor Guts himself! How could Bilquìs have resisted such a one? She was conquered in double-quick time.

During their days in the fort, the pouch-eyed Captain visited Bilquìs regularly, always bringing with him some item of clothing or beautification: blouses, saris, sandals, eyebrow pencils with which to replace the lost hairs, brassières, lipsticks were showered on her. Saturation bombing techniques are designed to force an early surrender . . . when her wardrobe had grown large enough to permit the removal of the military overcoat, she paraded for him in the hall. 'Come to think of it,' Bilquìs told Good News, 'maybe that was when he made that dressing-up remark.' Because she remembered how she had replied: lowering her eyes in the elite actressy manner which her father had once praised, she said sadly, 'But what husband could I, without hope of dowry, ever find? Certainly not such a generous Captain who outfits strange ladies like queens.'

Raza and Bilquìs were betrothed beneath the bitter eyes of the dispossessed multitudes; and afterwards the gifts continued, sweetmeats as well as bangles, soft drinks and square meals as well as henna and rings. Raza established his fiancée behind a screen of stone lattice-work, and set a young foot-soldier on guard to defend her territory. Isolated behind this screen from the dull, debilitated anger of the mob, Bilquìs dreamed of her wedding day, defended against guilt by that old dream of queenliness which she had invented long ago. 'Tch tch,' she reproached the glowering refugees, 'but this envy is a too terrible thing.'

Barbs were flung through the stone lattice: 'Ohé, madam! Where do you think he gets your grand-grand clothes? From handicraft emporia? Watch the mud-flats of the river beneath the fortress walls, count the looted naked bodies flung there every night!' Dangerous words, penetrating lattice-work: scavenger, harlot, whore. But Bilquìs set her jaw against such coarseness and told herself: 'How bad-mannered it would be to ask a man from where he brought his gifts! Such cheapness, I will never do it, no.' This sentiment, her reply to the gibes of her fellow refugees, never actually passed her lips, but it filled up her mouth, making it puff up into a pout.

I do not judge her. In those days, people survived any way they could.

The Jami-Masjid

[26] Aurungzeb goes to prayer; from *Travels in the Mogul Empire (1659–67)* by François Bernier.

The principal mosque is visible at a great distance, being situated on the top of a rock in the centre of the town. The surface of the rock was previously levelled, and around it a space is cleared sufficiently large to form a handsome square, where four fine long streets terminate, opposite to the four sides of the *Mosquée*; one, opposite to the principal entrance, in front of the building; a second, at the back of the building; and the two others, to the gates that are in the middle of the two sides. The ascent to the three gates is by means of five-and-twenty or thirty steps of beautiful and large stones, which are continued the whole length of the front and sides. The back part is cased over, to the height of the rock, with large and handsome hewn stone, which hides its inequalities, and tends to give a noble appearance to the building. The three entrances, composed of marble, are magnificent, and their large doors are overlaid with finely wrought plates of copper. Above the principal gate, which greatly exceeds the others in grandeur of appearance, there are several small turrets of white marble that produce a fine effect; and at the back part of the *Mosquée* are seen three large domes, built also of white marble, within and without. The middle dome is much larger and loftier than the other two. The end of the *Mosquée* alone is covered: the space between the three domes and the principal entrance is without any roof; the extreme heat of the climate rendering such an opening absolutely necessary. The whole is paved with large slabs of marble. I grant that this building is not constructed according to those rules of architecture which we seem to think ought to be implicitly followed; yet I can perceive no fault that offends the taste; every part appears well contrived, properly executed, and correctly proportioned. I am satisfied that even in *Paris* a church erected after the model of this temple would be admired, were it only for its singular style of architecture, and its extraordinary appearance. With the exception of the three great domes, and the numerous turrets, which are all of white marble, the *Mosquée* is of a red colour, as if built with large slabs of red marble: although it consists of a species of stone, cut with great facility, but apt to peel off in flakes after a certain time. The natives pretend that the quarries from which it is taken reproduce the stone by degrees: this, if true, is very remarkable; but whether or not they rightly attribute it to the water which fills the quarries every year, I cannot decide.

The King repairs to this *Mosquée* every *Friday*, for the purpose of prayer, that day corresponding in *Mahometan* countries to our *Sunday*. The streets through which he passes are watered to lay the dust and temper the heat: two or three hundred musketeers form an avenue from the gate of the fortress, and as many more line both sides of a wide street leading directly to the mosque. The muskets of these soldiers are small but well finished, and have a sort of large scarlet covering with a little streamer on the top. Five or six horsemen, well mounted, are also ready at the fortress gate, and their duty is to clear the way for the King, keeping, however, at a considerable distance in advance, lest he should be incommoded by their dust. These preparations completed, his Majesty leaves the fortress, sometimes on an elephant, decorated with rich trappings, and a canopy support-ed by painted and gilt pillars; and sometimes in a throne gleaming with azure and gold, placed on a litter covered with scarlet or brocade, which eight chosen men, in handsome attire, carry on their shoulders. A body of *Omrahs* follow the King, some on horseback, and others in *Palekys*; and among the *Omrahs* are seen a great number of *Mansebdars*, and the bearers of silver maces.

[27] 'Five thousand pairs of shoes'; from the *Journal* of Lady (Emily) Bayley in *The Golden Calm* edited by M.M. Kaye.

Emerging from the Palace, there was a large open space planted with trees, as a great many of the old houses and streets had been destroyed in this quarter to improve the sanitary condition of the city, and thus a clear view was obtained of the Great Mosque, the Jumah Musjid, a most glorious building. Indeed, I think I know none in India to equal it. It stands on an eminence, whether natural or artificial I am not certain, and is approached on three sides by the most superb flights of steps, all of cut red sandstone,

The Jami-Masjid (the Great Mosque) at Delhi; miniature painting on ivory from the second half of the nineteenth century

which lead from the level of the road up to the plateau on the top, the courtyard being entered through three magnificent red sandstone gateways, with galleries on the top.

As you enter at the principal gateway you find yourself within a superb courtyard capable of holding five thousand people at once, and at the further end rises a noble Mosque with three most beautiful domes of great size and graceful curves, made of white marble intersected with black lines. The courtyard too is paved with white marble panelled with lines of black, and the tall minarets which flank the mosque are a mixture of red sandstone and white and black marble. A beautiful wall of cut red sandstone surrounds the courtyard and unites the gateways to the mosque.

I have been up to one of the galleries in the Gateway to see the great crowd that assembles in that courtyard on the last day of the Great Mohammedan Fast, the Ramadan. On that occasion nearly five thousand people stood shoulder to shoulder in the courtyard in pure white dresses and turbans, and not a sound was to be heard save the voice of the officiating priest or Mullah who, standing in the mosque, sung out his address so that it could be heard at the furthest limit of the courtyard. When the call to prayer came, the whole of that vast crowd threw themselves on their knees and bowed their heads to the ground, as if they had been one man, and remained motionless until the prayer was ended.

It was a wonderful sight and a thrilling one, and when the crowd broke up and rushed out of the different gateways, no longer silent but jabbering at the pitch of their voices, another wonderful sight presented itself, for all these five thousand worshippers had left their leather shoes on the broad flights of steps outside the courtyard, and now they reclaimed them. It was always a puzzle to me how they could ever find their own footwear again, as the shoes lay side by side from the top to the bottom of the steps, and were almost all of the same pattern.

[28] Impressions of an artist; from *Imperial India: an artist's journals* by Valentine Prinsep.

(Val Prinsep (1838–1904) was born in Calcutta, his father being in the Indian Civil Service. His family retired to Kensington and

cultivated the society of artists, especially the Pre-Raphaelites
and G.F. Watts. In 1876 Prinsep went to India to paint Lord
Lytton's Durbar.)

Of Delhi itself I have now seen something. The Jumma Musjid,
or Mohammedan cathedral, has frequently been described; but
no one in writing can convey the impressions it produces on the
artistic mind. I say this advisedly, for the Anglo-Indian goes by
general report, and never troubles himself with artistic impressions, nor does he see the beauties close under his Anglo-Indian
nose. I am sore on the subject, and naturally so. Here these
people could have chosen the front of the Jumma Musjid, about
forty steps rising to a magnificent plateau, which overlooks a
wide *maidán* or plain, backed by the ancient fort containing the
palace of the old Mogul Emperors. From this position the
Viceroy could indeed declare the commencement of the new
'Raj'! But the Anglo-Indian has chosen a bare plain, and builds
his Brummagen daïs with no surroundings or any historical
associations. Well, perhaps it is a type of the new Raj – this daïs –
cold, new, flaunting, and bare, without a rag of sentiment or
beauty; but let us hope the Raj will prove stronger than that
abominable erection, which nearly fell down the other day. But
to return to the Musjid. Ascending by broad steps – of which
there are three flights, one in front and one on each side – one
climbs to the inside courtyard, rising high above bazaar and
crowd, and open to the blue heaven above, as though lifted from
the earth and things earthly. The architecture is not so fine, or
rather, not of so fine a period, as (I am told) the Taj. Yet the dirty
red is just the colour to relieve against the sky, and the warm
white of the marbles let in gives wonderful variety. I did not go
into the mosque proper, which occupies one side of the square,
for people were praying. I saw it was only a shallow building,
while the square is 150 yards across. The mosque proper is open
to the air, of course, and the altar is a wonderful kind of mother-
of-pearl colour. It is only alabaster, but this effect is produced by
the friction of human bodies and the fall of the light. The people
standing in rows before this were something to see.

I feel in writing home that my continual gush will perhaps
bore. I write, however, my own impressions as an artist, and I
wish rather to dwell on these things than to mention the horrors
my countrymen have stuck up. Everything fine that I have seen

has been so 'rummy' and *bizarre*, and unlike anything else, – a continual surprise, in fact. Yet all this sense of beauty is to be found in this people even now; and we have left it unacknowledged, to almost die out. I know it exists, for the other day in a poky little lane out of the *Chandnee Choke*, or principal street, attracted by a fine door, I looked into an Indian house, and beheld a kind of small *taj*, all white marble, worked and carved into all kinds of traceries, and really fine; yet this has been done within the last forty years.

From the Jumma Mushjid was preached the holy war against the English; and the sanctity of the mosque was so great, that after the Mutiny many were for entirely destroying it, as a warning. Happily Lord Lawrence was wise enough not to give way to the clamour of the many, and the advice of some high up in the service. The mosque was, however, used as a storehouse for years; and even now, though we have restored it to the Mohammedans, the great bronze central gate is never allowed to be opened, except by permission.

[29] A Prussian view in 1910; from *A German Staff Officer in India* by Count Hans von Königsmarck.

(Count Hans von Königsmarck was in the circle of Prince William of Prussia, and visited India in anticipation of the Crown Prince's tour of India in 1911.)

The Jama-Masjid has room for ten thousand worshippers. It is the biggest mosque in India, the goal of every pious Mussulman's aspiration. Saracenic in conception, it betrays Indian art in its execution. Shah Jehan, it is true, based its plans on the religious ordinances of Islam, but the artists who brought it into being were Hindoos.

Broad flights of stairs ascend on three sides to the platform of rock that supports the Jama-Masjid in proud isolation. Splendid portals, slender minarets, prepare one for the magnificence of the interior of the main building. Colonnades enclosing a court of two hundred square yards throw the view open in endless vistas. Turned towards Mecca rises the red sandstone mosque. As an architectonic whole an overpoweringly impressive picture.

Refreshing coolness greets one in the sacred courts. Designed to inspire a joyous note of exaltation is the majestic harmony of its lines, the airy grace of the arches striving heavenwards. Enthralled, one's eyes feast on the alabaster embrasures of the windows, on the ornamentation of the marble recesses and columns elaborated as delicately as jewellery. Admirable indeed is the art that contrives to fashion dead matter to a semblance so full of life.

At the portals of the shrine beggars stretched their skinny arms out towards me. They live on the strangers; for there is no living to be made out of the lachrymal ducts of their compatriots. India's soil has never been productive of the tender plant of pity, and like overfed gods the rich Hindoos pass the misery of their fellowmen by on the other side; the British intruder ministers to it.

Indian mendicancy is innocent even of rags – it is naked. Skin and bones tell their dumb tale eloquently – only the infant whimpers softly at the shrivelled breast. They do their begging with their emaciated bodies, these figures of misery, with their hollow eyes that mirror a world of woe.

Fakirs, those excrescences of Brahminical idolatry, those repulsive representatives of the blackest pessimism, desecrate the exultant note of the shrine. Here in the forecourt of the mosque you see them in the full flower of their degradation, the hideous ascetics who embody the warfare between the material and the spiritual into a repellent spectacle – rude turnkeys of the torture-chamber, who insensately kill the divine spark of warm, glad, sensuous joy, who degrade body and soul to expressionless, pallid phantoms.

Wholly naked, face and body overlaid with a deposit of ashes, dust, and sweat, hair rolled up into hideous knots, they hardly retain any semblance of the Divine image, not even of a Brahmin divinity. The ingenuity they devote to the invention of ever new tortures is amazing. Not only do they pierce their tongues with red-hot irons, perforate their limbs with iron hooks and hang suspended head downwards in pendent agony, they have themselves buried out of hand to the neck in earth, or chained for their lifetime to a stake. Others, again, see particular merit in the oath never to use their legs for locomotion and thenceforward to move about, supported in squatting posture, on hands and arms. To take one's walk abroad with peas in one's footgear has its devotees too. For the most part, however, the holy men – women are not worthy of these intelligent exercises – lie dully huddled up, immobile as pagodas, on dirty heaps of ashes. Without the quiver of an eyelash they stare into the blinding sun, or into the flaring fire, which, to ensure enhanced chastisement, is kept up even on the hottest day. One asks oneself whether these handfuls of fleshless bones, of vanished limbs, are in reality already dead to all bodily feeling while here on earth? Half extinct, their glance strays unintelligently over the gaping crowd that surrounds them in reverent admiration; only every now and then a word forces itself from their bloodless lips – mildew, falling like poison on the teeming earth.

Sick at heart at the repulsiveness of these idle parasites, who, in the misery of their own making, insensately and without purpose, sacrifice their bodies to the worms, I turn away indignantly from the unworthy spectacle that none the less seems to elicit the enthusiastic approval of the passers-by.

'Only stupidity and curiosity pay them any attention nowadays,' says my amiable companion soothingly, who had only a smile and a shrug of his shoulders to waste on the repulsive exhibition of his co-religionists. 'And the outlook for religion in India is unfortunately not much more promising,' continues the Hindoo aristocrat. 'If, indeed, its outer forms are still preserved, the whole rotten structure must sooner or later fall in on itself, worm-eaten and undermined, as in any case it already is.'

'Take the wholesome policy of English government into consideration, the individual superiority – in physique and morale – of the Briton in comparison with your conquerors hitherto,' I urge. Why? 'Because the Englishman does not settle here permanently, does not propagate his race in this country. Arabians, Persians, and Mongols, Spaniards and Portuguese, gave up returning home to their household gods. They founded new homes here, blended themselves with the native population into a new race, and cut themselves adrift from the motherland for all time. The native manner of life usurped the place of home customs. The soil of India, which proffers to mankind all the means of existence in luxuriant abundance and without effort, in course of time sapped their energy and crippled their spirit of enterprise. The Briton escapes these dangers. He recruits his family stock with new blood from home, and the time-expired Anglo-Indians, who bring the evening of their days to its close on their native heath, are replaced in continuous succession by uncontaminated newcomers. The Englishman preserves his nationality even in foreign lands. In his customs and habits, views and sentiments, he remains body and soul the son of the motherland through thick and thin. Physically as well as socially he contrives to maintain his unique position uncontaminated, even in foreign lands. He never suffers his iron limbs to relax in sloth; by his sports and his work he stimulates his hardy, enterprising spirit. By these means the Britons keep themselves tuned up to concert pitch, at the height of their powers – weighty factors which will enable them to master the treacherous, infectious diseases of young India's infancy, just as they succeeded in nipping similar ferments in the bud in the year 1857.'

[30] Friday at the Mosque in the early twentieth century; from *Indian Pages and Pictures* by Michael Myers Shoemaker.

Delhi's Juma Masjid is most beautifully placed. One approaches it over a wide green meadow and no other structures detract from its graceful majesty. Behind, as the courtiers should attend the king, marshals the fantastic Indian city, – but the mosque stands well to the front and alone. Its wide and lofty steps rise upward from the green of the grass to the stately portals. Its walls stretch away on either hand, while two towering minarets guard its white domes, which, balloon shaped, give the whole a lifting, floating appearance. In fact, one would not be greatly amazed to see the structure separate from this earth and float away like Aladdin's palaces.

The Italian dome is of the earth earthy, but those of Russia and India are most ethereal in appearance, probably owing to the contraction of their lines at the base. Certainly the effect is marvellous and seems especially noticeable here to-day.

So a bell clangs, and the people – all men, as no women may enter this section – form in long lines extending from side to side of the court, and reaching half-way towards us, bow, and prostrate themselves in prayer. Beyond and above rises the arcade-like mosque with its glistening domes and minarets against the blue enamel of the sky. The whole is a picture of wondrous beauty and richness in colour and movement, and the

most impressive I have ever seen in any of the mosques of Islam
lands.

Passing inward with the multitude we are waved by a grave-
faced old man to the arcades which surround the court, for today none but the faithful may approach the sanctuary or profane
by their nearer presence the sacred enclosure. So we mount to the
top of the walls. What a picture of oriental gorgeousness lies
spread out below us! The vast expanse of the court, which will
hold some thirty thousand people, is dotted with thousands who
crowd around the tank in its centre for the commanded ablution.
Stately white-robed figures with splendid coats and turbans,
gorgeous with every known shade and colour, grass green and
purple, blue and gold, magenta and yellow, deep reds, lilac and
pink, are reflected in the dazzling white marble pavement.
Beyond rises the arcade-like mosque with its domes and
minarets, while thousands of pigeons, those birds beloved of the
prophet and faithful Mohammedans all of them, make their
prostrations and fill the air with the melody of their voices.

This being Friday, the faithful are flocking to the mosque by
thousands and in company with white-robed and turbaned
Mohammedans we mount the great staircase to the main portal.
There occurs the wildest kind of an altercation at the gates
concerning our servant, whom they evidently believe is a Hindu
in disguise, and they are not satisfied until he has washed out his
mouth.

For some time the court seems one of social gathering as the
people move hither and thither chatting and laughing, and then
one sees that the crowd is composed of all the tribes of Asia.
Yonder is a group of warlike Afghans. Here comes a giant from
Beloochistan, all in white with a huge black beard. There are
some natives of the town, aristocratic and elegant in figure and
dress. The Thibetans and mountain people have their representatives and Persia sends her quota as one may note by the
Astrakan turbans and singsong nasal voice.

Children are just children the world over, no matter what the
faith of their elders. Here are some dozens, laughing, quarrelling,
fighting, with no consideration for the holiness of the spot.

To my amazement a bell calls the faithful to prayer. A bell in a
Mohammedan mosque! Times have changed. In other days,
nothing meaner than a creation of the Almighty was worthy to
call His children to His worship, hence the muezzin, but Ahmed,

our servant, says that 'This be very big mosque, and no man can make people hear.'

[31] E.M. Forster in his socks; from *The Hill of Devi* by E.M. Forster.

(E.M. Forster (1879–1970) first visited India in 1912. Returning in 1921, he became private secretary to the Maharajah of Dewas State Senior, a curious experience which he describes in *The Hill of Devi* (1953). *A Passage to India*, his masterpiece, was published in 1924.)

I stood on the high platform of the Great Mosque, one of the noblest buildings in India and the world. Profound thankfulness filled me. The sky was now intensely blue, the kites circled round the pearl-grey domes and the red frontispiece of sandstone, sounds drifted up from Delhi city, the pavement struck warm through the soles of my socks: I was back in the country I loved.

The Tomb of Humayun

[32] The *chubootra*; from *From New York to Delhi* by Robert B. Minturn.

Hoomaioon's tomb is a square building of red stone and marble, built upon a terrace about three hundred feet square, and twenty high, formed of the same materials. The architecture is in the purest and simplest form of Indian Moosulman art. Each side of the mausoleum is over a hundred feet long, and contains three deep arched recesses, almost the whole height of the building, within which are the windows. The arches are almost pure Gothic, but a little flattened. The dome is of white marble, and is considerably lower than those of the later Moosulman buildings.

Within the building, under the dome, is a large circular room, containing in its centre the simple, unadorned tomb of the Emperor. Hoomaioon was the son of Babur, and father of Akbur. He did not long enjoy the empire conquered by his father, for, having been deposed by a successful rebellion, he became a fugitive from one Indian court to another, and finally had to take refuge with the King of Persia. At length he treacherously got possession of a city belonging to his protector, and with the money and forces obtained by this act, he succeeded in overthrowing one of his most formidable opponents, his younger brother Kamran. Having put out Kamran's eyes he continued the reconquest of his empire, and at last reestablished his throne at Delhi, after sixteen years of exile. Six months afterwards he died, having fallen from the staircase of his library upon a marble floor. He was a great scholar, astrologer, and patron of literature, and is considered one of the finest characters in Indian history.

The two wives of Hoomaioon are also buried in this building, which contains besides the tombs of other members of his house; among them that of Dara Shéko, the eldest son of Shah Jehan, who was murdered by the command of his brother, the Emperor Aurungzeeb.

The terrace, or chubootra, on which this mausoleum is built is a distinctive feature of Moosulman art in India. It is always much broader than the building which it supports, and generally just so high that when the observer stands at the entrance of the

The Tomb of Humayun; watercolour by a Delhi artist, c. 1820

court-yard, the lower line of the building is apparently on a level with his eye. The effect of these chubootras is really wonderful, and is like that of a good frame to a picture, or a pedestal to a statue. The arched recesses which are spoken of above, are also peculiar to this architecture. They begin at the ground, and commonly cover nearly half the surface of the building. The doors and windows which are within them may be of any size, but these recesses are always as large as circumstances will permit, and are the grand feature of every façade.

[33] 'Matchlocks at the tassels'; from *Tours of Upper India* by Major Archer.

From this we proceeded to Homaion's tomb; he was of the Mogul dynasty, and died in 1555. This tomb is a grand monument of former times. Though by no means approaching the magnitude of Acbar's, it is yet, considered as a beautiful building, very far its superior. I do not know what edifice it can be compared to, the shape and construction of these fabrics being so essentially different from any thing we have in Europe. The dome is three-fourths as large as St. Paul's, I should conceive; the figure of the whole is a square, and at the four corners are smaller domes: the large one, which is in the exact centre of the building, was in the inside enriched with gilding and enamel; from the centre a tassel of gold-lace once depended; but when the Jauts, (those sworn foes to honesty and liberality) plundered Delhi, they amused themselves by firing their matchlocks at the tassels: the marks of the bullets in the dome and in other parts of this superb edifice, are very apparent. Several members of Homaion's family are interred in this spot; their tombstones are beautifully carved in marble.

[34] Reflections at the tomb of Humayun; from *Reminscences of Imperial Delhie* by Sir Thomas Metcalfe in *The Golden Calm* edited by M.M. Kaye.

(The Metcalfe family produced a number of distinguished civil servants, including Lord Metcalfe (pictured opposite) who was British Resident during the reign of Akbar II. Sir Thomas Metcalfe (father of Emily Bayley) went to India in 1813 and was

Akbar II with the British Resident, Lord Metcalfe

also British Resident in Delhi for a time. He died, reputedly of poison, in 1853.)

There is something in this place to which the mind cannot be indifferent. The ruins of grandeur that extend for miles on every side fill it with serious reflection. The palaces crumbling into dust, every one of which could tell many tales of royal virtue or tyrannical crime, of desperate ambition or depraved indolence . . . the myriads of vast mausoleums every one of which was intended to convey to futurity the deathless fame of its cold inhabitant, and all of which are passed by unknown and unnoticed . . . these things cannot be looked at with indifference.

[35] Death and decay in all around . . .; from *A Visit to India, China and Japan in the year 1853* by Bayard Taylor.

The tomb is on a grand scale, rising to the height of one hundred feet, from the noble terrace of solid masonry, but has a most wretched, forlorn air. The floors are covered with litter and filth, the marble screens broken and battered, the dome given to bats and owls, and the spacious garden has become a waste of weeds. From the terrace, I counted upwards of fifty similar palaces of the dead, several of them, if not on a scale of equal grandeur, yet even superior in design and in the richness of their decoration.

[36] 'One of the grandest piles in the world' in 1875; from *The Prince of Wales' Tour* . . . by Sir William Howard Russell.

(Sir William Howard Russell (1826–1907) was one of the most distinguished journalists of his day. He covered the Crimean War for *The Times* and his reports on the condition of the troops led to Florence Nightingale's reforms. He accompanied the Prince of Wales on his tour of India in 1875–6.)

The Prince, on his way back to the camp, stopped at Houmayoun's Tomb, where the Delhi princes surrendered to Hodson and met their death. This mausoleum struck me as one of the finest monumental buildings I had ever seen, when I visited it in 1858. Sombre, massive, vast, it is doubtless one of the grandest piles of the kind in the world; the effect of the red sandstone, relieved by the snow-white marble, the noble terraces, exquisite filigree windows, lofty walls, 290 yards long, is scarcely to be surpassed; but it is falling somewhat into decay.

[37] Blunt breakfasts at the tomb; from *India under Ripon, a secret diary* by Wilfred Scawen Blunt.

(Wilfred Scawen Blunt (1840–1922), traveller, politician and poet, visited India in 1878 and 1883–4. He was an outspoken anti-imperialist.)

To-day we spent in visiting the great monuments south of Delhi, in company with the Loharos and Prince Suliman Jah, who organized the expedition. We breakfasted at Humayum's tomb, over whom our friends the Loharos said prayers, he being their ancestor, not Prince Suliman's. It was touching to see this, and to notice a little offering of withered flowers on the tomb of a man so long dead. We went to the top of the monument. Prince Suliman, who is well read, or rather well learned, in history, gave us the story of Humayum and his dynasty, and pointed out to us on the Hindu fort the tower from which his great ancestor fell while looking at the stars. They brought him here and buried him, and his widow raised this pile, under which the rest of the members of his family lie. Thirty-five emperors and kings of Delhi lie buried, he told us, within sight of where we stood. Parrots were building in the chinks of stone; but there are guardians still of the tomb. It was here that later the last King of Delhi fled, and was taken by Hodson, with his two sons, while they were praying, and on the way back from here that he shot the young princes, our friends' uncles. We asked him whether they had been brought back here to be buried, and he smiled sarcastically. They were thrown like the corpses of dogs into the street in Delhi, and none knows where they now lie. The King himself lies buried in Rangoon. From this we went across to the beautiful mosque and more beautiful tombs of other ancestors, and of a dead Persian poet, which we found decked with fresh flowers. Our friends talked all the while of these dead heroes as still living, and, when the young Loharo exclaimed 'This country is full of poets and kings and learned men,' I, for a moment, though he meant at the present day. But it was of those under ground he was talking. The living people of the place are only poor guardians of the tombs who live on alms.

[38] Turnips round the tomb: Lord Curzon writing to Lady Curzon in 1905; from *The Life of Lord Curzon* by the Earl of Ronaldshay.

(George Nathaniel, Lord Curzon of Kedleston (1859–1925) was Viceroy of India from 1899 to 1905. The Durbar of 1903 marked the zenith of his splendour. He took a great interest in the restoration of Mogul (as opposed to Hindu) ruins in Delhi and Agra. Following the arrival of Kitchener as army commander, he left India an angry and embittered man.)

You remember Hamayun's tomb? I had the garden restored, the water channels dug out and refilled and the whole place restored to its pristine beauty. I went to England last summer and, the eye of the master being away, the whole place has been allowed to revert. The garden has been let to a native and is now planted with turnips and the work of four years is thrown away! I shall drive out there, and woe betide the Deputy Commissioner whose apathy has been responsible.

Chandni Chowk

[39] At the market; from *Travels in the Mogul Empire (1659–67)* by François Bernier.

There is, indeed, a fruit-market that makes some show. It contains many shops which during the summer are well supplied with dry fruit from *Persia, Balk, Bokara,* and *Samarkande*; such as almonds, pistachios, and walnuts, raisins, prunes, and apricots; and in winter with excellent fresh grapes, black and white, brought from the same countries, wrapped in cotton; pears and apples of three or four sorts, and those admirable melons which last the whole winter. These fruits are, however, very dear; a single melon selling for a crown and a half. But nothing is considered so great a treat: it forms the chief expense of the *Omrahs,* and I have frequently known my *Agah* spend twenty crowns on fruit for his breakfast.

In summer the melons of the country are cheap, but they are of an inferior kind: there are no means of procuring good ones but by sending to *Persia* for seed, and sowing it in ground prepared with extraordinary care, in the manner practised by the grandees. Good melons, however, are scarce, the soil being so little congenial that the seed degenerates after the first year.

Ambas, or *Mangues,* are in season during two months in summer, and are plentiful and cheap; but those grown at *Dehli* are indifferent. The best come from *Bengale, Golkonda,* and *Goa,* and these are indeed excellent. I do not know any sweetmeat more agreeable.

Pateques, or water-melons, are in great abundance nearly the whole year round; but those of *Dehli* are soft, without colour or sweetness. If this fruit be ever found good, it is among the wealthy people, who import the seed and cultivate it with much care and expense.

There are many confectioners' shops in the town, but the sweetmeats are badly made, and full of dust and flies.

Bakers also are numerous, but the ovens are unlike our own, and very defective. The bread, therefore, is neither well made nor properly baked. That sold in the Fort is tolerably good, and the *Omrahs* bake at home, so that their bread is much superior. In its composition they are not sparing of fresh butter, milk, and eggs; but though it be raised, it has a burnt taste, and is too much like cake, and never to be compared to the *Pain de Gonesse*, and other delicious kinds, to be met with in *Paris*.

In the *bazars* there are shops where meat is sold roasted and dressed in a variety of ways. But there is no trusting to their dishes, composed, for aught I know, of the flesh of camels, horses, or perhaps oxen which have died of disease. Indeed no food can be considered wholesome which is not dressed at home.

Meat is sold in every part of the city; but instead of goats' flesh that of mutton is often palmed upon the buyer; an imposition which ought to be guarded against, because mutton and beef, but particularly the former, though not unpleasant to the taste, are heating, flatulent, and difficult of digestion. Kid is the best food, but being rarely sold in quarters, it must be purchased alive, which is very inconvenient, as the meat will not keep from morning to night, and is generally lean and without flavour. The goat's flesh found in quarters at the butchers' shops is frequently that of the she-goat, which is lean and tough.

But it would be unreasonable in me to complain; because since I have been familiarised with the manners of the people, it seldom happens that I find fault either with my meat or my bread. I send my servant to the King's purveyors in the Fort, who are glad to sell wholesome food, which costs them very little, at the high price I am willing to pay. My *Agah* smiled when I remarked that I had been for years in the habit of living by stealth and artifice, and that the one hundred and fifty crowns which he gave me monthly would not otherwise keep me from starving, although in *France* I could for half a *roupie* eat every day as good meat as the King.

As to capons, there are none to be had; the people being tender-hearted toward animals of every description, men only excepted; these being wanted for their *Seraglios*. The markets, however, are amply supplied with fowls, tolerably good and cheap. Among others, there is a small hen, delicate and tender, which I call *Ethiopian*, the skin being quite black.

Pigeons are exposed for sale, but not young ones, the *Indians* considering them too small, and saying that it would be cruel to deprive them of life at so tender an age.

There are partridges, which are smaller than ours, but being caught with nets, and brought alive from a distance, are not so good as fowls. The same thing may be remarked of ducks and hares, which are brought alive in crowded cages.

The people of this neighbourhood are indifferent fishermen; yet good fish may sometimes be bought, particularly two sorts, called *sing-ala* and *rau*. The former resembles our pike; the latter our carp. When the weather is cold, the people will not fish at all if they can avoid it; for they have a much greater dread of cold than *Europeans* have of heat. Should any fish then happen to be seen in the market, it is immediately bought up by the eunuchs, who are particularly fond of it; why, I cannot tell. The *Omrahs* alone contrive to force the fishermen out at all times by means of the *korrah*, the long whip always suspended at their door.

You may judge from what I have said, whether a lover of good cheer ought to quit *Paris* for the sake of visiting *Dehli*.

[40] Flies; from *Excursions in India* by Captain Thomas Skinner.

(Captain Thomas Skinner (1800–43) was stationed at Hardwar on the upper Ganges, and travelled widely in India. He commanded the 31st Foot in the 1842 expedition to relieve Kabul.)

I found my tent pitched immediately under the castle walls, and opposite the Chandery Choke, or principal street. I was in the centre of bustle, but smothered by dust and tortured by flies. It is impossible to convey an idea of the numbers of these insects, and the intolerable nuisance attending them; they are quite enough to keep you in a perpetual fever, and I have not yet arrived at that state of dignity or luxury to enjoy the constant attendance of an automaton, with a feather-fan, to keep my august person from being offended by their approach. I have frequently been amused by the unconsciousness of the men whose duty it is to procure a 'gentle air' for their languid masters, or to exercise the more exalted office of controller of flies about the person; they stand like statues by your side, their arms waving the fan up and down as if they had been set in motion by machinery. They often fall asleep in their office, but continue to perform its duties as if they had been wound up for a certain time. If you move from your position, though scarcely awake, they continue to follow

you, and it seems as difficult to throw them off, as it was for
Sinbad to release himself from the old man of the sea.

[41] 'The gayest scene in India'; from *From New York to
Delhi* by Robert B. Minturn.

I drove in a buggy through the Chandee chôk, or Silver market,
which is altogether the handsomest street in India. It is about a
mile in length, extending from the great western entrance of the
palace, to the Lahóree gate of the city. Its breadth is one hundred
and twenty feet, and an open aqueduct bordered by rows of trees
runs through its centre. The houses on each side are mostly of
pukka, and not over two stories high. Their roofs are tiled, and
they have light wooden balconies in front, which add much to
the appearance of the street. The ground floor of these houses is
commonly used for shops; the upper stories are often inhabited
by what the natives call 'scarlet ladies,' and by other 'great evils
of great cities' in the East. When I was at Delhi, Chandee chôk
was the gayest scene in India. Every native who could muster a
conveyance of any description betook himself thither in the cool
of the afternoon. Some came on elephants, which were magnificently caparisoned, and painted with bright colours around the
eyes and on the trunk. Others rode milk-white horses, the tails of
which were dyed scarlet, and which were decorated with
housings of fine cloth and gold embroidery. Others rode in
bailees, or two-wheeled carts covered with red canopies, and
drawn by neat teams of bullocks. A few preferred palkees, or ton-
jons, a vehicle very like the jan-pan of the hills. But at least half
had abandoned oriental fashions, and adopting the manners and
customs of their conquerors, drove on the chôk in graceful
English phaetons or buggies, drawn by well-groomed and well-
harnessed Arab steeds. All had as many followers as possible,
who ran ahead armed with sword, spear and shield, shouting out
their master's titles, and clearing the way, with words and blows,
through the closely packed crowd. The dress of the inhabitants of
Delhi is very gay. The tight-fitting cassock (chupkun) is of some
dark cloth or flowered cotton, and the turban and kummurbund
are of scarlet or some rich colour, often fringed with gold.
Sometimes Cashmeer shawls, or the imitation ones made at
Delhi, are worn around the head, waist or shoulders. Some of the

Chandni Chowk (Silver Street), Delhi; from the *Illustrated London News*, 1857

costumes are very rich and costly, but most of them are tawdry, and decorated with spangles and artificial jewellery. In Delhi there are a great number of 'dandy Moosulmans.' They are frequently sepoys, who pass their spare time as 'coureurs d'aventures.' Their dress is as showy as their limited means will allow, and they wear a natty little skull-cap, cocked on one side of the head, from which their long, straight, greasy hair hangs down upon their neck. Their appearance is altogether far from respectable, and they interchange salutations with the young ladies of the market, who sit at the windows of the upper stories, or parade their charms in open bailees. Now and then one may see an Afghan, a short, thick-set man, with loose grey woollen clothes, broad, heavy features, a dirty face, of the colour of leather, and brown tangled locks. He evidently looks with the utmost contempt on the unmanly foppery of the effeminate race whom his ancestors have conquered and spoiled whenever they chose; and if asked his opinion, will express it in no measured terms, and in language far different from the courtly euphemisms of the Hindoostanee.

Half way down the Chandee chôk is a pretty little mosque, with three gilt domes, where, scarcely more than one hundred years ago, Nadir Shah, the Persian conqueror, sat with drawn sword, looking on while his troops sacked the city. The slaughter lasted from morning till night, and was accompanied by all the horrors of unrestrained lust, rapine and vengeance. Over a hundred thousand of the inhabitants perished, and the aqueduct in the Chandee chôk ran red with blood.

[42] Walks through the Chandni Chowk; from *The Gorgeous East* by Rupert Croft-Cooke.

Through the heart of Old Delhi ran one of Asia's most notable streets, Chandni Chowk, the Street of Silver. I learned more of India from its pavements than from all the rest of the city.

It had a history. The street of the silversmiths had been made a wide processional highway before the Moguls came and said to be the richest street in the world it had been sacked four times, by Timur, Nadir Shah, Ahmad Shah and the Mahratta chief Holkar whom the British finally expelled in 1804. It had seen processions under four dynasties, and under the British, viceroys had ridden down its length on elephants attended by cavalry. It was on one of these occasions in December 1911 [*sic*] that a bomb in Chandni Chowk wounded the Viceroy Lord Hardinge of Penshurst.

Now it seemed to me to be a microcosm of India and I would walk from the Red Fort to the cool fruit market at the far end of it several times a week and never grow tired of it. The airless brilliance of the sunlight was blinding but I was accustomed to that now and it did not disturb me as I idled, observed, stopped to talk or to buy, until I reached shade and a cool drink among the polychromatic fruit stalls.

It was crowded and not since my first days in Bombay when I had been shocked by the streets' over-population had I felt the press of people so pungently as here. Like ants, I thought, using the ancient simile with a new intent, like ants they seemed to have no order or design in their activities, yet to the individual these were full of lazy purpose and perhaps even in mass they were moving towards some end, something dictated by race or species for which they would do anything but hurry.

There was so much to see and every few paces would bring me to the unexpected. The pavements were wide and the open-fronted shops spread over them, while down the central avenues the traffic was not then the furious bedlam of today with the din of scooter taxis never ceasing to buzz and whistle in one's ears. It was noisy in a more haphazard way, trams beating insistently on their bells at a group of ambling donkeys heavily laden, an occasional army truck sounding its horn at an indifferent Brahminy bull munching vegetables, shouts and hand-bell ringing from the *tonga* men or the esoteric calls understood by their charges of goatherds driving a flock.

On the pavements the vendors' cries rose above these, or the squeals of small boys playing catch-as-catch-can among the pedestrians. The crowd here was more varied than in the south with a higher proportion of Muslims and frontier people. I could pick most of the races and types but not infallibly and only after the perplexities of my first thirty months in India. Here more frequently than in Bombay were mountain-bred Pathans swinging along with their walking-sticks and their dirty-white baggy trousers, their coloured waistcoats and their almost Nordic faces; a few Dravidians from the south delicately made with keen dark faces and exquisite profiles; Brahmins from everywhere, pale and

Indian craftsman stamping gold and silver lace; pencil and wash
drawing by John Lockwood Kipling (father of Rudyard), 1870

intelligent; young students cool and talkative; Sindhi Hindus in
their money-changing shops; shopkeepers squatting patiently,
ready to bargain but without the volubility of an Italian market-
place; Punjabis, Gujaratis, sallow Garhwalis, and others from
the Himalayan foothills with smiling Mongolian features; tough
coolies from these very United Provinces, neat Bengalis, sinewy
Balachis, and from everywhere Hindu *banyas* and *babus* in their
dhotis and little folding black or white caps. A handsome race, I
thought once again as I watched them, and at their slim tall best
having great physical strength and grace. Yet there were plenty
of signs of undernourishment among them and childhood
diseases neglected through poverty showed cruelly now. There
were thin weak legs and arms, old bony knees which knocked
painfully, young bodies twisted with rickets. An ancient Hindu

would totter past me with every rib of his chest a sharp ridge of
bone visible under the poor flesh and his arms like lengths of
tobacco twist. But so many, particularly the old men, were of
positive beauty, that they could still be called a handsome,
perhaps the most handsome, race. These white-bearded patri-
archs with the dim, restless eyes had faces so delicately modelled
that they might have been ancient ascetics who had given their
lives to contemplating the Infinite; yet they were still, probably,
in their fifties and illiterate as likely as not, their only study the
soil and their life's work the driving of a few cattle, ploughing a
dusty patch, and raising a family to follow them in the business of
keeping alive.

But the women I saw in the Chandni Chowk in those days
were the wives of labourers, themselves field-workers perhaps,
and though they moved with a youthful rhythm their faces even
in early middle age were toil-worn and prematurely wrinkled.
Their saris had lost their gay colours through recurrent washing
and their bangles were mostly of glass.

There was little to buy in the shops which were as usual in
India in batches – a dozen silversmiths, a row of cloth stores, two
or three grain shops together, all with identical wares. On the
pavement were the smaller vendors, some displaying no more
than a square yard of seemingly valueless bits of old metal, rusty
springs, a tin spoon or two, bent nails and screws. There were
shops selling *ganja* and opium; one or two cafés with wireless
screaming Indian music at full blast making a contradiction and
cacophany, for by its very nature it comes gently in tides of sound
advancing or retreating like the sound of the sea. There were
bangle shops, too, with a thousand almost identical rings of
coloured glass; stationers in which the shoddy ill-printed
booklets in Hindi and Urdu were sold along with slates and
precious pieces of paper. Best of all were the toyshops at which for
a few annas I could buy the hesitating children tawdry things of
painted wood, or crude clay figures roughly daubed with gilt and
colours. The fortune-tellers sold from the pavement and shoemakers sat cross-legged, repairing sandals while their would-be
wearers waited barefoot.

Sometimes a wedding procession would pass and the bride-
groom, wearing the costume and stage jewellery of a rajah,
would go by on a tired hack, to the music of a raucous little band
– all hired from a contractor for the day. Sometimes a funeral

with a corpse flower-covered on a shoulder-borne bier. But mostly their private occasions would be sufficient to keep that crowd on the pavement in ceaseless movement.

Here was a street-smell which differed from that of Bombay though both were essentially Indian. I should like to think that an expert on oriental smells could distinguish his city or region blindfold, as it were, from the heavy spice-laden air of the south, to the sharper aroma of Delhi and the thick stench of Calcutta. In Chandni Chowk there was less stress on cooking food than I had known in my first days in Bombay, and more wood-smoke in the clear light atmosphere, but common to both was an elemental muskiness never absent from an Indian street. Compounded from many sources, few distinguishable from the rest except at moments when one or another may be uppermost, it fills the nostrils in the sunlight and grows sharper at night. Spices are always there and dried herbs, wood-smoke and the scented smoke rising from *agar-batties* (incense sticks), fruit, jasmine petals threaded to make a garland, bottled perfumes, animal smells from horses or cattle in the street, the bonfire smell of little paperless *birris* which the poorer smoked, spices again, flowers again and the sharp sweetish smell of oriental bodies.

As inescapable was the dust. It never rests, it permeates everywhere, it rises again from the ground a week or two after the rainy season, undaunted by the torrential months which have won a temporary victory over it. It is this dust which belies the European dream of the jewelled East, which mocks the coloured sheen on our pictures of Hindustan, for in some seasons the dust of India clouds everything, destroys freshness and verdure, robs the trees of their brightness and grass of its gaiety. Dust dulls the very colours, coats the furniture, soils the windows, fills the nostrils. Out of the cities a man's life is lived with dust, down the long earthy roads he seems to move like Jehovah in a cloud, and across his fields it rises about him as he works. In Chandni Chowk at that time I could feel it in my throat and nose, and I used to pity wives out from England who tried to fight it off in the dry season, dreaming of their tidy English homes.

With the dust were the flies in their crawling millions, blackening the sticky sweetmeats in the open shops. I would see a man waving an ineffectual fan over his sugary wares – with each motion the flies were dispersed and had time to settle again before the fan returned. Still the half-naked salesman would wave rhythmically, pausing only to sell an anna's worth of coloured sugar to a small boy. If life seemed dangerous in Chandni Chowk because of the flies and dust I would remember that behind it was a rigid system of hygiene old as the Brahmins and calculated to defeat all but the most out-of-hand epidemics. And if the rags on passers-by looked soiled and their feet were earthy, their bodies were as clean as their minds, and cleanliness was to them part of their creed which came before food or propagation.

In those memorable walks through Chandni Chowk, I would be approached, perhaps, by a beggar-woman with a child at her breast. She would clutch at my coat and demand two annas for food. A rickety infant of two years would stumble after her. She would smile in a mechanical parody of winningness, all expression leaving her face as I gave her a coin. She would already be approaching another man before my hand was back in my pocket. The Indian beggar, I used to think, had none of the artistry of the Spaniard. But what persistence! I have been followed for a mile before now by a woman mendicant because she had known that her will would be stronger than mine and that finally she would win.

In Chandni Chowk there was no sense of time, no urgency to be anywhere at a given moment. The sun told the people as much about time as they needed to know for even the richest of them lived with a simplicity which made the clockwork elaborations of the West seem fussy, the complicated possessions, the gadgets and mechanism, the comforts and etceteras which the Europeans and Americans called necessities. Eating from a polished metal tray, without utensils but with his whole body washed and his street-soiled shoes removed in preparation for it; sleeping on a mattress on the ground, maybe, or on a cot of rope and wood, free of furniture; bathing at a tap or with a brass pot of water; combing his hair with a comb carved from wood; eating simply; drinking only water; ready to move with all his earthly possessions by train or bullock-cart at an hour's notice, the Indian sets an example to the world in dismissing the non-essentials. Yet his luxuries, as I knew, could be pleasantly sybaritic. In Chandni Chowk I stood more than once by a scent stall watching a grave Hindu business man, perhaps, or a Muslim shopkeeper choosing oil with which to have his body massaged, the stall-keeper spooning up drops for him to sniff from the back of his hand. I knew too that the Indian's feeling for fine textures near his skin, his garlands and formal bouquets of flowers, the nuts and seeds he chewed between his strong teeth after eating, his love of embroidery and carving were proof that although he loved simplicity he had polished his tastes and cared for luxuries that were not cumbrous.

I would stop beside a fortune-teller and discuss horoscopes knowing that the stories of Indian astrology which had reached me in England were unexaggerated and no one, Hindu, Muslim or Christian, went far without advice from the stars. It was not the only legend of India which had turned out to be coldly factual nor the only picture-book promise which had been fulfilled. In nearly all the clichés I had found an element of truth and with my own eyes seen the over-painted pictures brought home since the nabobs' days. The temple bells, the sacred Ganges, the caller from the minaret, the holy men, the fabulously rich princes living in mediaeval strongholds and receiving the horizontal homage of their subjects, the peacocks on the castle walls, the flights of green parrots round ancient courtyards, the lavish and intricate jewellery, the endless garlands of flowers, the incense, the veteran scholar at a house door intoning the Koran, the leopards and pythons, the ceremonial elephants with glittering trappings, the turbaned men with fans and fly-whisks, the deft craftsmen, the watermen who never ceased their sad chanting at the oars, the pearl mosques against the setting sun, the gods and goddesses, the purple hills, and the groups of women gossiping at the well. All these lengendary and over-written things I had known with my own senses and I recognized that the most gushing descriptive writer on India was not always a liar.

The Observatory

[43] The Maharajah of Jaipur's Observatory described in 1844; from *Reminiscences of Imperial Delhie* by Sir Thomas Metcalfe in *The Golden Calm* edited by M.M. Kaye.

The Observatory at Delhi denominated the 'Juntur Muntur', literally witchcraft, was constructed by the Maha Raja Jey Singh of Jeypoor who succeeded to the inheritance of his father about 1693 of the Christian era.

It is situated without the Walls of the City at a distance of $1\frac{1}{4}$ mile SW and consists of several detached Buildings.

The principal ones are the Gnomon, a large Equatorial Dial, and a Circular Building designed for the purpose of observing the Altitude and Azimuth of the heavenly Bodies.

The two former do not require particular notice, but on the third of which there are two and exactly similar close to each other and intended not as duplicates but as supplementary to each other – a Pillar rises in the Centre of the same height with the Building itself, which is open at the top.

From this Pillar at the height of about three feet from the bottom proceed Radii of Stone horizontally to the circular Walls of the Building.

These Radii are thirty in number – the spaces between them are equal to the Radii themselves so that each Radius and each intermediate Space forms a Sector of Six Degrees.

The parts in the Centre Pillar opposite to the Radii and in the intermediate Spaces, in all sixty, are marked by lines reaching to the top, and were painted of different Colours. As no observation could be made in the one Building when the Shadow fell on the space between the Stone Radii or Sector, it was found requisite to construct the Second on which the Radii or Sector corresponds with the vacant Spaces of the other – so that in one or the other, an observation of any body visible above the Horizon might at any time be made.

St James's Church

[44] The English church; from *Up the Country* . . . by Emily Eden.

Yesterday we went to the church built by Colonel Skinner. He is a native of this country, a half-caste, but very black, and talks broken English. He has had a regiment of irregular horse for the last forty years, and has done all sorts of gallant things, had seven horses killed under him, and been wounded in proportion; has made several fortunes and lost them; has built himself several fine houses, and has his zenana and heaps of black sons like any other native. He built this church which is a very curious building, and very magnificent – in some respects; and within sight of it there is a mosque which he has also built, because he said that one way or the other he should be sure to go to heaven. In short, he is one of the people whose lives ought to be written for the particular amusement of succeeding generations. His Protestant church has a dome in the mosque fashion, and I was quite afraid that with the best dispositions to attend to Mr. Y., little visions of Mahomet would be creeping in. Skinner's brother, Major Robert Skinner, was the same sort of melodramatic character, and made a tragic end. He suspected one of his wives of a slight *écart* from the path of propriety – very unjustly, it is said – but he called her and all his servants together, cut off the heads of every individual in his household, and then shot himself. His soldiers bought every article of his property at ten times its value, that they might possess relics of a man who had shown, they said, such a quick sense of honour.

[45] Colonel James Skinner and his church; from the *Journal* of Lady (Emily) Bayley in *The Golden Calm* edited by M.M. Kaye.

The next house to the Treasury was a very pretty one in which my friends the John Gubbins' lived, and next to that was the office of the Delhi Press. In the large open space in front of these buildings was the English church, built at the sole expense of

St James's Church; engraving by R.G. Reeve
after a drawing by Lieutenant Tremenheere, c. 1839

Colonel James Skinner, and it is in the churchyard surrounding
it that my beloved Father was buried. There is also in this
enclosure the grave of Mr William Fraser, who was murdered in
Delhi in 1835, a circumstance I perfectly remember.

There is a tablet to my Mother's memory in this church, and
Colonel Skinner who built the church and who raised the
regiment known as Skinner's Horse, is buried in the chancel. The
church had then porticoes north, south and west, and was
surmounted by a dome, with a gilt cross on the summit. The
church was generally painted pink and was a strange piece of
architecture, but it was well suited to the climate, and is full of
sacred and happy memories to me. Here I was married on
March 6th 1850, and Emmie was baptized there in the February
following, and the funeral service for my Father was read here on
November 4th 1853.

On the opposite side of the church to the houses already
described stood a palatial building called Skinner's House, the
house of the numerous Skinner family, and adjoining it was a
mosque built by Colonel Skinner for his Mohammedan friends.

Colonel Skinner was a man of dark blood, and his wife was a

native lady, and their children were all, of course very dark in complexion, and spoke English with an extraordinary accent, and the whole family was a marvellous revelation to anyone fresh from England. Now it would be almost impossible to find a family of the same type in India, for although they looked upon themselves as English people and held a prominent position in Delhi society they had very little education and were more native than English in their ways.

My Father had a great regard for Colonel Skinner himself, as a warm-hearted friend and a very fine soldier, but it was difficult to say what the religion of the family was. I knew only two of the sons and one daughter. One son called Joe Skinner was a marvellous creation, as you may imagine when I tell you that his visiting dress consisted of a green cloth cutaway coat, with gilt buttons (or possibly gold as they were very pretty), very light claret-coloured trousers, patent leather boots, white waistcoat and gilt buttons, and a white necktie. He always carried a gold-mounted Malacca cane, with which he incessantly tapped his boot, and talked of the time when he was in the Guards, though he had never been out of India.

Another son was called Aleck Skinner, and when I went to call upon his wife, who was supposed to be educated 'English fashion', she offered to sing to me, and thereupon sat herself down at the piano and sang a song, playing the accompaniment herself; but both words and tune were unknown to me until I looked at the title page and found it was 'Villikins and his Dinah', totally metamorphosed by her playing and accent, and perfectly unrecognizable.

This Aleck Skinner had a large family of sons and daughters, who have, I suppose, succeeded to the large family property. He sent me their photographs some time ago, and most of them were named after the Royal Family, but they were all black.

[46] Mutiny memorials; from *Picturesque India* by W.S. Caine.

The Memorial Church of St. James is in the same neighbourhood, in a charming and well-kept garden. It was built by Colonel Skinner, at his sole cost, as stated on a tablet facing the altar, 'in fulfilment of a vow made, while lying wounded, on the field of battle, in grateful acknowledgment of the mercy of Divine Providence, and in testimony of his sincere faith in the truth of the Christian religion.' Round the walls of the church are many memorial tablets, chiefly to those who were murdered during the horrors of the mutiny.

The Indian Mutiny

[47] The Guard Commander at the Fort meets the mutineers; from the narrative of Munshi Jeewan Lal in *Two Native Narratives of the Mutiny*.

(Munshi Jeewan Lal, 'an educated native gentleman', was writer to Sir David Ochterlony and Sir Charles Metcalfe. Familiar with palace intrigues, he was basically loyal to the British though he spent the Mutiny in the Fort.)

Very early in the morning of the 11th of May [1857], the attention of Captain Douglas was called to the burning bungalow across the river. Information of the arrival of troopers from Meerut had reached the Commandant, as also of the disturbances in the city. Boorun 'Chobdar' (a silver stick in waiting) Bukar Sing, Kishen Sing, messengers, reported that the residence of the Toll-Collector had been fired, and the officer in charge killed, and that the mutineers were making for the city, killing people here and there. At this moment one of the Sowars presented himself at the foot of the stairs, and told the sentry he wished to speak to Captain Douglas.

It was reported that the man was waiting below. Captain Douglas then came to the top of the stairs and inquired what he wanted. The man replied: 'We have come from Meerut, where we have killed our officers, because they insisted on our using cartridges smeared with the fat of cows and pigs, and an attempt has been made to destroy our caste. Hindus and Mahommedans conjointly have created a mutiny (*bulwa*). There has been a fight; both Europeans and natives have fallen, and we have come here as complainants, seeking justice from the King. Advise us what we shall do, otherwise as we have been ordered, so we must do.'

Captain Douglas' orderly states that the man spoke as if he were in a fury, and the gleam of bloodshed was in his eyes. Captain Douglas replied: 'You have committed a great crime in killing your officers, and unless you at once cease from bloodshed in the city, you will be severely punished, as I have four companies of Gúrkhas.'

As the Commandant ceased speaking the Sowar mounted his

horse, and rode off to join his companions. Immediately after this a 'Chobdar' (an attendant bearing a silver-handled *chourie* to keep off flies) came running with a message from the King, requiring the attendance of Captain Douglas, who went to the Dewan-i-Khás, where the King awaited him. On the way he met Ahsanúllah Khán and the King's Vakíl. From them he learned that a large force of mutineers had arrived in front of the city walls and were gathered on the city sands, raising loud cries. They urged the Commandant at once to take steps to restore order, as in the very presence of the King they were threatening, and dangerous. Captain Douglas found the King in the Dewan-i-Khás (Hall of Private Audience), and in reply to the King's questions as to what all this meant, he narrated what he had heard that morning – that a few of the troops at Meerut had mutinied and had fled to Delhi. He begged the King not to be anxious, as European troops from Meerut would assuredly be pursuing the mutineers, and must shortly arrive, and there were the regiments at Rajpúr besides. His Majesty might rest assured that the authorities had already taken steps to dispose of these men. From time to time during the interview, the loud cries of the mutineers penetrated the Audience Chamber. Captain Douglas asked permission to open the Water Gate leading to the river, with a view to calling some of the men into the presence of the King. The Vakíl and Ahsanullah Khán advised that this should not be done, and that Captain Douglas should not expose himself to the fury of the soldiery, who were already inflamed with bloodshed, and moreover, if they once obtained admission, they might plunder the Palace.

It was agreed that Captain Douglas should speak to the men from the river wall of the Palace. He did so, and called towards him two of the officers from among the mutineers. They saluted the Commandant, and said: 'The English tried to make Christians of us, and gave us these cartridges with that object; for this reason we have come to the King for protection, as we have been attacked, and some of us killed, by the English soldiers.' Captain Douglas replied: 'This place is under the private apartments (zenana) of the King; it is not the place for you to make a disturbance. Encamp somewhere on the riverbed, and the King will afterwards listen to your complaints.' The men moved off towards the Rájghaut Gates of the city. As Captain Douglas was about to leave, after giving assurances to His

Majesty, the King expressed great anxiety for the safety of himself and his family, and claimed the protection of the British Government. Captain Douglas again assured him he had no grounds of apprehension, and hurried to his house. There he learned that the Commissioner, Mr. Simon Fraser, was waiting for him at the bastion of the Calcutta Gate of the city. Stopping the buggy of Captain Dildar Khán, which was passing at the time, he drove on in it to the river-side bastion, where he found Mr. Simon Fraser, Mr. Hutchinson, and Mr. Charles Le Bas, the judge, with other gentlemen. Having joined them, he produced a letter which he had in his pocket. He gave it to Mr. Fraser to read, who returned it. Captain Douglas again read it. They then all conversed in English. While so doing a chaprassie of the Camel Department delivered a letter from the wife of the Toll-Collector, who had been murdered, asking for some arrangements to be made for the burial of her husband. Captain Douglas replied: 'Under the circumstances of this mutiny I can now make no arrangements.' At this moment five troopers came galloping up and fired a volley from their carbines. One shot, striking Captain Douglas on the foot, quite disabled him. He then slipped down into the fort ditch, where some of the budmashes (scoundrels) attempted to attack him, but they were deterred by the presence of Kishen Sing, Kúrmi Jat, and others attached to the office of the Fort Commandant, who carried him safely to the door of the Fort on a roughly improvised litter of sticks. After reaching the Gate, Mukhun Sing and Kishen Sing and others who were present carried him upstairs. He asked for some water, which he drank. He addressed the soldiers at the Gate, and said: 'If you will shut the gates and exclude the mutineers, and will stand by the Europeans, I will promote one of your number to be a subahdar.' The chaprassie then carried him upstairs to his room, where there were Mr. Jennings, the chaplain, and two ladies – Miss Jennings and Miss Clifford – who helped to bandage the foot. Captain Douglas fainted several times. On regaining consciousness he called out: 'I left my sword on the open plain.' Mukhun Sing, under the orders of Captain Douglas and of the other gentlemen, then closed the doors. A noisy set of ruffians, chiefly sweetmeat-sellers and Mogul residents of the Fort, with other seditious and murderous persons, crying, 'Yá Allah! Yá Allah!' rushed up the stairs and called to Mukhun Sing to open the doors, else they would kill him as well. Mr. Jennings ordered the door to be opened, when the murderers rushed in, and with their swords released the life of each. The ladies had taken refuge in a mahogany wardrobe, and were dragged out. Mr. Jennings charged the men, and fell outside on the landing. The only one spared was Munshi Rám Lál, who was wounded. He was an officer of the King's household. It is believed he was knocked down with the butt end of a gun out of malice by one of the shopkeepers, who then escaped.

[48] The mutineers beard the king; from the narrative of Munshi Jeewan Lal in *Two Native Narratives of the Mutiny*.

When the King returned to the Palace, he found the courtyard of the Dewán-i-Khás crowded with troopers and their horses. They assailed him with loud cries, complaining that the men of the regiment which had mutinied at Delhi had possessed themselves of the treasure from the Delhi collectorate, intending to keep it, and had refused to share it with the Meerut mutineers. The King, utterly distracted and bewildered in the conflicting counsels, ordered the Princes, who had been appointed to the command of the troops, to send every mutineer out of the city, locating regiments in separate places, and leaving only one regiment in the Palace for the defence of the city, and another on the sands in front of the Palace, between the fort and the river. The King pointed out to some of the Subahdars present that the Dewán-i-Khás had hitherto been an enclosure sacred to Royalty alone, and had never before been forcibly entered by armed men. Another regiment was ordered to hold the Ajmere Gate of the city, a fourth the Delhi Gate, a fifth the Cashmere Gate. These orders were partially carried out. From house to house the unwilling King was distracted by cries and petitions – now from the servants of Europeans who had been murdered, now from the shopkeepers whose shops had been plundered, now from the higher classes whose houses had been broken into – all looked to the King for immediate redress. Appeals were made to him to repress the plunder and rapine now common throughout the city.

The King, in a Persian *rubakari*, beautiful with flowing language, called on all the Subahdars to remember that such a state of things was most unbecoming in the reign of a

Mahommedan king who was a bright light in the histories of the world, and at whose feet all other kings and monarchs waited with bended knee; and that it must be suppressed. Towards evening a number of his native regimental officers came and again represented the difficulty they experienced in getting rations. Forgetful of the lofty tone of the morning's order, and of the high-toned phraseology expressive of the King's dignity, they addressed him with such disrespectful terms as, 'I say, you King! I say, you old fellow!' 'Listen,' cried one, catching him by the hand. 'Listen to me,' said another, touching the old King's beard. Angered at their behaviour, yet unable to prevent their insolence, he found relief alone in bewailing before his servants his misfortunes and his fate. Again summoned by loud cries from outside the Palace gates, he passed a second time in procession through the city, calling on the shopkeepers to open their shops and resume trade. Throughout this eventful day he was distraught, perplexed, and cowed at finding himself in a position which made him the mere puppet of those who had formerly been only too glad humbly to obey his orders, but who now, taking advantage of the spirit of insubordination which was rife in all classes of the city in this day of ruin and riot, were not ashamed to mock and humiliate him.

[49] Hard times at Flagstaff Tower; from a statement by Captain Robert Tytler in the India Office records.

I was in Delhi on the 10th of May last. About 3 p.m. on Sunday, the 10th of May, I heard a bugle and the sound of carriage wheels pass my door. This being very unusual where I resided, I told a servant of mine to run out and see if any one was coming to my house. He went and returned immediately, and said it was a carriage with natives going towards the lines. My house being a corner one, the carriage was obliged to pass three sides of the grounds; so before it passed a second side, I directed the same servant to run to the lines, and give my salam to the subadar-major of the regiment, and say I wanted to see him, for it occurred to me that he and the other native officers of my regiment who had been to Meerut on court martial duty must be returning in this carriage. The servant returned shortly afterwards, and said there were a great number of natives in the

Repulse of a sortie by the Sepoys on the British troops before Delhi; lithograph, 1857. (Flagstaff Tower is on the escarpment, top right)

carriage from Meerut, but none belonging to our regiment, by which I distinctly understood he alluded to soldiers.

On the morning of the 11th of May, I think about 9 o'clock, one of my servants rushed into the room and said, Lieut. Holland had sent over to say that troops were marching on Delhi. I put on my uniform and went over to him. He joined me and we then went together to Lieut. Gambier, the Adjutant, where we met Colonel Knyvett, commanding the regiment, Captain Gardner and the Brigade Major, Captain Nicoll; and I then learnt the mutineers were marching from Meerut on to Delhi, and I was ordered at once to proceed to the lines and take my own Company along with Captain Gardner's, completing them to the strength of 200 men, with the usual allowance of ammunition in pouch. I was then ordered to proceed to a house on the ridge above the new powder magazine outside the city, and to be very particular that no body of men crossed over from the opposite side of the river. Captain Gardner and I went immediately to the lines; we found the men of our companies rather excited, and it was with some slight difficulty that we succeeded in completing each of our companies to 100 strong. A slight delay now took place in serving out the ammunition, and after sending repeatedly to the magazine to ascertain the cause, I went myself, and the khalassies said, 'what can we do? the sepoys about here who have come for ammunition are quarrelling and squabbling with us about the cartridges and caps, and we cannot give either without counting them.' I hurried the work and returned to the company. When the cartridges and caps were being served out, many of the men seized more bundles than they were entitled to; therefore to prevent further delay at the time I had these men marked, that I might punish them afterwards. Captain Gardner also remarked to me that the men of his company showed the same anxiety to secure more ammunition than they were entitled to. The order was now given to the companies to march. Both Captain Gardner and myself remarked the excited manner in which the men left the lines, shouting vehemently every now and then, and which neither of us could prevent. I wish here to record a circumstance that occurred on the morning of the 11th, but which I have omitted mentioning. There was a Brigade parade that morning to hear the sentence of a general court martial read regarding a native officer Ishwari Pandè at Barrackpore, when I remarked a murmur of disapprobation throughout the whole regiment. Though it lasted but a few seconds, it struck me forcibly as something extraordinary, never having witnessed any thing like it before. When we arrived at the house over the magazine, I placed sentries at different points which commanded the bend of the river. The rest of the men after piling arms, I took into the house; it was a very hot day, and as some of our men had procured water-melons and some sweetmeats they brought them to us, and insisted on our partaking of them; both Captain Gardner and myself remarked the great attention our men were paying us. In the meantime we were called out to see fires that were every now and then appearing in the city. Shortly after this we heard a report of cannon. All this we could not account for. Captain Gardner remarked to me how lucky it was that our men seemed so well disposed, as we were convinced that there was something serious going on in the city, particularly as we remembered the fires that had broken out in Umballa and other places. We now remarked that our men were forming small groups in the heat of the sun. I ordered them to come in and not expose themselves thus. They said, 'we like being in the sun.' I ordered them in again. When I went into one of the rooms, I remarked for the first time, a native from his appearance a soldier, haranguing the men of the companies and saying that every power or Government existed its allotted time, and that it was nothing extraordinary that that of the English had come to an end, according to what had been predicted in their native books. Before I could make a prisoner of him the magazine in the city exploded, and then the men of the two companies with a tremendous shout took up their arms and ran off to the city exclaiming, 'Prithiviraj ki jai!' or 'Victory to the sovereign of the world.'

On the men running off towards the city, and yelling out like fiends, *Prethiviraj ke jai*, both Captain Gardner and myself rushed after them, and ordered those within reach of hearing to return to their post; when orders failed, entreaties were resorted to, but proved of no avail; however thirty or forty men of my own company and about an equal number from Captain Gardner's returned; these were chiefly old soldiers that had served with me in Affghanistan. My men having thus deserted, I felt quite at a loss how to act and what to do, for we were perfectly ignorant that there was a mutiny and massacre in Delhi, so strictly did the sepoys keep all information from us, isolated as we were at this out-post. When shortly afterwards Lieutenant Mew of the 74th native infantry came to my post and said, that the Brigadier required a hundred of my men to take up a position near the rear guard of the 38th native infantry, I replied we had not a hundred men with us, and now for the first time learnt that there was a general mutiny and massacre of all Christians in the city, and that the officers, ladies and children were assembled at the flag-staff tower on the ridge. On hearing this, in a moment I formed my plan, collected my men and marched to the flag-staff tower, picking up all the troops in the shape of guards I could find on the way. On arriving at the flag-staff tower I found the tower full of ladies, children and servants; the Brigadier, European officers and civilians were congregated in front of the door facing the road leading to the Cashmere Gate of the city, from whence they expected momentarily an attack to be made on them by the mutineers in the city; in front of this body of officers, were the only two remaining guns of the Delhi brigade in position, and to their left was a cart containing the mangled remains of the officers murdered in front of the church in the city, chiefly officers of the 54th native infantry. The remnants of the native infantry regiments were to the right of the tower, sitting and standing in groups in a most sulky mood, whilst in rear of the tower stood some of the carriages and horses of the officers. After reporting the arrival of my party I made enquiries about my wife and children, for I had given Mrs. Tytler positive instructions not to leave on any account our house till I returned for her, and I dreaded to hear the worst, for had she remained in the bungalow, as I had asked her to do, she would have been murdered in cold-blood, as will be shewn hereafter; but the Almighty had willed it otherwise, and she was with the rest of the ladies in the flag-staff tower. On returning to the groups of officers I shall never forget the sad and unhappy but resigned countenances of all. Gardner and myself were, comparatively speaking, fresh, for we knew nothing of the horrors of the mutiny till Lieutenant Mew told us of it, whereas those we now saw had felt all the pangs of an anticipated speedy massacre, and seemed patiently waiting with resigned Christian fortitude the result of their fate, and that from about twelve o'clock noon, the hour they had assembled at the flag-staff. The smile and scornful look of defiance and exultation in the looks of the natives were unmistakeable and unbearable, contrasted with the meek resigned Christian fortitude of our men, women and even children. The manner in which our ladies helped in passing up to the top of the tower, the muskets and amunition, and in their entire bearing and presence of mind, showers the greatest credit on all present. No women in such peril and imminent danger, could ever have been expected to act in the praiseworthy manner, that those assembled in the flag-staff tower did. When I went into the tower, I found that for their better security, they had been sent into the narrow confined stair-case leading to the top, which added to their misery and discomfort, from the suffocating heat of the day. Seeing the helpless position we were all in, I at once decided that an immediate retreat was absolutely necessary; and particularly after hearing that the cavalry mutineers had left the city and were approaching cantonments from the Subzeemundee side, I went to the Brigadier, and apologizing to him for the liberty taken, recommended and begged for an immediate retreat to Meerut by a ford on the right of cantonments, which I was well acquainted with, having often been there whilst out shooting. The proposition of a retreat appeared to take all by surprise, and whilst it cheered and held out hopes to many, the majority strongly opposed it, considering it would be an act of insanity leaving the tower, feeling convinced that I had been talked over by the men, who, they said, were anxious to get us away from this position, to fall on us at once; and that we ought to stop, and defend it to the last. My views however differed, and I earnestly urged on the Brigadier the necessity for an immediate retreat, pointing out to him that the few men of the 38th that were left, were composed of the best men in the regiment, and that I felt convinced they would protect us and cover our retreat. The Brigadier, overwhelmed as he was with anxiety, fatigue and the responsibility of his painful situation, listened to my request and told me to ascertain the feelings and disposition of the sepoys of the 38th. I accordingly went to them, they were about 150 or 200 strong, besides men of the other two regiments. I begged of our sepoys not to deceive us but to tell me, would they cover our retreat to Meerut or elsewhere whichever the Brigadier might think most advisable; they solemnly declared they would. I pointed out to them that we had been upwards of twenty-three years together, serving in Affganistan and several other places, the character our corps had always borne, and why should they now disgrace that regiment we had always been so proud of, and join in such foul cold-blooded murders as had been perpetrated this day? I appealed to them as the best men of our regiment, telling them to tell me honestly and not to deceive us, for I stood amongst them, unarmed and in their power, would they, or would they not, protect us and cover our retreat? Most of the men came up to me and put their hands respectfully on my head, whilst with the most solemn oaths they swore they would protect us and cover our retreat, in which declaration all joined, but begged that I should take personal command of them, and that the two guns now with us should be kept in advance of, and near the infantry, for being as they declared they were disaffected, they would seize the first favourable opportunity of firing into them for protecting us. They also entreated to be taken where water could be had, as they had not tasted water since the morning. All this I promised should be done, reminding them of their solemn oath to be faithful to us. I hurried back and reported the result to the Brigadier, begging of him as it was nearly evening, that we had not one moment to lose, but to retire at once, for I had heard that the troopers of the cavalry from Meerut glutted with their spoil and blood-thirsty deeds, had left the city and were then resting themselves and horses near Subzeemundee, prior to their intended attack on cantonments, which would take place the moment they were refreshed. The number of voices which opposed this movement exceeded those who agreed with me, thus naturally causing the Brigadier to doubt how to act, for the responsibility of his position was fearfully great. I again and again entreated and urged the necessity for our immediate retreat, a second and a third time he sent me to ascertain the real feelings and disposition of our men, and the result was the same, and my opinion each time strengthened, that we had not one moment to lose, and that the men would protect us. Still hope clung to that solitary tower in the breasts of many, it seemed to them their only safety, and they could not be persuaded to leave but to remain, defend and die in it. What a helpless situation to be murdered in, which it would have been, had not the Almighty willed it otherwise. A small solitary building isolated from all others built on a ridge, a conspicuous object from every side, full of men, women and children, without a drop of water, or a particle of food, a frail piece of brick and mortar suffocating in itself from the intense heat in the month of May. The Brigadier, thank God! saw the necessity of acceding to my request, and said, 'Well, what is to be done?' I replied, 'Put all the ladies and children in every available carriage, the guns to follow with the infantry close behind them, the latter I will take command of'; at the same time I proposed that it would be advisable, if the European officers would keep with the infantry, thus shewing a degree of confidence in the men. This however would not be listened to, for none had any faith in the sepoys with us, having seen during the day the treachery of the others, and which I was, comparatively speaking, ignorant of. All the officers of the 38th remained with me, as well as several Civilians, and we left the flag-staff tower as proposed, when I had put Mrs. Tytler, my children and Mrs. Gardner into my palanquin-carriage. My pay havildar Omrow Sing, and a sepoy Thakoordeen, both men that I had every confidence in, came to the carriage, and with tears in their eyes, entreated of me to make my family over to them, and that they would take them to Meerut, by hiding them from village to village amongst their people, and thus protect them. They begged and implored of me to listen to them, for they said, we had not five minutes to live, and that an escape was impossible, for that the sowars had sworn to take the blood of every Christian. I said, 'No, I am perfectly satisfied that the men of my regiment will protect us.' They then entreated of Mrs. Tytler, to get me to listen to them, she spoke to me, and talked of our children, but I was too resolved; if we were to be destroyed, God's will must be done, but I would not hear of their plan faithful as I then considered them, still I doubted their power of assistance in a case and trial of this nature. I now returned to the infantry column, reminded the men of their sacred pledged oath, and gave the word, 'sections right shoulders forward quick march,' the sepoys moved off, steadily enough till we reached the bottom of the ridge in cantonments, when two men of our regiment, that had been on duty at the magazine in the city, at the time it was blown up, joined our party, scorched in a frightful manner, a group of at least one-third of our men surrounded them, innumerable questions were put, and replied to, the purport of which was that the English had designedly blown up the magazine for the wilful destruction of the natives, and of the native guard, and that the whole of the 38th guard were destroyed, they only having escaped. I now heard a murmur of disgust and disapprobation, and could plainly hear words to this effect uttered, 'let it be so, we will see and taste the blood of the English yet.'

[50] An officer's account of the storming of the Kashmir Gate; from a letter signed 'Felix' to the Editor of the *Lahore Chronicle*, dated 30 September 1857.

On the 11th our batteries opened fire, a salvo from the nine 24-pounders opening the ball, and showing by the way it brought down the wall in huge fragments what effect it might be expected to produce after a few hours. The Kashmir Bastion attempted to reply, but was quickly silenced, and both portions of No. II went to work in fine style, knocking the bastion and adjacent curtains to pieces. Majors Campbell and Kaye, Captain Johnson and Lieutenant Gray had charge of No. II. No. III, however, did not commence fire till the following day, when the full power of our artillery was shown, and the continuous roar of fifty guns and mortars pouring shot and shell on the devoted city, warned the enemy that his and our time had at length come. Night and day, until the morning of the 14th, was this overwhelming fire continued. But the enemy did not let us have it all our own way. Though unable to work a gun from any of the three bastions that were so fiercely assailed, they yet stuck to their guns in the open, which partially enfiladed our position; they got a gun to bear from a hole broken open in the long curtain wall; they sent rockets from one of their martello towers, and they maintained a perfect storm of musketry from their advanced trench, and from the city walls.

On the night of the 13th the engineers stole down and examined the two breaches near the Kashmir and Water Bastions; and both being reported practicable, orders for the assault were at once issued, to take place at daybreak the following morning.

At 4 a.m. [*on 14th September*] the different columns fell in, and were marched to their respective places, the heads of Nos. 1, 2, and 3 Columns being kept concealed until the moment for the actual assault should arrive.

The signal was to be the advance of the Rifles to the front to cover the heads of the columns by skirmishing.

Everything being ready, General Nicholson, whose excellent

arrangements elicited the admiration of all, gave the signal, and the Rifles dashed to the front with a cheer, extending along and skirmishing through the low jungle, which at this point extends to within fifty yards of the ditch. At the same moment, the heads of Nos. 1 and 2 Columns from the Kudsia Bagh, advanced steadily towards the breach[*es*]. Our batteries had maintained a tremendous fire up to the moment of the advance of the troops, and not a gun could the enemy bring to bear on the storming columns; but no sooner did these emerge into the open, than a perfect hailstorm of bullets met them from the front and both flanks, and officers and men fell fast on the crest of the glacis. For ten minutes it was impossible to get the ladders down into the ditch to ascend the escarp; but the determination of the British soldier carried all before it, and Pandy declined to meet the charge of the British bayonet. With a shout and a rush the breaches were both won, and the enemy fled in confusion.

Meanwhile the explosion party advanced in front of the 3rd column straight upon the Kashmir Gate. This little band of heroes (for they were no less) had to advance in broad daylight to the gateway in the very teeth of a hot fire of musketry from above, and through the gateway and on both flanks; the powder bags were coolly laid and adjusted, but Lieutenant Salkeld was by this time *hors de combat* with two bullets in him. Sergeant Carmichael then attempted to fire the hose, but was shot dead. Sergeant Burgess then tried and succeeded, but paid for the daring act with his life. Sergeant Smith, thinking that Burgess too had failed, ran forward, but seeing the train alight had just time to throw himself into the ditch and escape the effects of the explosion. With a loud crash the gateway was blown in, and through it the 3rd Column rushed to the assault, and entered the town just as the other columns had won the breaches. General Wilson has since bestowed the Victoria Cross on Lieutenants Home and Salkeld, on Sergeant Smith, and on a brave man of Her Majesty's 52nd [*Bugler Hawthorne*], who stood by Lieutenant Salkeld to the last, and bound up his wounds.

General Nicholson then formed the troops in the Main Guard inside, and with his Column proceeded to clear the ramparts as far as the Mori Bastion. It was in advancing beyond this [*from the Kabul Gate*] towards the Lahore Gate that he met the wound which has since caused his lamented death – a death which it is not too much to say has dimmed the lustre of even this victory –

as it has deprived the country of one of the ablest men and most gallant soldiers that England anywhere numbers among our ranks.

The 4th Column, I regret to say, failed; but as it was too far for me to know anything of its real progress, I prefer leaving its story to be told by another instead of sending you a vague and imperfect account. Had this Column succeeded, its possession of the Lahore Gate would have saved much subsequent trouble.

Mr Editor, I regret that my account must stop here, as, being wounded myself at this stage of the proceedings, I was unable to witness the subsequent capture of the magazine, the Burn Bastion, the palace, and finally of the whole city. Some one else will doubtless conclude my story in a more worthy manner than I have told it.

Thus terminated the siege of Delhi. Our loss during the actual siege was about 300 men. On the day of the assault it was 61 officers and 1178 men killed and wounded, being nearly one-third of the whole number engaged. The loss of the enemy is never likely to be correctly ascertained; but at the end of the operations it is probable that at least 1500 men must have been killed between the 7th and 20th, and a very large number wounded, who were carried away ... The plan of attack was bold and skilful, the nature of the enemy we were contending with was exactly appreciated, and our plans shaped accordingly. Pandy can fight well behind cover; but here he was out-manoeuvred, his attention being diverted from the real point of attack till the last, and then the cover which might have proved such a serious obstacle to us was seized at the right moment without loss and all its advantages turned against him. With plenty of skilled workmen the siege works might have been more speedily constructed, but with the wretched means at our disposal the wonder is that so much was done with so little loss.

If the siege of Delhi was not a regular siege in the same sense with that of Bhurtpore or Seringapatam, it may yet bear a fairer comparison with a greater than either – that of Sebastopol. In both the strength of the fortifications was as nothing; it was the proportion of besieged to besiegers, the magnitude of the arsenal inside, and the impossibility of a thorough investment that constituted the real strength of the place; in fact, neither were, properly speaking, sieges, but rather attacks on an army in a strongly intrenched position.   (Signed) FELIX.

[51] Hodson – right or wrong?; from *Indian Reminiscences* by Colonel S. Dewé White.

(Colonel S. Dewé White wrote his bitter reminiscences (published in 1880) while in retirement at Southsea. An over-zealous Christian, he was unpopular with his brother officers.)

The importance of securing the principal members of the Royal Family was pressed upon the General by Chamberlain and Hodson, who both urged that the victory would be incomplete if the King and his male relatives were allowed to remain at large. Wilson would not consent to any force being sent after them, and it was with considerable reluctance that he agreed to Hodson going on this hazardous duty with some of his own men only. The last of the Moghul Emperors had taken refuge in Humayun's tomb, about seven miles from Delhi, where, on the afternoon of the 21st, he surrendered to Hodson on receiving a promise from that officer that his own life and the lives of his favourite wife and her son should be spared. Hodson brought them all into Delhi and placed them under a European guard in a house in the Chandni Chauk, thus adding one more to the many valuable services he had rendered throughout the siege.

I went with many others the next day to see the King; the old man looked most wretched, and as he evidently disliked intensely being stared at by Europeans, I quickly took my departure. On my way back I was rather startled to see the three lifeless bodies of the King's two sons and grandson lying exposed on the stone platform in front of the *Kotwali*. On enquiry I learnt that Hodson had gone a second time to Humayun's tomb that morning with the object of capturing these Princes, and on the way back to Delhi had shot them with his own hand – an act which, whether necessary or not, has undoubtedly cast a blot on his reputation. His own explanation of the circumstance was that he feared they would be rescued by the mob, who could easily have overpowered his small escort of 100 sowars, and it certainly would have been a misfortune had these men escaped. At the time a thirst for revenge on account of the atrocities committed within the walls of Delhi was so great that the shooting of the Princes seemed to the excited feelings of the army but an act of justice; and there were some men, whose opinions were entitled to the greatest respect, who considered the safety of the British force would have been endangered by the escape of the representatives of the house of Taimur, and that for this reason Hodson's act was justified.

My own feeling on the subject is one of sorrow that such a brilliant soldier should have laid himself open to so much adverse criticism. Moreover, I do not think that, under any circumstances, he should have done the deed himself, or ordered it to be done in that summary manner, unless there had been evident signs of an attempt at a rescue.

But it must be understood that there was no breach of faith on Hodson's part, for he steadily refused to give any promise to the Princes that their lives should be spared; he did, however, undoubtedly by this act give colour to the accusations of bloodthirstiness which his detractors were not slow to make.

[52] An awful aftermath; from *Red Year* by Michael Edwardes.

When the news reached Lord Canning that Delhi had been recaptured, he wrote to General Wilson: 'In the name of outraged humanity, in memory of innocent blood ruthlessly shed, and in acknowledgement of the first signal vengeance inflicted on the foulest treason, the Governor-General in Council records his gratitude to Major-General Wilson and the brave army of Delhi.'

The signal vengeance was by no means over, nor was there any cessation in the amount of innocent blood ruthlessly shed, for the city of Delhi was put to the sword, looted and sacked with the ferocity of a Nazi extermination squad in occupied Poland.

After the capture of the palace, Colonel Bourchier had looked out from its walls over the devastated city. 'The demon of destruction,' he wrote in his diary, 'seemed to have enjoyed a perfect revel. The houses in the neighbourhood of the Mori and Kashmir bastions were a mass of ruins, the walls near the breaches cracked in every direction, while the church was completely riddled by shot and shell.' Most of the city, however, was not badly damaged, at least until the soldiers got at it. Maddened by a heady mixture of fatigue, liquor and bloody rumour, they turned violently on the city and its inhabitants. 'All the people found within the walls when our troops entered were bayoneted on the spot, and the number was considerable as you may suppose, when I tell you that in some houses forty and fifty persons were hiding. These were not mutineers, but residents of the city who trusted to our mild rule for pardon. I am glad to say they were disappointed.' The writer exaggerated, for by no means all the inhabitants were murdered, but no one cared to compute the total.

The authorities were not much concerned with what happened to the male citizens, but they did think that women and children should be spared. General Wilson issued an order strictly forbidding violence against women and children, but few obeyed it, especially after a soldier observed, under the veil of a 'girl' he had caught, the beard of a rebel sepoy.

The fear of people who were as yet unmolested was such that men killed their women and then themselves. One writer reported that he had 'given up walking about the streets of Delhi, as yesterday an officer and myself had taken a party of twenty men out patrolling, and we found fourteen women with their throats cut from ear to ear by their own husbands, and laid out on shawls. We caught a man there who said he saw them killed, for fear they should fall into our hands; and showed us their husbands, who had done the best thing they could afterwards, and killed themselves.'

When rough order had been imposed, old men, women (subject to some inspection) and children were on the whole left untouched. Sensibly, most of them chose to leave the city and were brutally encouraged to do so by the British. Frederick Roberts, the future Field Marshal, felt some regret. 'I have wished these last few days,' he wrote to his father on 26 September, 'that there were no such things as women where war was. Kicking men out of house and home matters little, but I cannot bear seeing unfortunate women suffering, and yet it can't be helped.'

Perhaps the most revolting aspect of the violence was that the executioners seemed to enjoy what they were doing. Within a few days of the capture of the city, the provost marshal had officially hanged between four and five hundred, and it was said on good authority that the soldiers had bribed the executioners 'to keep them a long time hanging, as they liked to see the criminals dance a "Pandies" hornpipe, as they termed the dying struggles of the wretches.' When a great multiple gallows was erected in a square in the city, 'English officers used to sit by it, puffing at their cigars, and look on at the convulsive struggles of the victims.'

If there was much indiscriminate terrorising, there was also a kind of institutional violence. The magistrate, Sir Theophilus Metcalfe, reopened his court. In it prosecution was swift, and a decision of 'not guilty' so rare that few noticed it. Lesser princes of the royal family were charged with conspiring with the rebels, on evidence that was dubious to say the least. But they *were* members of the royal family and therefore, without question, guilty. They were 'all condemned, hanged, and carted off the same day' Metcalfe, for sound reasons, was held in dread by the citizens of Delhi. When a jeweller appeared to be asking too much for his wares, his British customer threatened: 'I shall send you to Metcalfe Sahib.' The man bolted in such a hurry that he left his treasures behind, and never again showed his face. Certainly, there was little possibility of escaping alive from Metcalfe's justice. His victims usually ended up swinging from the beams of burnt-out Metcalfe House.

Life was cheap now in Delhi, but there was no squandering of property. Everyone except the most senior officers plundered whatever could be found before the official Prize Agents seized everything. Houses were attacked, their walls ripped down and their floors ripped up in the search for buried treasure. And there was a great deal to be found. 'The plunder being daily found in the city is more than enormous; it is almost incredible. I fancy every officer present at the siege might be able to retire at once.' It was not only officers who benefited. One recalled later that when his regiment returned to England an unusually large number of men and non-commissioned officers bought their discharge from the army. They had succeeded in keeping their plunder from Delhi for nearly three years, and had then sold it. 'Many jewellers' shops in the town in which we were quartered exposed for sale in the windows, ornaments and trinkets of unmistakable Eastern workmanship.'

When the Prize Agents took over they were no less rapacious, but much of the cream had gone. Even so, when the government of India decided not to divide the prize money but to give the captors of Delhi only the equivalent of six months' pay, there was such an outcry that the government surrendered. The sum involved was between half and three-quarters of a million sterling, at the then rate of exchange. It represented only a fraction of what had actually been taken from the city.

Between the private plunderers and the Prize Agents, Delhi had been very thoroughly ransacked. But although the Prize Agents had their methods, they were not as good as the Sikhs who had joined the British on the Ridge. In an attempt to fix their loyalty, before the city was captured, they had been reminded, deliberately, that there existed a prophecy which foretold the sacking of Delhi by men of their faith. 'Like hounds drawing a cover, they took street by street, and entering one deserted house after another, tapped each wall or panel with the delicate touch of an artist, poured water over the floors observing where it sank through fastest, and then, as though they had been gifted with the eye of an eagle, the ear of the Red Indian, or the nose of the bloodhound, cut their way straight through to the cranny or the cupboard, or the underground jars which contained the savings of a lifetime or of generations.'

So Delhi suffered its reign of terror. The poet Ghalib mourned: 'Here is a vast ocean of blood before me, God alone knows what more I have to behold . . . Thousands of my friends are dead. Whom should I remember and to whom should I complain? Perhaps none is left even to shed tears upon my death . . . My pen dare not write more.' Poet or Christian, trusted Indian assistant to a Prize Agent, it mattered nothing to the British. Professor Ramchandra of the Delhi College, a Christian employed by the Prize Agents, was forced to leave his house. He was abused in the street and on at least one occasion attacked by an officer who did not care whether he was a Christian or not – for he 'was as black as jet'.

It took many weeks before the truth about what was going on inside Delhi reached the ears of responsible authority outside. John Lawrence reacted strongly against indiscriminate vengeance, and so did Lord Canning. But they were crying against the strongest of winds. As late as 4 December, Lawrence was writing to Canning: 'I do not know what your Lordship has resolved to do with Delhi. But if it is to be preserved as a city, I do hope that your Lordship will put a stop to the operations of the Prize Agents. I also recommend that it be free from martial law. What Delhi requires is a soldier of energy, spirit and character to keep the troops in order, and a strong police and a magistrate to maintain the peace. Until there be some security for the lives and property of the natives, tranquillity will not be restored. I am a strong advocate for prompt and severe punishment when such has been deserved. But the systematic spoliation which I understand goes on at Delhi cannot fail to exasperate the natives, and render more wide and lasting the breach which has taken place between them and us.'

[53] Some verses inspired by the Munity; quoted in *Red Year* by Michael Edwardes.

Avenge O Lord thy slaughtered saints by Martin Tupper, published in the *Naval and Military Gazette*, 5 September 1857.

> And, England, now avenge their wrongs by vengeance deep and dire,
> Cut out this canker with the sword and burn it out with fire;
> Destroy these traitor legions, hang every Pariah-hound,
> And hunt them down to death, in all the hills and cities round.

Lines on the death of John Nicholson 'from a Punjabi ballad recently sung in the streets of Delhi' by L.J. Trotter.

> John Lawrence sent a missive to Britain's gracious Queen,
> Recounting first proud Delhi's fall, and the great hero's mien,
> How gallantly he stormed the breach, above the Kashmir gate,
> And ever foremost in the van, had met a soldier's fate.
> The Queen, with gentle sympathy, in tears this letter read,
> And then her chieftain's mother called, whose only son was dead.
> She soothed the mother's bitter grief, and from her royal neck,
> Weeping, a priceless necklet took, her sobbing guest to deck;
> Oh! mother's heart, be comforted, nor mourn thy soldier son;
> God owns thy child, in England's Queen thou has a mother won.

New Delhi

[54] So why build New Delhi? Thoughts from the mid-nineteenth century; from *The Travels of a Hindoo* . . . by Bholanauth Chunder.

The public works of a people embody the form and pressure of their age. The public works of the Hindoos were royal roads, rows of trees, canals and bridges, topes of mango and peepul, tanks and wells, rest-houses for the night, *durmshalas* or inns, hospitals, bathing-ghauts, and temples – all public works for the comforts only of the physical man. The Mahomedans nearly trod in the footsteps of their predecessors. Their reservoirs, aqueducts, canals, gardens, serais, and mosques, exhibit but the same cares for the material well-being of a people, without any progress made by humanity towards the amelioration of its moral condition. Far otherwise are the public works of the English. Their schools and colleges, literary institutes, public libraries, museums, and botanic gardens, are proofs of a greater intellectual state of the world than in any preceding age. It is not suited to the genius or inclination of the Europeans to build churches and temples. The age would not tolerate such a costly sentimentality as the Taj. It would be an anachronism now. The generations of the present day say that 'they are not called upon to do anything for posterity – posterity having done nothing for them?' Supposing the English were to quit India, the beneficence of their rule ought not to be judged of by the external memorials of stone and masonry left behind them, but by the emancipation of our nation from prejudices and superstitions of a long standing, and by the enlightened state in which they shall leave India. In the words of De Quincey, 'higher by far than the Mogul gift of lime-stone, or travelling stations, or even roads and tanks, were the gifts of security, of peace, of law, and settled order.'

[55] An event of 'Periclean importance'; from an article by Robert Byron in *Architectural Review*, January 1931.

(Robert Byron (1905–47) travelled to India in 1929 as special correspondent for the *Daily Express*. His well-received *The Road to Oxiana* (1937) was a somewhat light-hearted travelogue overlaid with a significant enquiry into the origins of Islamic art. The Eton and Oxford of the aesthetes may be said to have influenced his attitudes.)

That New Delhi exists, and that, twenty years ago, it did not exist, are facts known to anyone who is at all aware of the British connection with India. It is expected, and assumed, that the representatives of British sovereignty beyond the seas shall move in a setting of proper magnificence; and that in India, particularly, the temporal power shall be hedged with the divinity of earthly splendour. To satisfy this expectation, New Delhi was designed and created. But that the city's existence marks, besides an advance in the political unification of India, a notable artistic event, has scarcely been realized. Nor is this surprising in a generation which has been taught by painful experience to believe architectural splendour and gaiety inseparable from vulgarity. Of the city's permanent value as an aesthetic monument, posterity must be the final judge. But to contemporaries, and in the darkness of contemporary standards, the event shines with a Periclean importance.

    The surprise which awaits the traveller on his first view of the imperial capital will be proportionate to the fixity of his previous ideas about it. Primarily, his conception has been political. The very words 'New Delhi' suggest a Canberra in Asia, a hiving of black-coated officials in a maze of offices. True, there have been photographs; but these have been either of the worse buildings, which were finished first, or, if of the better, of structures in disarray, confused with scaffolding, and offset by no proper layout. Nor can, nor ever will, any photograph convey the colour of the scheme and the part played by colour in the unity and proportion of the architecture. Again, the traveller may already have assessed the worth of the architects from their buildings in London. He may have recalled Britannic House at Finsbury Circus, the little bank abutting on St. James's, Piccadilly, and the cenotaph in Whitehall, from the hand of Sir Edwin Lutyens;

together with the Ninth Church of Christ Scientist, India House, and the new Bank of England, from that of Sir Herbert Baker. And he must confess that, whatever the merits of these buildings compared with those around them, judged by universal standards they display little distinction and no genius. Finally, before he reaches Delhi, the traveller must necessarily have observed the scale and variety already employed by English enterprise to embellish the chief towns of India; and he must have found himself, in the process, not merely depressed, but tempted to regret our nation's very existence. For it has been our misfortune to have impressed on the length and breadth of the country an architectural taste whose origin coincided with the sudden and complete enslavement of European aesthetics to the whims of literary and romantic symbolism. The nineteenth century devised nothing lower than the municipal buildings of British India. Their ugliness is positive, daemonic. The traveller feels that the English have set the mark of the beast on a land full of artistry and good example. Here and there, in the large commercial towns, a new dawn is breaking. But the traveller remembers anxiously that the greater part of New Delhi was designed before the War. Only in the unremitting abuse lavished on the new city by resident Englishmen and occidentalized Indians does a perverse hope seem to linger.

I must here interpolate a personal experience. I had reached this point in my observations when a company of Scottish soldiers, heralded by bagpipes, marched through the stone railings on to one end of the Great Place, and threading past the three fountains reached a point between the Secretariats. Here they wheeled sharply to the left and went at a smart pace up the asphalt gradient in the direction of the central dome. The dramatic value of Scottish kilts and Scottish music in foreign countries is fully realized by the authorities, who always use it to give point to 'forceful demonstrations'; nor is that value lessened by the presence of a khaki coal-scuttle on each man's head. But in this setting, beneath this range of towering buildings multi-coloured in the blue sky, amidst all this decorated space, the apparition of these troops defiling up that mysterious trough between the Secretariats towards the glowing dome beyond, their accoutrements flashing in the Indian sun, and only a crawling ox-cart to deflect the attention, was more than merely theatrical. The emotion of time and circumstance, third dimension of true splendour, was evoked. The whole history of civilized man, of all his politics, empires, thrones, and wars, of all his effort to govern and be governed, followed in the soldiers' wake. That the entire spectacle, men and buildings, was the symbol of English dominion, seemed merely incidental. But that the evolution of government could demand, and create, in its everyday course, such a spectacle, seemed to postulate an apotheosis of human order. Indian nationalists, should they see them, will detect a propagandist ring in these words, and will point my attention from gaudy display to the rights of man. To which it must be answered that beauty is infallible, and confers a measure of right on its creators, whatever their sins.

[56] Robert Byron loves Lutyens . . . and bashes Baker; from an article by Robert Byron in *Architectural Review*, January 1931.

In 1911, Sir Edwin Lutyens, at once architect and humanist, but fettered (so it seems to many) by the powerful and admirable tradition of eighteenth-century building in his own country, was commissioned to design a city in Asia. Before him lay an arid plain; above, a fierce sun and a blue sky; near by, the ghost of an ancient imperial capital; and on every side a people who, from prince to coolie woman, possess an innate and living desire for what is proper and best. Behind him stood an imposing political organization, a superb product of the European genius. The mainspring of this organization must be housed. Its housing must be both convenient and magnificent.

Like all humanists, Sir Edwin Lutyens had drunk of the European past, and he now drank of the Indian. He borrowed themes and inventions from both. But he used them as Beethoven used snatches of popular songs in his symphonies, or Shakespeare old legends in his plays.

In so doing, he has accomplished a fusion between East and West, and created a novel work of art. But the fusion between East and West is only incidentally one of architectural motives. It is a fusion also of tastes, comforts, and conceptions of beauty, in different climates. The Mogul Emperors, behind their gorgeous façades, lived in rooms like housemaids' closets – though set with pearls and rubies. Lutyens has combined the gorgeous façade, coloured and dramatic, of Asia, with the solid habit, cubic and intellectual, of European building. Taking the best of East and West, bests which are complementary, he has made of them a unity, and invested it with a double magnificence. That his scheme will ever be haunted by the ghosts of lost possibilities, is a tragedy which he shares with all the great architects of history.

But above all, in every rib and moulding, in every block of stone, he has revealed and given life that perfectly balanced sanity and proportion which is the distilled essence of beauty, and which Europe calls the humanist ideal. Sometimes, even, he has shouted for joy in his earth, conjuring rays from a dome, fountains from a roof, a glass star from a column, and smoke from an arch.

Geoffrey Scott, addressing those who term the baroque style of architecture ostentatious, asks if they find ostentation in the shout of an army. 'Other architectures,' he says, 'by other men, have conveyed strength in repose. . . . But the laughter of strength is expressed in one style only; the Italian baroque architecture of the seventeenth century.' New Delhi has caught the echo of that laughter. It peals over the land, mitigating for those who hear it, the steel fury of the sun and the tragedy of conflicting effort. But those who hear it are few. The majority are deaf to all but the 'rights of man' – whether to give or to withhold them. They forget that one of those rights is beauty. This at least the English have given. And for this at least the English will be remembered. The Council Chamber has been Sir Herbert's unhappiest venture. Its effect from a distance has been described. It resembles a Spanish bull-ring, lying like a mill-wheel dropped accidentally on its side.

The exigencies of constitutional discussion have obliged Sir Herbert Baker to divide the interior of the Council Chamber into three courtyards of peculiar, and indeed fantastic, shape, each of which discloses a section of a pivotal circular building in the centre. They deserve careful study. For they epitomize all that New Delhi might have been; and all that New Delhi, owing to Sir Edwin Lutyens, is not.

Surmounting the cupola of the central building, the wartlike cupola already observed from without, the royal crown of England is reared into the sky on a red stalk. We shall see this again; and also the white bowler hat, flat-brimmed like that of a foreign Jesuit, from which it rises. This hat is Sir Herbert's adaptation of the roof of a Mogul *chattri* into a more European form. It is here supported by a ring of decorated pillars hung with stone pants. The whole rests on an eye, which balances precariously on a grooved white drum. This dome, which forms the entire roof of the plaster gasometer beneath it, rises from within a heavy parapet-cornice, accompanied by a spawn of subsidiary *chattris*. Below the cornice falls a heavy shadow, which, with various ribs, emphasizes the circular character of the supporting wall. The latter's bottom zone has been dented with classical niches, between which are placed a series of front doors in Kensington.

[57] Connaught Place lacks grandeur; from *Indian Summer* by Robert Grant Irving.

R.T. Russell, Chief Architect to the Government of India, and his office prepared the detailed designs for Connaught Place along lines which Nicholls had advocated before leaving Delhi in 1917. Airy stuccoed colonnades, punctuated by Palladian archways, afforded protection to shoppers from sun and rain alike, and the elegant, understated classicism prompted admiring comparisons with terraces at Bath and Cheltenham. Built only two stories tall, however, the blocks failed to achieve the intended effect of urban enclosure, even before trees in the central park grew to obscure views across the circus. Furthermore, as Nicholls had feared, the sheer width of avenue entrances interrupted the desired circular continuity and rendered the boundaries of the plaza ambiguous. But these visual defects did not hamper the magnetic popularity of the stylish shops, which eventually eclipsed fashionable Chandni Chauk in Old Delhi. Indeed forty years after its first bricks were laid, one Indian planner recorded that Connaught Place, full of hustle and glamor, had become the Delhiwallah's abiding image of his city far more than even that widely recognized symbol, the historic Qutb Minar.

[58] Life at the Viceroy's House; from *Palaces of the Raj* . . .
by Mark Bence-Jones.

The Viceroy's House knew the full splendours of the Raj for a
mere ten years, until the Second World War put an end to grand
entertainments. It was a swansong, and a brief one; yet
magnificent for all that. A visiting French nobleman has left an
account of a State Ball in the Willingdons' time. He was escorted
by one of the ADCs – 'fair-haired youngsters who looked
charming in their dress suits faced with sky-blue lapels' – to the
foot of the open staircase, which seemed to him 'the most
handsome staircase in the world'. There were two of the
Bodyguard on each step, 'motionless as two grim giants hewn in
stone'; the gold costumes of the maharajas mingled with the
shining lustre of saris, the red, blue and silver of uniforms, the
glitter of diadems and the 'flaxen coiffures of the young
Englishwomen'; while high overhead was the 'starlit splendour
of the Indian night'. Ascending the stairs, he found himself
advancing across the marble floor of the Durbar Hall, 'highly
polished as a mirror', to where, flanked by *chobdars* with maces,
stood the Viceroy, 'a charming representative of the English
aristocracy who looked his royal part to proud perfection', and
'his smiling vivacious wife, who with prodigious sleight of mind
found something to say – infallibly the right and fitting thing – to
every one of us'. Then on into the ballroom, with 'sweet wafts of
orange blossom' coming through the open windows.

Even more splendid was the scene when the elderly
Willingdons had been replaced by the towering figure of Lord
Linlithgow, immensely handsome and in the very prime of life,
with his tall and graceful consort by his side. For an Investiture,
they entered the Durbar Hall to a fanfare of trumpets, preceded
by their Staff in scarlet and gold and followed by solemn little
Indian boys, sons of maharajas or nawabs, carrying their trains.
The corridors beyond the apses were lined with the Bodyguard;
there were 600 people in the hall itself, waiting to be invested,
together with 400 spectators.

Then there were the banquets held during sessions of the
Chamber of Princes, when every other guest at the long table was
the ruler of a State. The gold plate glittered in its crimson-lined
niche, the lustres glinted, the scarlet and gold *khitmagars* moved
deftly against the teak-panelled walls, and from an adjoining

The Viceroy, Lord Curzon, with Lady Curzon,
entering Delhi at the Durbar of 1903

room came the music of the Viceroy's Band. The Band played every night, even when there was only a small party in the Semi-State Dining room downstairs, and by a long-standing custom, the company always went into dinner to the strains of *The Roast Beef of Old England*, which Lord Linlithgow and his family used to sing in a rousing chorus when there were no official guests.

Whatever might have been said about Lutyens' palace being only suited to great occasions, it provided a pleasant enough background for the day-to-day life of the Viceregal family, as well as for the party of handsome and high-spirited young ADCs in attendance on them. 'In spite of its size, it was essentially a liveable-in house,' recalled Lord Halifax, the former Lord Irwin, shortly before his death. 'Admiration and affection for it steadily grew together, and every day that we lived there, we came to love it more.' The Irwins had watched the house growing to completion during the first three years of their Viceroyalty; they had helped to furnish it, and had supervised the planting of the garden. In their day, the trees were still small and the creepers had not yet covered Lutyens' stone pergolas, but they were able to enjoy 'the riot of colour from the best of Western flowers' which grew in tropical profusion, softening the formal pattern of lawns and waterways in the main Mogul garden, running wild in the more English setting of the walled garden beyond. During the spring and autumn months, luncheon was served out of doors in the shadow of the house, or beneath the colonnade of the swimming pool, and there would also be dinner under the stars. Although Delhi could at times be very hot – a perspiring Lutyens had once suggested that the new capital should be called Oozapore – it was a dry heat, far less enervating than the humidity of Calcutta. In winter, the climate was crisp and bracing; log fires crackled in Lutyens' elegant fireplaces.

If the climate of Delhi was pleasanter than that of Calcutta, so was the atmosphere. One did not feel oppressed by the ghosts of the past, even though the surrounding plain was strewn with crumbling tombs. Lord Irwin and the Commander-in-Chief, Sir Philip Chetwode, would go for early morning rides across the plain, accompanied by their respective daughters, and with a single Indian ADC in attendance. In November, the mimosa trees and tamarinds were in flower; in spring, the corn was green; but at other times, the plain was burnt brown by the sun. They would pass the bullocks turning their wheels, and the processions of camels bringing in the crops. Sometimes they would have their breakfast among the fallen masonry of one of the tombs. That there was open country immediately beyond the Viceregal Estate was not the least of the advantages possessed by New Delhi over Calcutta, where, for many years, the inhabitants of Government House had only been able to ride on the Maidan. These morning rides, and a game of tennis in the afternoon, provided the Viceroy with much-needed exercise, for as often as not he spent the rest of the day and the greater part of the night at his desk, pausing only for meals. Lord Linlithgow even worked at breakfast, which he had with his Private Secretary; and he would retire after dinner to his study on the ground floor overlooking the garden and stay there till the small hours.

During the War years, and the couple of years that followed, life at the Viceroy's House went on as before, though it had lost much of its glitter. There were still the luncheon and dinner parties of fifty or a hundred, but with fewer courses and no band after 1942. Galaxies of Princes still came to stay, including the elderly Maharaja of Kapurthala, who was so punctilious about his appearance that he had men stationed at intervals along the corridors to dust his shoes as he walked from his bedroom in the south-west wing to join the assembled company for dinner. There were also periodic house-parties of Governors, who came to confer with the Viceroy, and there were important personages from England who had to be put up, notably the Cabinet Delegation which descended on Lord and Lady Wavell in 1946 and stayed for several weeks. During those weeks, the Viceroy not only had to cope with the machinations of Sir Stafford Cripps, but every evening after dinner he was obliged to listen to A.V. Alexander singing his way solo through a repertoire that consisted of music hall ditties such as *Lady of Laguna* [sic] and *My Old Dutch*, interspersed with revivalist hymns. It was very different from Harcourt Butler's cheery sing-songs of twenty years earlier.

One at least among the numerous adherents of Mr Attlee who flocked to the Viceroy's House during the fevered months before Independence managed to endear himself to the overworked Viceroy and his household. This was the Governor-designate of Bengal, the former railwayman, Sir Frederick Burrows, who, together with his wife, was stranded here for some days owing to riots in Calcutta. The absence of afternoon tea, which the Wavells and their household had given up as a good example,

India being then in the throes of a food shortage, proved so great a hardship to Lady Burrows that a kind young ADC took her to the tea-shop in Connaught Circus and plied her with tea and cakes. He was worried, however, lest someone should recognize the Viceregal car and put it about that the self-denial which the inmates of the Viceroy's House pretended to practise was mere hypocrisy. As a further piece of self-denial, Their Excellencies and the rest of the party adopted an exclusively vegetarian diet when Congress Hindus came to luncheon or dinner. With the worsening of the political situation, Congress supporters absented themselves altogether from the Viceroy's House – it must have been some small consolation to Wavell, in the midst of all his troubles, to be spared those highly-coloured dishes composed mainly of chopped-up nuts that stuck in the throat.

Though Congress stayed away, there were plenty of other Indians at Their Excellencies' hospitable board. In March 1946, a Tibetan mission, which had come to present gifts to the Viceroy and Vicereine, was entertained to luncheon. The presentation took place beforehand; the Tibetans, nine colourful figures in robes and head-dresses, accompanied by sixteen retainers bearing the carpets and vessels of silver that were to be offered, made their way with dignity up the great steps and advanced across the floor of the Durbar Hall to where Their Excellencies awaited them on their thrones. It was a scene that would have been familiar to Emily and Fanny Eden; it had been enacted countless times in the past. But it was a scene that would hardly ever be witnessed again.

Within less than twenty years after Lord Irwin had taken up residence in the newly-completed Viceroy's House, the last Viceroy, Lord Mountbatten, had departed. Nevertheless, in the India that replaced the Raj, Lutyens' palace has managed to keep some of its glory. A reigning Queen of Great Britain has even stayed beneath its roof, an honour not vouchsafed to it in the days when Her Majesty's father and grandfather were Emperors of India. As the home of a modern democratic President, it is certainly on the large side, but the Indians have been wise enough to maintain a Presidential establishment worthy of the setting. Scarlet-clad guards still sit on their chargers beneath the stone sentry boxes, *khitmagars* in white, red and gold line the corridors.

When I visited the house in 1967, it was easy to imagine myself back in Viceregal days. I did, however, notice certain differences. The President's throne stood solitary in the Durbar Hall where formerly there were two; and as though to provide him with the feminine support which his Viceregal predecessors had derived from Her Excellency, there was the statue of a Hindu goddess standing behind it. In the adjoining corridors, there was a faint smell of joss-sticks. And in the State Dining Room, portraits of Gandhi and former Presidents had ousted a few of the Viceroys. But those responsible for the house had, with rare good sense, left the rest of the gallery of Lord Sahibs intact. There was Hardinge of Penshurst, but for whom New Delhi might never have been; there was Willingdon, 'the eternal Head of Pop', resplendent in grey frock coat and spats, the Star of India on his breast. There was even Ellenborough, the only one of the whole long line who could in fairness have been called bombastic. The idea of that Governor-General, who wanted to turn the old royal family out of the Palace at Delhi and 'come Aurungzeb' in it himself, sharing a room with the Mahatma, was just the sort of thing that would have appealed to Lutyens. And there, not far away, was the bust of the 'architect of this house', as the inscription modestly called him, standing in the sunlight, against the glowing red stonework of the open staircase. After the faces in the portraits – the self-assured solemnity of the British, the slightly worried earnestness of the Indians – he seemed to be chuckling.

[59] Violence (September 1947); from *Freedom at Midnight* by Larry Collins and Dominique Lapierre.

Gandhi would never complete his trip to the Punjab. A new outburst of violence interrupted him in mid-journey. This time the mania erupted in the vital nerve center from which India was governed, the proud and artificial capital of the extinct raj, New Delhi itself. The city that had witnessed so much pomp and pageantry, the sanctuary of the world's vastest bureaucracy was not to be spared the poison afflicting the slums of Calcutta and Lahore.

Set at the limits of the Punjab, once the citadel of the Moguls, Delhi was still in many ways a Moslem city in 1947. Most domestics were Moslems. So, too, were most of its tonga drivers, fruit and vegetable peddlers, the artisans of its bazaars. The riots had jammed its streets with thousands of Moslems from the surrounding countryside searching for shelter and safety. Inflamed by the horror stories told by Hindu and Sikh refugees pouring into the city, angry at the sight of so many Moslems in their new nation's capital, the Sikhs of the Akali sect and the Hindu fanatics of the R.S.S.S. launched Delhi's wave of terror on the morning of September 3, the day Gandhi ended his fast in Calcutta.

It began with the slaughter of a dozen Moslem porters at the railroad station. A few minutes later, a French journalist, Max Olivier-Lecamp, emerged into Connaught Circus, the commercial heart of New Delhi, to discover a Hindu mob looting its Moslem shops and butchering their owners. Above their heads, he saw a familiar figure in a white Congress cap whirling a *lathi*, beating the rioters, showering them with curses, trying by his actions to arouse the dozen indifferent policemen behind him. It was Jawaharlal Nehru, the prime minister.

Those attacks were the signal for commandos of Akali Sikhs in their electric-blue turbans and the R.S.S.S. with white handkerchiefs around their foreheads to unleash similar attacks all across the city. Old Delhi's Green Market with its thousands of Moslem fruit and vegetable peddlers was set ablaze. In New Delhi's Lodi Colony near the marble-domed mausoleum of the Emperor Humayun and the red-sandstone tomb of Akbar's greatest general, Sikh bands burst into the bungalows of Moslem civil servants, slaughtering anyone they found home.

By noon, the bodies of their victims were scattered about the green expanses ringing the buildings from which England had imposed her Pax Britannica over the subcontinent. Driving from Old to New Delhi for dinner that night, the Belgian consul counted seventeen corpses along his route. Sikhs prowled the darkened alleys of the Old City flushing out their quarry by shouting: '*Allah Akhbar*,' then beheading those Moslems unfortunate enough to answer their call.

R.S.S.S. bands kidnapped a Moslem woman shrouded in her *burqa*, soaked her in gasoline and set her ablaze at the gate of Jawaharlal Nehru's York Road residence as a protest against their prime minister's efforts to protect India's Moslems. Later, guarded by a squad of Gurkha soldiers, a score of Moslem women took refuge in Nehru's garden.

Warned by Sikh bands that any house sheltering a Moslem would be burned, hundreds of Hindu, Sikh, Parsi and Christian families turned their faithful servants into the streets, condemning them to the Sikh's swords or a hasty flight to an improvised refugee camp.

The only beneficiaries of Delhi's wave of atrocities were the spindly horses of the city's Moslem tonga drivers who had fled or been massacred. Turned loose, they joyously celebrated their freedom on the greensward of those immense spaces with which the British had ventilated their imperial capital beside another species of animal, the Sacred Cow.

Delhi's Moslems, most of whom now wanted to flee to Pakistan, were assembled in a series of refugee camps, where they could wait in relative safety for transportation to Mr Jinnah's Promised Land. Cruel irony, those Moslems were herded into two magnificent monuments of that brief era when their Mogul forebears had made Delhi the most splendid city in the world, Humayun's Tomb and the Purana Qila ('Old Fort'). Between 150,000 and 200,000 people were going to live in those relics of Islam's ancient grandeur in conditions of undescribable filth, without shelter from the sun or the monsoon's cataracts. So terrified were those wretches by the thought of leaving their protective walls that they refused to venture out even to bury their dead. Instead, they threw them from the ramparts to the jackals. Initially, the Purana Qila had two water taps for 25,000 people. One visitor noted its inmates defecating and vomiting in the same pool of water in which women were washing their cooking pots.

Sanitation was by open latrine and the constraints of India's society remained in vigor. Despite the growing filth, the refugees in Purana Qila refused to clean their latrines. At the height of Delhi's troubles, the Emergency Committee had to send a hundred Hindu sweepers under armed guard into the fort to perform the chores its Moslem inmates refused to carry out.

Another of Delhi's curses, its bureaucracy, remained unmoved by the catastrophe. When the refugees in Humayun's Tomb began to dig additional latrines, a representative of the New Delhi High Commissioner's office promptly protested that 'they were spoiling the beauty of the lawns.' Inevitably, cholera broke out. Sixty people died of the dread disease in forty-eight hours at Purana Qila. The Health Department chose to give the cause of their deaths as 'gastroenteritis' to cover their failure to provide serum in time. When the Department's representative finally arrived with it, he brought 327 batches of serum and no needles or syringes.

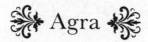

Agra

(with excursions to Fattephur Sikri and Sikandra)

Agra and the Red Fort

[60] Babur's Begs long for the cool of Afghanistan, 1525; from Babur's *Memoirs* edited by F.G. Talbot.

When I came to Agra it was the hot season. All the inhabitants fled from terror, so that we could not find grain nor provender, either for ourselves or our horses. The villages, out of hostility and hatred to us, had taken to rebellion, thieving, and robbery. The roads became impassable. I had not had time, after the division of the treasure, to send proper persons to occupy and protect the different pergannas and stations. It happened too that the heats were this year uncommonly oppressive. Many men about the same time dropped down, as if they had been affected by the Simûm wind, and died on the spot.

On these accounts, not a few of my Begs and best men began to lose heart, objected to remaining in Hindustân, and even began to make preparations for their return. If the older Begs who were men of experience, had made these representations, there would have been no harm in it; for if such men had communicated their sentiments to me, I might have got credit for possessing at least so much sense and judgment as, after hearing what they had to urge, to be qualified to decide on the expediency or inexpediency of their opinions; to distinguish the good from the evil. But what sense or propriety was there in eternally repeating the same tale in different words, to one who himself saw the facts with his own eyes, and had formed a cool and fixed resolution in regard to the business in which he was engaged? What propriety was there in the whole army, down to the very dregs, giving their stupid and unformed opinions? It is singular that when I set out from Kâbul this last time, I had raised many of low rank to the dignity of Beg, in the expectation that if I had chosen to go through fire and water, they would have followed me back and forward without hesitation; and that they would have accompanied me cheerfully, march where I would. It never surely entered my imagination, that they were to be the persons who were to arraign my measures, nor that, before rising from the council, they should show a determined opposition to every plan and opinion which I proposed and supported in the council and assembly. From the time we left Kâbul, till we had defeated Ibrâhim and taken Agra, Khwâjeh Kilân had behaved admirably, and had always spoken gallantly, giving such opinions as befitted a brave man; but a few days after the taking of Agra, all his opinions underwent a complete change. Khwâjeh Kilân was now, of all others, the most determined on turning back.

I no sooner heard this murmuring among my troops, than I summoned all my Begs to a council. I told them that empire and conquest could not be acquired without the materials and means of war: That royalty and nobility could not exist without subjects and dependent provinces: That, by the labours of many years, after undergoing great hardships, measuring many a toilsome journey, and raising various armies; after exposing myself and my troops to circumstances of great danger, to battle and bloodshed, by the divine favour, I had routed my formidable enemy, and achieved the conquest of the numerous provinces and kingdoms which we at present held: 'And now, what force compels, and what hardship obliges us, without any visible cause after having worn out our life in accomplishing the desired achievement, to abandon and fly from our conquests, and to retreat back to Kâbul with every symptom of disappointment and discomfiture? Let not any one who calls himself my friend ever henceforward make such a proposal. But if there is any among you who cannot bring himself to stay, or to give up his purpose of returning back, let him depart.' Having made them this fair and reasonable proposal, the discontented were of necessity compelled, however unwillingly, to renounce their seditious purposes. Khwâjeh Kilân not being disposed to remain, it was arranged, that as he had a numerous retinue, he should return back to guard the presents; I had but few troops in Kâbul and Ghazni, and he was directed to see that these places were all kept in proper order, and amply supplied with the necessary stores. I bestowed on him Ghazni; I also gave him the district of Kehrâm in Hindustân, yielding a revenue of 30,000*l.* Khwâjeh Kilân, who was heartily tired of Hindustân, at the time of going, wrote the following verses on the walls of some houses in Delhi:—

> (*Tûrki*)—If I pass the Sind safe and sound,
>   May shame take me if I ever again wish for Hind.

When I still continued in Hindustân, there was an evident impropriety in his composing and publishing such vituperative verses. If I had previously cause to be offended at his leaving me, this conduct of his doubled the offence. I composed a few extempore lines, which I wrote down and sent him.

> (*Tûrki*)—Return a hundred thanks, O Baber! for the bounty
> of the merciful God
> Has given you Sind, Hind, and numerous
> kingdoms;
> If unable to stand the heat, you long for cold;
> You have only to recollect the frost and cold of
> Ghazni.

[61] No place for gardening; from Babur's *Memoirs* edited by F.G. Talbot.

It always appears to me that one of the chief defects of Hindustân is the want of artificial water-courses. I had intended, wherever I might fix my residence, to construct water-wheels, to produce an artificial stream, and to lay out a regularly planned pleasure-ground. Shortly after coming to Agra, I passed the Jumna with this object in view, and examined the country, to pitch upon a fit spot for a garden. The whole was so ugly and detestable, that I repassed the river quite repulsed and disgusted. In consequence of the want of beauty, and of the disagreeable aspect of the country, I gave up my intention of making a garden; but as no better situation presented itself near Agra, I was finally compelled to make the best of this same spot. I first of all began to sink the large well which supplies the baths with water; I next fell to work on that piece of ground on which are the tamarind trees, and the octangular tank; I then proceeded to form the large tank and its inclosure; and afterwards the tank and grand hall of audience that are in front of the stone palace. I next finished the garden of the private apartments, and the apartments them-selves, after which I completed the baths. In this way, going on, without neatness and without order, in the Hindu fashion, I, however, produced edifices and gardens which possessed consid-erable regularity. In every corner I planted suitable gardens; in

Babur enthroned in his garden:
a page from the Babur-nama, late sixteenth century

every garden I sowed roses and narcissuses regularly, and in beds corresponding to each other. We were annoyed with three things in Hindustân: one was its heat, another its strong winds, the third its dust. Baths were the means of removing all three inconveniences. In the bath we could not be affected by the winds. During the hot winds, the cold can there be rendered so intense, that a person often feels as if quite powerless from it. The room of the bath, in which is the tub or cistern, is finished wholly of stone. The water-run is of white stone; all the rest of it, its floor and roof, is of a red stone. Several other people, who procured situations on the banks of the river, made regular gardens and tanks, and constructed wheels, by means of which they procured a supply of water. The men of Hind, who had never before seen places formed on such a plan, or laid out with so much beauty, gave the name of Kâbul to the side of the Jumna on which these palaces were built.

[62] Akbarabad at Agra, 1563. Towers of Rajput heads; from *Storia do Mogor* by Niccalao Manucci.

Akbar resolved to found a city as a memorial of his victories, and gave to it the name of Fateabad – that is to say, 'Peopled by victory.' In this city he lived for some time. Then, for certain reasons, chiefly in order to reduce some rebellious Rājput villagers, who objected to pay tribute until they had been overcome by force of arms, he (Akbar) decided to leave Fathābād and found another city twelve leagues off, on the bank of the river Jamana. For this purpose he selected the village called Āgrah in the year one thousand five hundred and sixty-three. After the foundation of the city, it was renamed Akbarābād – that is to say, 'Built by Akbar.' Thus Fathābād became uninhabited. In spite of this, the rebellious villagers did not desist from their risings, chiefly round about the town of Matora, to which Aurangzeb gave the title of Essalamabad – that is to say, 'Peopled by the Faithful.' Mathurā is twenty leagues from Āgrah in the direction of Dihlī, and on the same side of the river Jamnah. The chief cause of these risings is their not wishing to pay the customary tribute.

When Akbar decided to build the city of Akbarābād, he gave an order that his palaces should be made of copper. But they represented to him that this could not be done. Enough metal could not be procured to erect lofty palaces such as the king desired. Another reason was that they would not be habitable in the hot season on account of the high temperature, or in the winter, from the great cold. Thus he abandoned this project, and built his palace and the fortress of red hewn stones of great size.

During the time that the said city was being brought to perfection the king's amusement was to mount on a mad elephant, simply to make it combat with another one. This is a very dangerous affair, for many elephant-drivers lose their lives in this amusement, and thus their wives, when drivers mount their elephants for a combat, break their bracelets and take off their jewels as a sign that they are widows.

It happened that the villagers, of whom I have spoken before, raised such a great rebellion that Akbar was obliged to go against them in person. He surrounded a fort into which many of them had retired, a place that it was impossible to escalade. Therefore orders were given that the most courageous of the elephants should be sent to batter in the gate. He (Akbar) disguised himself, and at dawn appeared near the gate, and, mounting upon a very bold elephant, attacked the gate. In the first assault the animal was not able to knock it down; it was driven to the assault once more, the gate fell, and the fortress was taken. The driver of the elephant asked the pretended elephant-driver what his name was, as he was anxious to report his bravery to the king and announce that he was the cause of the victory. Akbar replied that before giving his name he wanted to know that of the elephant. The driver said the elephant was called the 'Active'; thereupon Akbar said that his name was 'Breaker-in of Gateways.' The following day, when the elephants were paraded before him, he gave to 'Active' the title of 'Active, Breaker-in of Gateways,' and made him captain of all the elephants, with an increase of pay. He rewarded the elephant-driver by a *sarāpā*, whereby the man learnt that the 'Breaker-in of Gateways' was the very king himself.

He had a great deal of trouble with these rebels, and after returning home victorious he was forced to order his captains to go against them several times. These officers, on reaching the rebel villages, carried out their orders to slay and behead (the only remedies he applied, and after him the other Mogol kings did the same). In order to defend themselves these villagers hid in the thorny scrub or retired behind the slight walls surrounding their villages. The women stood behind their husbands with spears and arrows. When the husband had shot off his matchlock, his wife handed him the lance, while she reloaded the matchlock. Thus did they defend themselves until they were no longer able to continue. When reduced to extremity, they cut their wives' and daughters' throats, then in desperation they threw themselves against the enemy's ranks, and several times they succeeded in gaining the day by mere reckless courage.

Every time that a general won a victory the heads of the villagers went sent as booty to the city of Āgrah to be displayed in the royal square before all the people as a proof of their success. After twenty-four hours the heads were removed to the imperial highway, where they were hung from the trees or deposited in holes on pillars built for this purpose. Each pillar could

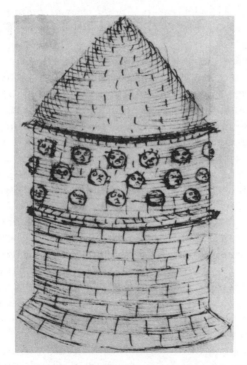

A tower of heads, 'mortered and plaistered in, leaveinge out nothing but their verie faces'; drawing by Peter Mundy in his *Travels in Europe and Asia*

accommodate one hundred heads. Many a time have I seen in
the city piles of these villagers' heads. Once I saw ten thousand of
them; they could be recognised by their being shaven, with huge
moustaches, mostly reddish in colour. In the thirty-four years
that I dwelt in this Mogul kingdom I travelled often from Āgrah
to Dihlī, and every time there was a number of fresh heads on the
roadside and many bodies of thieves hanging from the trees, who
were punished thus for robbing on the highway. Thus passers-by
are forced to hold their noses on account of the odour from the
dead, and hasten their steps out of apprehension of the living.
The villagers were not able to take vengeance on their first
enemy, Akbar, in his lifetime, but how they avenged themselves
on his bones after his death I shall tell hereafter.

[63] Akbar's chronicler glorifies the Fort; from the
Akbarnama of Abu-l Fazl in *The History of India as told by its
own Historians* edited by Sir H.M. Elliot and J. Dowson.

Five or six days after his recovery he proceeded towards Agra,
and in a fortunate hour, which was a chosen one of stars and
horizons, he cast his light and his shadow on that fortunate city.
   Among the principal events of the year was the founding of the
fort of Agra. It is not concealed from the minds of the
mathematical and the acquainted with the mechanism of the
spheres that since the world-adorning creator hath decked Time
and the Terrene with the existence of the Shāhinshāh in order
that the series of creations might be perfected, that wise-hearted
one has exercised himself in bringing each individual life from
the secrecy of potentiality to the theatre of performance. At one
time he has prepared the constituents of rule by perfecting the
earth for animated nature by improving agriculture by
irrigation and the sowing of seeds. At another time he stablishes
spiritual and temporal dominion by building fortresses for the
protection of products and the guarding of honour and prestige.
Accordingly, he at this time gave directions for the building in
Agra – which by position is the centre of Hindustan – of a grand
fortress such as might be worthy thereof, and correspond to the
dignity of his dominions. An order was then issued that the old
fort which was built on the east bank of the Jamna, and whose
pillars had been shaken by the revolutions of time and the shocks

of fortune, should be removed, and that an impregnable fort should be built of hewn stone. It was to be stable like the foundation of the dominion of the sublime family and permanent like the pillars of its fortunes. Accordingly, lofty-minded mathematicians and able architects laid the foundations of this great building in an hour which was supreme for establishing a fortress. The excavations were made through seven strata of earth. The breadth of the wall was three yards and its height sixty yards. It was provided with four gates whereby the doors of the dominion were opened towards the four quarters of the world. Every day 3 to 4,000 active builders and strong-armed labourers carried on the work. From the foundations to the battlements, the fortress was composed of hewn stone, each of which was polished like the world-revealing mirror, and was ruddy as the cheek of fortune. And they were so joined together that the end of a hair could not find place between them. This sublime fortress, the like of which had never been seen by a fabulous geometrician, was completed with its battlements, breastwork, and its loop-holes in the space of eight years under the faithful superintendence of Qāsim K̲h̲ān Mīr Barr u Baḥr.

[64] Akbar's Red Fort; from the *Journal 1608–11* of William Finch in *Early Travels in India* edited by William Foster.

(A servant of the East India Company, William Finch arrived in India in 1610 to buy indigo. He kept a detailed journal which, according to Purchas, 'was supplied in substance with more accurate observations of men, beasts, plants, cities, deserts, castles, buildings, regions, religions, than almost any other; as also of waies, wares, warres.')

Agra hath not been in fame above fiftie yeeres, being before Acabars time a village; who removed from Fetipore for want of good water. It is spacious, large, populous beyond measure, that you can hardly passe in the streets, which are for the most part dirty and narrow, save only the great bazar and some few others, which are large and faire. The citie lyeth in manner of a halfe-moone, bellying to the land-ward some 5 c. in length, and as much by the rivers side, upon the bankes whereof are many goodly houses of the nobility, pleasantly over-looking Gemini, which runneth with a swift current from the north to the south, somewhat easterly, into Ganges. Upon the banke of this river stands the castle, one of the fairest and admirablest buildings of the East, some three or foure miles in compasse, inclosed with a faire and strong wall of squared stone; about which is cast a faire ditch, over it draw-bridges. The walles are built with bulwarkes, somewhat defensible, regalled, with a counter-scarfe or front without, some fifteene yards broad. Within this are two other strong walls and gates. To the castle are foure gates, one to the north, by which you passe to a rampire with great peeces; another west to the Bazar, called the Cichery gate, within which, over against the great gate, is the Casi his seat of Chiefe-Justice in matters of law, and by it two or three murtherers very great (one three foot in the bore and fifteene long) of cast brasse. Over against this seat is the Cichery or Court of Rolls, where the Kings Viseer sits every morning some three houres, by whose hands passe all matters of rents, grants, lands, firmans, debts, etc. Beyond these two gates you passe a second gate, over which are two Rajaws in stone, who were slaine in the Kings derbar before the Kings eyes, for being over-bold in speech; they selling their lives bravely, in remembrance of which they are heere placed. Passing this gate you enter into a faire streete, with houses and munition all alongst on both sides. At the end of this street, being a quarter of a mile, you come to the third gate, which leads to the Kings Derbar; always chained, all men but the King and his children there alighting. This gate is to the south, called Acabar Drowage, close within which is the whores child, many hundreds of which attend there day and night, according as their severall turnes come every seventh day, that they may bee ready when the King or his women shall please to call any of them to sing or dance in his moholl, he giving to every one of them stipends according to their unworthy worth. The fourth gate is to the river, called the Dersane, leading into a faire court extending alongst the river, in which the King lookes forth every morning at sun-rising, which hee salutes, and then his nobles resort to their tessillam. Right under the place where he lookes out is a kind of scaffold whereon his nobles stand, but the addees with others awayt below in the court. Here also every noone he looketh forth to behold fighting of elephants, lyons, buffles, killing of deare with leopards; which is a custome on every day of the weeke, Sunday excepted, on which is no fighting; but

Tuesday on the contrary is a day of blood, both of fighting beasts and justiced men, the King judging and seeing execution.

To returne to the thirde gate: within it you enter into a spacious court with atescanna's round about, like shops or open stalls. A little further you enter within a rayle into a more inward court, within which none but the Kings addees and men of sort are admitted, under paine of swacking by the porters cudgells, which lay on load without respect of persons. Being entred, you approach the Kings derbar or seat, before which is also a small court inclosed with railes, covered over head with rich semianes to keepe away the sunne; where aloft in a gallery the King sits in his chaire of state, accompanied with his children and Chiefe Vizier (who goeth up by a short ladder forth of the court), no other without calling daring to goe up to him, save onely two punkaw's to gather wind; and right before him below on a scaffold is a third, who with a horse taile makes havocke of poore flies. On the right hand of the King, on the wall behind him, is the picture of our Saviour; on the left, of the Virgin. Within these railes none under the degree of foure hundred horse are permitted to enter. On the further side of this court of presence are hanged golden bels, that if any be oppressed and can get no justice by the Kings officers, by ringing these bels when the King sits, he is called, and the matter discussed before the King. But let them be sure their cause be good, least he be punished for presumption to trouble the King. Here every day, betweene three and foure a clocke, the King comes forth (and many thousands resort to doe their duties, each taking place according to his degree); where hee remaines hearing of matters, receiving of newes by letters read by his Vizier, graunting of suites, etc., till shutting in of the evening, the drumme meanewhile beating, and instruments playing from a high gallery on the next building opposite; his elephants and horses passing by in brave fashion, doing their tessillam and being perused by officers to see if they prosper. In the castle are two high turrets, over-laid with pure massie gold, which may be seen from farre, one over his mohol, the other over his treasury. After his going in from the derbar in the evening, some two houres after he comes out againe, sitting forth in a small more inward court behind the other, close to his moholl, into which none but the grandes, and they also with tickets to be renewed with every moone, are permitted to enter; where he drinkes by number and measure, sometimes one and thirtie, and running over, mixing also among severe judicatures. From this court is his privy passage into a curious garden, and to his barge, by which he often passeth the river to an other garden opposite. It is remarkeable that, both in court and here in these gardens, no courtiers or gardeners are tied to attendance, but by their seventh dayes turne.

Some adde that the citie hath no walls, but a ditch round about, not broad, and dry also; adjoyning to the ditch without the citie are very large suburbs. The city and suburbs are one way seven mile in length, three in breadth. The noble mens houses and merchants built with bricke and stone, flat roofed; the common sort, of mudde walls, covered with thatch, which cause often and terrible fires. The citie hath sixe gates. The adjoyning river Gemini being broader then the Thames at London, on which are many boats, some of one hundred tunnes, but these cannot returne against the streame. Most of the noble mens houses are by the rivers side. From Agra to Lahor sixe hundred miles. The way is set on both sides with mulbery-trees.

[65] Jahangir's day; from the *Journal 1608–13* of William Hawkins in *Early Travels in India* edited by William Foster.

(William Hawkins carried a letter from James I to the new emperor Jahangir requesting 'such liberties of traffique and privilidges as shall be reasonable both for securitie and proffitt'. He reached Agra in 1609, but was dismissed from the court for 'having liquor on his breath' during one of Jahangir's occasional attempts to abstain.)

Now here I meane to speake a little of his manners and customes in the court. First, in the morning about the breake of day he is at his beades, with his face turned to the west-ward. The manner of his praying, when he is in Agra, is in a private faire roome, upon a goodly jet stone, having onely a Persian lamb-skinne under him; having also some eight chaines of beads, every one of them containing foure hundred. The beads are of rich pearle, ballace rubyes, diamonds, rubyes, emeralds, lignum aloes, eshem, and corall. At the upper end of this jet stone the pictures of Our Lady and Christ are placed, graven in stone; so he turneth over his beads, and saith three thousand two hundred words, according to the number of his beads, and then his prayer is ended. After he hath done, he sheweth himselfe to the people, receiving their salames or good morrowes; unto whom multitudes resort every morning for this purpose. This done, hee sleepeth two houres more, and then dineth and passeth his time with his women, and at noone hee sheweth himselfe to the people againe, sitting till three of the clocke, viewing and seeing his pastimes and sports made by men, and fighting of many sorts of beasts, every day sundry kinds of pastimes. Then at three of the clocke, all the nobles in generall (that be in Agra and are well) resort unto the court, the King comming forth in open audience, sitting in his seat-royall, and every man standing in his degree before him, his chiefest sort of the nobles standing within a red rayle, and the rest without. They are all placed by his Lieutenant-Generall. This red rayle is three steppes higher then the place where the rest stand; and within this red rayle I was placed, amongst the chiefest of all. The rest are placed by officers, and they likewise be within another very spacious place rayled; and without that rayle stand all sorts of horsemen and souldiers that belong unto his captaines, and all other commers. At these rayles there are many doores kept by many porters, who have white rods to keepe men in order. In the middest of the place, right before the King, standeth one of his sheriffes, together with his master hangman, who is accompanied with forty hangmen wearing on their heads a certaine quilted cap, different from all others, with an hatchet on their shoulders; and others with all sorts of whips being there, readie to doe what the King commandeth. The King heareth all causes in this place, and stayeth some two houres every day (these Kings of India sit daily in justice every day, and on the Tuesdayes doe their executions). Then he departeth towards his private place of prayer. His prayer beeing ended, foure or five sorts of very well dressed and roasted meats are brought him, of which, as hee pleaseth, he eateth a bit to stay his stomacke, drinking once of his strong drinke. Then hee commeth forth into a private roome, where none can come but such as himselfe nominateth (for two yeeres together I was one of his attendants here). In this place he drinketh other five cupfuls, which is the portion that the physicians alot him. This done, he eateth opium, and then he ariseth; and being in the height of his drinke he layeth him downe to sleepe, every man departing to his owne home. And after he hath slept two houres, they awake him and bring his supper to him; at which time he is not able to feed himselfe, but it is thrust into his mouth by others; and this is about one of the clocke, and then he sleepeth the rest of the night.

Now in the space of these five cups he doth many idle things; and whatsoever he doth, either without or within, drunken or sober, he hath writers who by turnes set downe everything in writing which he doth, so that there is nothing passeth in his lifetime which is not noted, no, not so much as his going to the necessary, and how often he lieth with his women, and with whom; and all this is done unto this end, that when he dieth these writings of al his actions and speeches which are worthy to be set downe might be recorded in the chronicles. At my being with him he made his brothers children Christians; the doing whereof was not for any zeale he had to Christianitie, as the Fathers and all Christians thought, but upon the prophecie of certain learned Gentiles, who told him that the sonnes of his body should be disinherited and the children of his brother should raigne; and therefore he did it to make these children hatefull to all Moores, as Christians are odious in their sight, and that they beeing once Christians, when any such matter should happen, they should find no subjects. But God is omnipotent and can turne the making of these Christians unto a good ende, if it be His pleasure.

[66] Tom Coryat has his picture; from *Observations (1616)* by Thomas Coryat in *Early Travels in India* edited by William Foster.

(Thomas Coryat, a famous butt at the Mermaid Tavern, was determined to make his name as a traveller and went to India on foot. He made a speech in Persian to the Great Mogul and loudly denounced Mahomet from a minaret. Thought to be mad, he set off, 'all afoote, with most unwearied leggs' (Sir Thomas Roe), for Samarkand but died on the way in 1617 of dysentery and an excess of sack.)

The King [*Jahangir*] presenteth himselfe thrice every day without faile to his Nobles, at the rising of the Sunne, which he adoreth by the elevation of his hands; at noone, and at five of the clocke in the evening: but he standeth in a roome aloft, alone by himselfe, and looketh upon them from a window that hath an embroydered sumptuous coverture, supported with two silver Pillasters to yeeld shadowes unto him. Twice every weeke, Elephants fight before him, the bravest spectacle in the World; many of them are thirteene foot and a halfe high; and they seeme to justle together like two little Mountaines, and were they not parted in the middest of their fighting by certaine fire-workes, they would exceedingly gore and cruentate one another by their murdering teeth. Of Elephants the King keepeth thirtie thousand in his whole Kingdome at an unmeasurable charge; in feeding of whom and his Lions, and other Beasts, he spendeth an incredible masse of Money, at the least tenne thousand pounds sterling a day. I have rid upon an Elephant since I came to this Court, determining one day (by Gods leave) to have my Picture expressed in my next Booke, sitting upon an Elephant.

Tom Coryat on his elephant; woodcut from his *Travellers for the English Wits*

[67] A seventeenth-century visit to Agra; from *Indian Travels of Thévenot and Careri* edited by Surendranath Sen.

Before King Ecbar Agra was no more but a Bourg which had a little Castle of Earth, and pretended to no privilege over its Neighbours upon account of Antiquity; and indeed, there were never any marks of that to be found.

The Prince being pleased with the seat of it, joyned several Villages thereunto: He gave them the form of a town by other buildings which he raised, and called it after his own Name *Ecbar-Abad* the habitation of *Ecbar*, where he established the seat of his Empire, in the year One thousand five hundred threescore and six. His declaration of that was enough to People it; for when the Merchants came to understand that the Court was there, they came from all parts, and not only the *Banian* Traders flocked thither, but Christians also of all Perswasions, as well as Mahometans, who strove in emulation who should furnish it with greatest variety of Goods; and seeing that Prince called the *Jesuits* thither, and gave them a Pension to subsist on, Catholick Merchants made no scruple to come and live there, and to this day these Fathers take the care of Spirituals, and teach their Children.

Though this Prince pretended to make *Agra* a place of consequence, yet he Fortified it not neither with ramparts, Walls, nor Bastions, but only with a Ditch, hopeing to make it so strong in Soldiers and Inhabitants, that it should not need to fear the attempts of any Enemy. The Castle was the first thing that was built, which he resolved to make the biggest at that time in the *Indies*; and the situation of the old one appearing good and commodious, he caused it to be demolished, and the foundations of the present to be laid. It was begirt with a Wall of Stone and Brick terrassed in several places, which is twenty Cubits high, and betwixt the Castle and River a large place was left for the exercises the King should think fit to divert himself with.

The Kings Palace is in the Castle. It contains three Courts adorned all round with Porches and Galleries that are Painted and Gilt; nay there are some peeces covered with plates of Gold. Under the Galleries of the first Court, there are Lodgings made for the Kings Guards: The Officers Lodgings are in the second; and in the third, the stately appartments of the King and his Ladies; from whence he goes commonly to a lovely Divan which looks to the River, there to please himself with seeing Elephants fight, his Troops exercise, and Plays which he orders to be made upon the Water, or in the open place.

Now after all the Air of Agra is very incommodious in the Summer-time, and it is very likely that the excessive heat which scorches the Sands that environ this Town, was one of the chief causes which made King *Cha-Gehan* change the Climate, and chuse to live at *Dehly*. Little thought this Prince that one day he would be forced to live at *Agra*, what aversion soever he had to it, and far less still, that he should be Prisoner there in his own Palace, and so end his days in affliction and trouble. That misfortune though befel him, and *Auran-Zeb* his third Son, was the cause of it, who having got the better of his Brothers, both by cunning and force, made sure of the Kings Person and Treasures, by means of Soldiers whom he craftily slipt into the Palace, and under whose Custody the King was kept till he died.

The Town of *Agra* is Populous as a great Town ought to be, but not so as to be able to send out Two hundred thousand fighting men into the Field, as some have written. The Palaces and Gardens take up the greatest part of it, so that its extent is no infallible Argument of the number of its Inhabitants. The ordinary Houses are low, and those of the commoner sort of People are but Straw, containing but few People a piece; and the truth is, one may walk the Streets without being crouded, and meet with no throng but when the court is there: But at that time, I have been told there is great confusion, and infinite numbers of People to be seen; and no wonder indeed, seeing the Streets are narrow, and that the King besides his Household, (who are many,) is always attended by an Army for his Guard; and the *Rajas, Omras, Mansepdars* and other great Men, have great Retinues, and most part of the Merchants also follow the Court, not to reckon a vast number of Tradesmen, and thousands of followers who have all their subsistence from it.

Some affirm that there are twenty five thousand Christian Families in *Agra*, but all do not agree in that. This indeed is certain, that there are few Heathen and *Parsis* in respect of *Mahometans* there, and these surpass all the other Sects in power, as they do in number. The Dutch have a Factory in the Town; but the English have none now, because it did not turn to account.

There are a great many at *Agra*, who are curious in breeding up of Beasts, to have the pleasure to make them Fight together: But seeing they cannot reach to Elephants and Lions, because it costs dear to feed them, most part content themselves with He-goats, Weathers, Rams, Cocks, Quailes, Stags, and Antilopes, to entertain their Friends with the fightings of these Beasts.

The *Indian* Antilopes, are not altogether like those of other Countries; they have even a great deal more courage, and are to be distinguished by the Horns. The Horns of the ordinary Antilopes are greyish, and but half as long as the Horns of those in the *Indies*, which are blackish, and a large Foot and a half long. These Horns grow winding to the point like a screw; and the *Faquirs* and *Santons* carry commonly two of them pieced together; they are armed with Iron at both ends, and they make use of them, as of a little Staff.

When they use not a tame Leopard for catching of Antilopes, they take with them a Male of the kind, that is tame, and fasten a Rope about his Horns with several nooses and doubles, the two ends whereof are tied under his Belly; so soon as they discover a Heard of Antilopes, they slip this Male, and he runs to joyn them: The Male of the Heard advances to hinder him, and making no other opposition, but by playing with his Horns, he fails not to be pestered and entangled with his Rival, so that it being uneasie for him to retreat, the Huntsman cunningly catches hold on him, and carries him off; but it is easier so to catch the Male than the Females.

There are Pidgeons in that Country all over green, which differ from ours only in colour: The Fowlers take them with Bird-lime, in this manner; they carry before them a kind of light Shed or Screen, that covers the whole Body, and has holes in it to see through; the Pidgeons seeing no Man, are not at all scared when the Fowler draws near, so that he cunningly catches them, one after another, with a Wand and Bird lime on it, none offering to flie away. In some places Parrocquets are taken after the same manner.

The *Indians* are very dexterous at Game; they take Waterfowl with great facility, as thus: The Fowlers swim almost upright, yet so, that they have their Head above Water, which they hide with a Pot full of holes, to let in the Air, and give them sight. Besides, this Pot is covered with Feathers, to cheat the Ducks, and other Fowl; so that when the Fowler draws near them, they are not in the least scared, taking that floating head for a Fowl; and then the Fowler makes sure of them by the Feet, which he catches hold of under Water, and draws them down: The other Ducks seeing no body, think that their comrades have only dived, and are not at all scared; so that growing acquainted with the Feathered head, that still follows them, they are at length all taken, whil'st in vain they stay for the return of those who have dived, before they flie away to another place.

[68] 'Transport for great men' on the Jumna; from *Travels in Europe and Asia (1608–67)* by Peter Mundy.

(A Cornishman employed by the East India Company, Peter Mundy (1597–1667) came to Agra in 1632 during the time of Shah Jahan before his removal to Delhi. His copious journals are illustrated by his own line-drawings.)

The kings and great mens boates heere are such as are at Puttana, although not soe longe, this litle River Jemina not soe Capeable to navigate as the river Ganges. They are rowed with Padles.

   Heere are verie great lighters or Gabares, of 3, 4, or 500 Tonns each, serving for transportinge great men with their howshold and howshold stuffe downe the river to Etaya, Ellahabaz, Puttana, Dhacca etts. places on the river Ganges, haveing howses in the midle for the weomen, and many of them on their stemms the figures of the head of an Eliphant, Dragon, Tiger, etts., with double sternes. Others there are plaine, both ends alike, for Courser offices, as carryeinge of Timber, stones, etts. such as are att Etaya.

   I have heere [*see overleaf*] sett the figure of the first and best sorte of theis Lighters.

[69] Mogul gardening; from *Travels in Europe and Asia (1608–67)* by Peter Mundy.

The Gardens about Agra are many, but the cheifest are Darree ca baug and King Ecbars on this side the river and Mootee ca baag on the other side, the latter built by Nooremohol. As these are, soe are all the rest in generall, I meane the better sort,

A 'lighter' on the Jumna;
drawing by Peter Mundy in his *Travels in Europe and Asia*

although much inferior yett for the manner, *vizt.*, a great, high, large, faire, fower square brick wall, 4 Towers, att each Corner one, with their Copulaes, pillars and galleries, An arched gate; some have 2 and some 3 or 4. Theis comonly lead towards the midle (by long walks with rancks of Cypresse trees on each side), where is the cheife howse of pleasure and Tancke, haveing divers other roomes and tancks heere and there in the Garden, but this is the principall, which is curiously contrived, wrought and painted; and some Tancks of great compasse. This square Garden is againe devided into other lesser squares, and that into other like bedds and plotts; in some, litle groves of trees, as Apple trees (those scarse), Orenge Trees, Mulberrie trees, etts. Mango trees, Caco trees, Figg trees, Plantan trees, theis latter in rancks, as are the Cipresse trees. In other squares are your flowers, herbes etts., whereof Roses, Marigolds (theis scarse only in Mootte ca baag) to bee seene; French Mariegolds aboundance; Poppeas redd, carnation and white; and divers other sortes of faire flowers which wee knowe not in our parts, many groweinge on prettie trees, all watered by hand in tyme of drought, which is 9 monethes in the Yeare. This, I say, is the generall manner, but the former excell both in greatnes and curiositie of buildinge, painteing etts.; the carved worke off through Cutt redd stone much used in all their gardens and Tombes etts. In Mootee ca baag were many roomes painted, which wee might perceive to bee drawne from Europe prints (of which they make accompt heere). Alsoe there was the picture of Sir Thomas Roe, late Ambassadour heere, as it was told us.

[70] On produce and prostitutes; from *Travels in Europe and Asia (1608–67)* by Peter Mundy.

The Bazare [*at Agra*] affoards plentie of all things, as flesh, fish, graine, fruites, etts., as Beefe, Mutton, Partridge, quailes, pigeons, Turtle doves (Sometymes geese and ducks); Mangoes, Plantans, Ananesses, etts. [*and other*] fruites of this countrie (and out of Persia), Raysins, Almonds, Pistaches, walnutts, apples, orrenges, Prunes, prunellas or dryed Apricocks, Musk millions, although of the latter there bee much in this Countrie, as also of water millions; Fish of divers sorts out of the River, whereof one is very good called Roe, a great scaly Fish.

There is also another Bazare or Markett, which, although not soe Commendable, yett much frequented and allowed of, not only heere but all India over, namely the Common Stewes, of which there bee in divers places of Agra. Each of them every eveninge is like a faire, where they resort, make their bargaines, take and choose the whores sittinge and lyeinge on their Cotts att their balcones and doores.

There are also dauncinge wenches, of whome there are divers sorts, as Lullenees, Harcanees, Kenchanees and Doomenees (all whoores though not in soe publique a manner) beinge of severall Castes and use different manner of musick. Most comonly they are hired att solemne feasts, where they playe, singe and daunce, whilst they [*the guests*] eate, drinck and discourse. And there is scarse any meetinge of friends without them, where, when they are once warme with their meates, drinckes, gullees, etts. (I meane the Moores etts.), they take whome they have a minde to, either for the night or otherwise. These women buy litle slave Wenches and bringe them upp to their professions, sellinge their Maidenheads at first att deere rates, after prostituted for a small matter.

[71] Elephant-fighting viewed from the Fort; from *Travels in Europe and Asia (1608–67)* by Peter Mundy.

In India are used many other fightings of beasts, as of Eliphants, wild Buffaloes etts. The fighting of Eliphants is seldome seene but where the King is, and there often used, sometymes twice a weeke, in the afternoone att Agra. First the Elephants appoynted for the day, which are usually one Couple, other tymes there may be two and some tymes three Couple. The King cometh to the windowe, that looketh into the River, upon whose strand, right before the said Windowe, being the place appoynted, they are brought; with each a guide sitting on his Neck. Att the word given they are lett goe, and soe runninge one against the other with their Truncks aloft they meete head to head. There they with their Teeth lye Thrustinge and forceinge with all their strength, whoe are againe parted by their Keepers. But sometymes they will not be ruled by words. Then doe they apply fireworks on long Bamboes or staves betwene them, whose cracks and noyse, fire and smoake doe sever them (for they stand much in feare of it), soe lett them joyne againe; this as often as they please. Sometymes one getts the victorie by over bearing the other in strength till hee make him give way, which hee followes; and if the other bee not too light for him, overtakes and overthrowes him sometymes, then lyes over him, thrusting att him with his teeth, tramplinge and overlyeing him, for they can neither kick, bite nor Scratch. Theis fighting Eliphants are of the fairest bignesse and strongest, whose teeth are sawen off in the midle and then bound about with iron or Brasse for there more strength; for if they were left whole, they endaunger the breakeing att every encounter. Yett is there a sort called Muccan, of a very great body, whoe have but very litle and short Teeth, and comonly overcome the others. There Keepers or Guides are many tymes strucken of in the fight, but quickly gett up againe; but sometymes they are killed outright. Other tymes they are left to run after men on horseback, whoe are too nimble for him; for the Eliphant cannot gallop, only shoveling away hee may run somewhat faster then a man.

Also wilde Buffaloes and Bulls, other tymes Tigers and lyons fight: also the wilde boare and the Leopard. Our pastime of Cockfightinge is not heere in use; only among young men and boyes they have certen small black birds called bulbulls, and sometymes Quailes, which make some sporte.

Elephants, camels and wrestlers fighting at Agra;
from the Babur-nama, late sixteenth century

[72] Aurungzeb attempts to aggravate his father; from
Storia do Mogor by Niccalao Manucci.

Although Aurangzeb's illness was at a height for only a few days,
it took him a long time to become convalescent and to recover his
strength. The medical men recommended a change of air by a
visit to the province of Kashmīr. Aurangzeb was quite willing to
take the change of air, but the existence of Shāhjahān was like a
thorn piercing his heart, hindering him from resting or taking
the recreation demanded by nature. Therefore he now displayed
no increase of gentleness to his father; on the contrary, he decided
to aggravate the old man more and more. Of a truth, this was
never the inspiration of the angel during his illness nor the
teaching of God, but was arrived at from the perversity of his
own nature. In order to bring his father's life quickly to an end,
he sent orders to make his imprisonment more severe. He
ordered the bricking up of a window looking towards the river,
where Shāhjahān sat for recreation. A company of musketeers
was posted below the Āgrah Palace with orders by firing to
disturb the old man, and to shoot him if he appeared at the
window. In addition to this, to increase his despondency, the
greater part of the accumulation of gold and silver money was
carried away, making as much noise as possible, so that he
(Shāhjahān) might hear and be dejected in his mind. But
Shāhjajān, too, played a game of finesse, and made out he saw
nothing; responding to the cries, noise, and musket-shots by
music, dancing, and entertainments, and carried on a joyous life
with his wives and women. I'tibār K͟hān, who knew everything
that went on in the palace, wrote it all to the court, so that
Aurangzeb decided to take Shāhjahān's life by poison.

[73] 'The hottest place in India'; from *Up the Country . . .* by
Emily Eden.

Agra is avowedly the hottest place in India, and everybody says
this is the hottest house in Agra, so there is a whole army of
engineers now beginning to see what can be done to build up
verandahs, and to make ventilators and to pretend to make the
hot winds bearable. There are in India two regular parties, one
preferring Bengal with the hot days and the damp and the sea-

breeze blowing at night, and the other standing up for their hot winds, twenty degrees hotter, but dry. I have never varied in thinking the account of them terrific. From the end of March, to the middle of June, they blow unceasingly, night and day. Nobody stirs out, and all night the tatties are kept wet, and thermantidotes (great *winnowing* machines) are kept turning to make a little cool air. The windows are never opened, and they say that at midnight, if you were to go out, it feels like going into a furnace. However those who are all for the provinces say, the wind is dry and not unwholesome, and that as long as you do not attempt to go out of the house, you do not suffer from the heat. It is a regular strict imprisonment. Calcutta is bad, but there we had a regular evening drive, and Government House was really cool at night; then in case of illness there was the sea at hand, but here, if any of us are ill, of course, there is no escape. Even natives cannot travel in the hot winds. The discomfiture is general. Most of our goods are half-way to Calcutta. The native servants, who thought they were within reach of their wives and families after two years' absence, are utterly desperate.

The Pearl Mosque (Agra Fort)

[74] 'A perfect type of its class'; from *A Visit to India, China and Japan in the year 1853* by Bayard Taylor.

I visited the Motee Musjeed, or Pearl Mosque, as it is poetically and justly termed. It is, in truth, the pearl of all mosques, of small dimensions, but absolutely perfect in style and proportions. It is lifted on a sandstone platform and from without nothing can be seen but its three domes of white marble with their gilded spires. In all distant views of the Fort these domes are seen like silvery bubbles which have rested a moment on its walls, and which the next breeze will sweep away. Ascending a long flight of steps, a heavy door was opened for me, and I stood in the court-yard of the mosque. Here, nothing was to be seen but the quadrangle of white marble, with the mosque on its western side, and the pure blue of the sky overhead. The three domes crown a deep corridor, open toward the court, and divided into three aisles by a triple row of the most exquisitely proportioned Saracenic arches. The Motee Musjeed can be compared to no other edifice I have ever seen. To my eye it is a perfect type of its class. While the architecture is the purest Saracenic, which some suppose cannot exist without ornament, it shows the severe simplicity of the Doric art. It has, in fact, nothing which can be properly termed ornament. It is a sanctuary so pure and stainless, revealing so exalted a spirit of worship that I felt humbled as a Christian, to think that our nobler religion has so rarely inspired its architects to surpass this temple to God and Mohammed.

[75] The ladies' mosque and a heavy bath in the mid-nineteenth century; from *The Travels of a Hindoo* . . . by Bholanauth Chunder.

The *Mootee Musjeed*, built entirely of pure white marbles, that make the nearest approach to the colour and lustre of a pearl, is justly entitled to its name of the Pearl Mosque. It is a chaste, simple, and majestic structure of an oblong shape, well-proportioned in its dimensions, and uniting the most refined elegance with an exquisite simplicity. The finely swelling-out domes are a triumph of architecture. The topmost gilt culisses still retain their original brilliancy. The chaste white marbles lend, indeed, a most placid and immaculate appearance. There is a tranquil beauty pervading the whole conception of the building, on which you may look for ever without feeling the least satiety. The agreeable surprise with which it stands opened on the sight of the traveller, rivets his attention in a fervour of admiration. The marbled design seems to be instinct with life – to be endued with a dumb language. Running below the outer cornice is an inscription in Persian, which, as expounded to us by one of the Musulman attendants, records the mosque to have been built by Shah Jehan in 1656, for the private chapel of the ladies of the harem. The cost is mentioned in *ashrufees* as equivalent to the sum of sixty lacs of rupees.

Fronting the mosque, is a large stone-built square basin to hold water for ritual ablutions. The fountain in its middle is now dry. Turned back to take our last view of the Motee Musjeed. From a distance, it may be fancied as seeming to woo us like a Peri from heaven – as Tom Moore's Paradise-lost Houri.

The remarkable bath of Shah Jehan, hollowed out of one single block of white marble, and measuring forty feet in diameter, is no longer to be seen. This artistic curiosity had particularly attracted the notice of Lord Hastings, and he had caused it to be taken up for a present to George IV. of England, then Prince Regent. But it was found to make a too heavy freight for a native craft, and the idea of its removal was abandoned. The ultimate fate of this curious bath is unknown.

[76] The Pearl Mosque 'admired even more than the Taj'; from *Rambles and Recollections of an Indian Official* by Major-General W.H. Sleeman.

We visited the Motī Masjid or Pearl Mosque. It was built by Shāh Jahān, entirely of white marble; and completed, as we learn from an inscription on the portico, in the year AD 1656. There is no mosaic upon any of the pillars or panels of this mosque; but the design and execution of the flowers in bas-relief are exceedingly beautiful. It is a chaste, simple, and majestic building; and is by some people admired even more than the Tāj, because they have heard less of it; and their pleasure is heightened by surprise. We feel that it is to all other mosques what the Tāj is to all other mausoleums, a *facile princeps*.

Few, however, go to see the 'mosque of pearls' more than once, stay as long as they will at Agra; and when they go, the building appears less and less to deserve their admiration; while they go to the Tāj as often as they can, and find new beauties in it, or new feelings of pleasure from it, every time.

The Taj Mahal

[77] Building the Taj Mahal, 1632; from *Travels in Europe and Asia (1608–67)* by Peter Mundy.

This Kinge is now buildinge a Sepulchre for his late deceased Queene Tage Moholl (as much to say att the brightnes of the Moholl), whome hee dearely affected, haveing had by her 9 or 10 children, and thought in her life tyme to use noe other woman (which is strange if true consideringe their libertie in that kinde). He intends it shall excell all other. The place appoynted [is] by the river side where shee is buried, brought from Brampore where shee dyed accompanyinge him in his warrs, as shee did all the tyme of his troubles. It is reported that in tyme of his rebellion, being fledd to Decan, where hee had private intelligence from Asaph Ckaun of his fathers death, and not knoweing how to gett out of Decan if they should heere of it, but that hee should bee intercepted and brought to what composition they would, hee fained himselfe dead. Then shee desireinge leave to carry her husbands body to be buried in his owne Countrie, it was graunted her; and by that meanes, in a Coffin Covered with black, hee was conveyed out of their dominion, which was but 3 or 4 dayes Journeies distant from his owne, where beinge come, more people adhered to him, till hee came to Agra, and by strange Courses to the Crowne. There is alreadye about her Tombe a raile of gold. The buildinge is begun and goes on with excessive labour and cost, prosecuted with extraordinary dilligence, Gold and silver esteemed comon Mettall, and Marble but as ordinarie stones. Hee intends, as some thinck, to remove all the Cittie hither, cawseinge hills to be made levell because they might not hinder the prospect of it, places appoynted for streets, shopps, etts. dwellings, commaunding Marchants, shoppkeepers, Artificers to Inhabit [it] where they begin to repaire and called by her name, Tage Gunge.

The Taj Mahal, seen from the river;
aquatint by Thomas and William Daniell, 1789

[78] Who designed the Taj Mahal?; from *Travels of a Hindoo*
. . . by Bholanauth Chunder.

Undoubtedly, the Taj is the highest architectural triumph of
man. But the Europeans are little inclined to give the credit of its
execution to the Indians. They would fain believe, that a
Frenchman of the name of Austin de Bordeaux designed and
executed the Taj. This Frenchman was no apocryphal being. He
was a man of great talent, who held the office of the first *nuksha
nuvees*, or plan-drawer, in the court of Shah Jehan, on a salary of
one thousand rupees a month, with other occasional presents.
He was called by the natives Oostan Eesau, under which name
he stands in all the Persian accounts first among the salaried
architects. He was sent by the Emperor to settle some affairs of
great importance at Goa, and died at Cochin on his way back,
leaving a son by a native woman, called Mahomed Shureef,
who, too, was afterwards employed as an architect on a monthly
salary of five hundred rupees. The Taj is not more ascribed to
Austin de Bordeaux than are its mosaics to Genoese and other
Italian artists; – what share remains, then, to be attributed to the
Indian of the soil on which it stands? It must be none other than
that of having gazed at its progress in silent admiration. True,
there had abounded, in those days, a great many European
adventurers in the court of the Great Mogul. There were
Hawkins, a munsubdar, Tavernier, a jeweller, Bernier, a
physician – and there may have been an Austin, an architect.
True, that in the Roman Catholic burial-ground at Agra, there
are old tombstones inscribed with Genoese and other Italian
names. But when we see around us so many other magnificent
mosques and mausoleums cognate in expression, we should
either deny them all, or make no hesitation in acknowledging
this. It has been very truly observed by one, that 'the idea
stamped upon the building is intensely Mahomedan and
Oriental.' The Italians referred to were employed as mere
diamond-cutters; and Elphinstone thinks 'it singular, that artists
of that nation should receive lessons in taste from the Indians.'
Tavernier saw the Taj commenced and finished, and he does not
say a word about its execution by Austin. Bernier came to India
only five years after the Taj had been completed – and had it
been constructed by one of his countrymen, the fact would
assuredly have been commemorated in his writings. The noble

Tagra characters in which the passages from the Koran are inscribed upon different parts of the Taj had been executed by one Amanut Khan of Schiraz. The name of this man is found inscribed in the same bold characters on the right-hand side as we enter the tomb. It is after the date thus: – A.H. 1048 'The humble Fakir Amanut Khan of Schiraz.' In the same manner, Austin de Bordeaux would have been permitted to place his name, had he been the *bonâ fide* architect. But it matters little whether the Taj is of European or of Indian hands – suffice it, that it is a masterpiece of human architecture. The Taj is in architecture what the Venus de Medici is in sculpture, or Shakespeare in poetry.

[79] A painter's opinion of the Taj Mahal in 1786; from *Select Views in India Drawn on the Spot* by William Hodges.

The basest material that enters into this center part of it is white marble, and the ornaments are of various coloured marbles but there is no glitter: the whole together appears like a most perfect pearl on an azure ground. The effect is such as, I confess, I never experienced from any work of art. The fine materials, the beautiful forms, and the symmetry of the whole, with the judicious choice of situation, far surpasses any thing I ever beheld.

[80] First impressions; from *Rambles and Recollections of an Indian Official* by Major-General W.H. Sleeman.

On the 1st of January, 1836, we went on sixteen miles to Agra, and, when within about six miles of the city, the dome and minarets of the Taj opened upon us from behind a small grove of fruit-trees, close by us on the side of the road. The morning was not clear, but it was a good one for a first sight of this building, which appeared larger through the dusty haze than it would have done through a clear sky. For five-and-twenty years of my life had I been looking forward to the sight now before me. Of no building on earth had I heard so much as of this, which contains the remains of the Emperor Shāh Jahān and his wife, the father and mother of the children whose struggles for dominion have been already described. We had ordered our tents to be pitched in the gardens of this splendid mausoleum, that we might have our fill of the enjoyment which everybody seemed to derive from it; and we reached them about eight o'clock. I went over the whole building before I entered my tent, and, from the first sight of the dome and minarets on the distant horizon to the last glance back from my tent-ropes to the magnificent gateway that forms the entrance from our camp to the quadrangle in which they stand, I can truly say that everything surpassed my expectations. I at first thought the dome formed too large a portion of the whole building; that its neck was too long and too much exposed; and that the minarets were too plain in their design; but, after going repeatedly over every part, and examining the *tout ensemble* from all possible positions, and in all possible lights, from that of the full moon at midnight in a cloudless sky to that of the noonday sun, the mind seemed to repose in the calm persuasion that there was an entire harmony of parts, a faultless congrega-tion of architectural beauties, on which it could dwell for ever without fatigue.

After my quarter of a century of anticipated pleasure, I went on from part to part in the expectation that I must by-and-by come to something that would disappoint me; but no, the emotion which one feels at first is never impaired; on the contrary, it goes on improving from the first *coup d'œil* of the dome in the distance to the minute inspection of the last flower upon the screen round the tomb. One returns and returns to it with undiminished pleasure; and, though at every return one's attention to the smaller parts becomes less and less, the pleasure which he derives from the contemplation of the greater, and of the whole collectively, seems to increase; and he leaves with a feeling of regret that he could not have it all his life within his reach, and of assurance that the image of what he has seen can never be obliterated from his mind 'while memory holds her seat.' I felt that it was to me in architecture what Kemble and his sister, Mrs. Siddons, had been to me a quarter of a century before in acting – something that must stand alone – something that I should never cease to see clearly in my mind's eye, and yet never be able clearly to describe to others.

The Emperor and his Queen lie buried side by side in a vault beneath the building, to which we descend by a flight of steps. Their remains are covered by two slabs of marble; and directly over these slabs, upon the floor above, in the great centre room under the dome, stand two other slabs, or cenotaphs, of the same marble exquisitely worked in mosaic. Upon that of the Queen, amid wreaths of flowers, are worked in black letters passages from the Korān, one of which, at the end facing the entrance, terminates with, 'And defend us from the tribe of unbelievers;' that very tribe which is now gathered from all quarters of the civilized world to admire the splendour of the tomb which was raised to perpetuate her name. On the slab over her husband there are no passages from the Korān – merely mosaic work of flowers with his name and the date of his death. I asked some of the learned Muhammadan attendants the cause of this differ-ence, and was told that Shāh Jahān had himself designed the slab over his wife, and saw no harm in inscribing the *words of God* upon it; but that the slab over himself was designed by his more pious son, Aurangzēb, who did not think it right to place these holy words upon a stone which the foot of man might some day touch, though that stone covered the remains of his own father. Such was this 'man of prayers,' this 'Namāzī' (as Dara called him), to the last. He knew mankind well, and, above all, that part of them which he was called upon to govern, and which he governed for forty years with so much ability.

This magnificent building and the palaces at Agra and Delhi were, I believe, designed by Austin de Bordeaux, a Frenchman of great talent and merit, in whose ability and integrity the Emperor placed much reliance. He was called by the natives 'Ustān Isā, Nādir-ul-asr,' 'the wonderful of the age'; and, for his office of 'naksha navīs,' or plan drawer, he received a regular salary of one thousand rupees a month, with occasional presents, that made his income very large. He had finished the palace at Delhi, and the mausoleum and palace of Agra; and was engaged in designing a silver ceiling for one of the galleries in the latter, when he was sent by the Emperor to settle some affairs of great importance at Goa. He died at Cochin on his way back, and is supposed to have been poisoned by the Portuguese, who were extremely jealous of his influence at court. He left a son by a native, called Muhammad Sharīf, who was employed as an architect on a salary of five hundred rupees a month, and who became, as I conclude from his name, a Musalmān. Shāh Jahān had commenced his own tomb on the opposite side of the Jumna; and both were to have been united by a bridge. The death of

Austin de Bordeaux, and the wars between his [*Shāh Jahān's*] sons that followed prevented the completion of these magnificent works.

I asked my wife, when she had gone over it, what she thought of the building? 'I cannot,' said she, 'tell you what I think, for I know not how to criticize such a building, but I can tell you what I feel. I would die to-morrow to have such another over me.' This is what many a lady has felt, no doubt.

The building stands upon the north side of a large quadrangle, looking down into the clear blue stream of the river Jumna, while the other three sides are enclosed with a high wall of red sandstone. The entrance to this quadrangle is through a magnificent gateway in the south side opposite the tomb; and on the other two sides are very beautiful mosques facing inwards, and corresponding exactly with each other in size, design, and execution. That on the left, or west, side is the only one that can be used as a mosque or church; because the faces of the audience, and those of all men at their prayers, must be turned towards the tomb of their prophet to the west. The pulpit is always against the dead wall at the back, and the audience face towards it, standing with their backs to the open front of the building. The church on the east side is used for the accommodation of visitors, or for any secular purpose, and was built merely as a 'jawāb' (answer) to the real one. The whole area is laid out in square parterres, planted with flowers and shrubs in the centre, and with fine trees, chiefly the cypress, all round the borders, forming an avenue to every road. These roads are all paved with slabs of freestone, and have, running along the centre, a basin, with a row of *jets d'eau* in the middle from one extremity to the other. These are made to play almost every evening, when the gardens are much frequented by the European gentlemen and ladies of the station, and by natives of all religions and sects. The quadrangle is from east to west nine hundred and sixty-four feet, and from north to south three hundred and twenty-nine.

The mausoleum itself, the terrace upon which it stands, and the minarets, are all formed of the finest white marble, inlaid with precious stones. The wall around the quadrangle, including the river face of the terrace, is made of red sandstone, with cupolas and pillars of the same white marble. The insides of the churches and apartments in and upon the walls are all lined with marble or with stucco work that looks like marble; but, on the outside, the red sandstone resembles uncovered bricks. The dazzling white marble of the mausoleum itself rising over the red wall is apt, at first sight, to make a disagreeable impression, from the idea of a whitewashed head to an unfinished building; but this impression is very soon removed, and tends, perhaps, to improve that which is afterwards received from a nearer inspection. The marble was all brought from the Jeypore territories upon wheeled carriages, a distance, I believe, of two or three hundred miles; and the sandstone from the neighbourhood of Dhōlpur and Fathpur Sīkrī. Shāh Jahān is said to have inherited his partiality for this colour from his grandfather, Akbar, who constructed almost all his buildings from the same stone, though he might have had the beautiful white freestone at the same cost. What was figuratively said of Augustus may be most literally said of Shāh Jāhān; he found the cities (Agra and Delhi) all brick, and left them all marble; for all the marble buildings, and additions to buildings, were formed by him.

We were encamped upon a fine green sward outside the entrance to the south, in a kind of large court, enclosed by a high cloistered wall, in which all our attendants and followers found shelter. Colonel and Mrs. King, and some other gentlemen, were encamped in the same place, and for the same purpose; and we had a very agreeable party. The band of our friend Major Godby's regiment played sometimes in the evening upon the terrace of the Tāj; but, of all the complicated music ever heard upon earth, that of a flute blown gently in the vault below, where the remains of the Emperor and his consort repose, as the sound rises to the dome amidst a hundred arched alcoves around, and descends in heavenly reverberations upon those who sit or recline upon the cenotaphs above the vault, is, perhaps, the finest to an inartificial ear. We feel as if it were from heaven, and breathed by angels; it is to the ear what the building itself is to the eye; but, unhappily, it cannot, like the building, live in our recollections. All that we can, in after life, remember is that it was heavenly, and produced heavenly emotions.

[81] Emily Eden enthuses; from *Up the Country* . . . by Emily Eden.

The Taj is quite as beautiful as ever, even more so, and as we have never heard anything else, that just shows how entirely perfect it must be.

[82] The Prince of Wales visits the Taj in 1876; from *The Prince of Wales' Tour* . . . by Sir William Howard Russell.

January 27th. – The Prince paid return visits to the fourteen Chiefs. When these visits were over, his Royal Highness drove through the suburbs, and after dinner he went to see the Taj illuminated.

Most writers who have tried their hands at a description of the Taj set out with the admission that it is indescribable, and then 'proceed to give some idea' of it. I do not know how many of the fair ladies present agreed with Colonel Sleeman's wife, who said to him, 'I cannot criticise, but I can tell you what I feel. I would die to-morrow to have such a tomb!' Holy and profane men, poets, prosers, and practical people all write of the Taj in the same strain. 'Too pure, too holy to be the work of human hands!' – 'a poem in marble!' – 'the sigh of a broken heart!' – 'poetic marble arrayed in eternal glory!' – 'the inspiration is from heaven – the execution worthy of it!' But the Taj, with 7000 spectators – 7000 people who came to look at the Prince of Wales looking at the Taj! Well, it played its part to perfection.

Ascending the terrace, the Prince walked over to the shelter of the dark gateway of the mosque. Gradually there grew out, in all its fair proportions and beauty, framed in the purple of the starry heavens, the marble 'Queen of Sorrow,' which has power to dim every eye. Then trooping into the illuminated square came a band, and forthwith the soft tender notes of 'Vedrai carino' floated through the night air. It may be doubted if Moomtaz-i-Mahul, or 'the Exalted One of the Palace,' would have quite approved of the music. However, Mozart was better than the *maestro* whose compositions next challenged the ears of the company. But the eye mastered every sense, and the loveliness of the Taj stole over the soul. In spite of blue lights, and lime lights, of lively dance music, of clank of spurs and sabres on the complaining marble, there was not a point which the peerless mausoleum could make which was for an instant marred or lost. Entering the tomb itself – the culminating glory – the party stood and gazed, almost trembling with admiration. Presently a clear, sustained note rose up into the vaulted roof of the tomb, and there found its counterpart, and the two commingled, swept upwards, and soared away, 'till naught remained 'twixt them and silence.' Again and again the notes soared, and the auditors stood breathless. Then came a few chords in sweet unison from four or five singers, but to my ear the effect was not so impressive as that of an old Moulvie's voice reading prayers when last I was there. That grand, grumbling chant awoke echoes which sounded like the responses of some vast congregation. The interior has been swept, garnished, cleaned, and, as far as can be, restored. If Shah Jehan could come back to earth, it is not too much to suppose that he would thank Sir John Strachey for the labour of love which has stayed the hand of the spoiler.

Moomtaz-i-Mahul died in childbirth of her eighth child. People have taken lately to abusing her husband and his times; but it may be recollected that about that very period of the world's history England was not quite a paradise; that we had a Star Chamber and other comforts for the conscience; were busy persecuting people we did not like; were preparing for a civil war and for the execution of our King, and were by no means in a condition to justify us in throwing stones at the builder of the Taj. We have done better since; and if there be no Taj or Sikundra to be put to our account, we hope we can say that our rule has, in the words of De Quincey, conferred on India 'gifts higher by far than Mogul gifts of palace or serai, roads or tanks – the gifts of security, order, law, and peace.'

[83] 'A most distressing discord'; from *The Turks in India* by H.G. Keene.

Visitors will be disappointed by the celebrated echo from the dome if they attempt to play or sing any complicated melodies or roulades in it. The echo is so quick that it catches the notes and runs them into one another, so as to produce a most distressing discord, unless the notes chosen be such as to form a natural harmony. The chord of the seventh produces a very beautiful

effect. It is this that in the words of the American traveller
[*Bayard Taylor*], 'floats and soars overhead in a long, delicious
undulation, fading away so slowly that you hear it after it is
silent, as you see, or seem to see, a lark you have been watching
after it is swallowed up in the blue vault of heaven.'

[84] 'Many a visitor moved to modest verse'; quoted in
Travels of a Hindoo . . . by Bholanauth Chunder.

Lady Nugent, the wife of Sir George Nugent, Commander-in-Chief.
   O thou! whose great imperial mind could raise
   This splendid trophy to a woman's praise!
   If love or grief inspired the bold design,
   No moral joy or sorrow equall'd thine!
   Sleep on secure! this monument shall stand
   When Desolation's wing sweeps o'er the land,
   By time and death in one wide ruin hurl'd;
   The last triumphant wonder of the world.

*Mrs C. Fagan, the wife of Colonel C. Fagan, Adjutant-General, under
Lord Combermere.*
   Pure as Mumtaza's spotless fame,
      The unsullied marble shines;
   Rich as her lord's unrivall'd love
      The wreaths that deck their shrines.

   On fanes more glorious I have gazed,
      Witness St Peter's dome;
   And costlier gems shine bright around
      The Medician tomb.

   But this! Love's temple – beauteous pile,
      The pride of Eastern art!
   This boasts the present deity,
      That seizes on the heart.

   All ruling Power! to thee we bend,
      Thy potent charm we own –
   This structure, simple, graceful, pure,
      Oh! this is Love's alone.

Anonymous [*B. Chunder?*]
    No eastern prince for wealth or wisdom famed,
    No mortal hands this beauteous fabric framed,
    In death's cold arms the fair Mumtaza slept,
    And sighs o'er Jumna's winding waters crept,
    Tears such as angels weep, with fragrance fill'd,
    Around her grave in pearly drops distill'd.
    There fix'd for ever firm, congeal'd they stand,
    A fairy fabric, pride of India's land.

[85] Lord Curzon's lamp; from *The Life of Lord Curzon* by the Earl of Ronaldshay.

The model which Lord Curzon sought was hard to find. As a result of the enquiries which he made in Cairo, his decision was finally cast in favour of a lamp which was known to have hung in the mosque of Sultan Beybars II. The lamp itself had vanished and neither in the museums of Cairo, Paris nor London could the famous original be found. It had probably passed into some private collection where it was lost to the generality of mankind. Fortunately its features down to the minutest detail were well known; and having come to his decision Lord Curzon sought the advice of two expert counsellors, Herz Bey, Director of the Arab Museum at Cairo, and Mr. E. Richmond, of the Egyptian Public Works Department, as to the best means of giving effect to it. It appeared that there were but two men in the whole of Egypt who were considered capable of carrying out a work of so much delicacy. Choice fell upon Todros Badir, who, at the end of two years labour, produced a lamp in bronze, inlaid throughout with silver and gold, such as had not been seen since the period of the original many centuries before. It was typical of Lord Curzon's minute attention to detail that during this time he should have caused the inscription with which he desired to commemorate his gift – 'Presented to the Tomb of Mumtaz Mahal by Lord Curzon, Viceroy of India, 1906' – to be translated into Persian, converted by a calligraphist at Agra into one of the scripts employed on the tombs of Shah Jahan and his queen, returned to Cairo for such revision as might be necessary to bring it into harmony with the style of the lamp and finally cut in a belt of pierced metal round its circumference.

The scene on the occasion of its installation by Sir John Hewett, Lieutenant Governor of the United Provinces and a former colleague of Lord Curzon, was one which would have made a powerful appeal to Lord Curzon's ingrained love of romance. At sunset on February the 16th, 1908, evening prayer was intoned by the Imam in the mosque of the Taj in the presence of a vast congregation. Thereafter a gathering of two hundred of its leading members assembled in the tomb, the remainder to the number of 10,000 halting in the grounds outside the central building. The President of the Anjuman Islamia, Syed Ali Nabi, speaking to those present in Urdu, reminded them of the debt of gratitude which they owed to Lord Curzon for the restoration of their historic monuments –

'The Taj Mahal is for the perfection of Moslem artistic endeavour and the embodiment of all that was best in the lives and thoughts of the Moghuls. It is with feelings of intense gratification, therefore, that we have watched this cherished mausoleum rescued from neglect and decay, that we have seen the tomb, the mosque and the many other structures grouped around it all tenderly and reverently repaired, the gardens assuming once more their ancient charm, and the arcaded courts and approaches restored to their former majesty.'

[86] Mrs Roosevelt holds her breath; from *India and the Awakening East* by Eleanor Roosevelt.

I must own that by the time we got to Agra I was beginning to feel we had seen a great many forts and palaces and temples and mosques. I realized that I was no longer viewing them with the same freshness of interest and appreciation that I had felt during the early part of my visit. I think the others felt much the same way, which may have been one reason why we had all been talking more and more about the fact that no letters from home were reaching us. I had even cabled for news of my family. Therefore when we got back to Government House after our visit to Akbar's fort, though we knew we should leave immediately to get our first glimpse of the Taj Mahal at sunset, we all pounced on the letters we found waiting for us, and could not tear ourselves away until the last one had been read. Then, to our dismay, we found we had delayed too long; by the time we got to the Taj – about six-thirty – the light was beginning to fade.

What I have just said about feeling jaded cannot apply to the Taj. As we came through the entrance gallery into the walled garden and looked down the long series of oblong pools in which the Taj and the darkened cypresses are reflected, I held my breath, unable to speak in the face of so much beauty. The white marble walls, inlaid with semi-precious stones, seemed to take on a mauve tinge with the coming night, and about half-way along I asked to be allowed to sit down on one of the stone benches and just look at it. The others walked on, but I felt that this first time I wanted to drink in its beauty from a distance. One does not want to talk and one cannot glibly say this is a beautiful thing, but one's silence, I think, says this is a beauty that enters the soul. With its minarets rising at each corner, its dome and tapering spire, it creates a sense of airy, almost floating lightness; looking at it, I decided I had never known what perfect proportions were before.

Fattephur Sikri

[87] Babur's daughter accompanies her father in 1530; from the *Hamayun-nama* of Gul-Badan Begum edited by A. Beveridge.

(Gul-Badan Begum (1524–1603) was born two years before her father Babur set out from Kabul to conquer Hindustan. In the reign of Humayun she sent material for the *Humayun-nama*. 'There had been an order issued: write down whatever you know . . .' is her opening line. Gul-Badan is literally 'Rose-body'.)

We had been at Agra three months, the Emperor went to Dolphur. Her Highness Maham Begum and this lowly person also went. A tank has been made there, ten by ten, out of one piece of rock. From Dolphur his Majesty went on to Sikri. He ordered a great platform made in the middle of the tank, and when it was ready he used to go and sit on it or row about.

They also put a chaukandi in the Sikri garden, and my royal father put in it a tir-khana where he used to sit and write his book.

[88] 'Bliss is his advent': Akbar returns to his capital; from the *Akbarnama* of Abu-l Fazl.

A breeze of joy comes from Fathpūr,
For my King returns from the long journey.
What bliss is his advent, for from every heart
Thousands of rejoicings come forth.
O Faizī, glorious be his arrival to a world.
For a world comes into his presence.

On this day of joy the great officers, the loyal servants, and others were drawn up in two sides of the way for a distance of four *koss* from the city. The mountain-like elephants stood there in their majesty. The Khedive of the world proceeded on his way on a heaven-like elephant, attended by the 'Avaunt' of the Divine

Akbar I inspecting the building of Fattephur Sikri (1584); detail from the Akbar-nama

Halo. The obedient princes moved on in their order. Many
grandees proceeded in front of the mace-bearers. The panoply
was there in its splendour and was followed by various officers.
The noise of the drums and the melodies of the magician-like
musicians gave forth news of joy. Crowds of men were gathered
in astonishment on the roofs and at the doors. At the end of the
day he sate in the lofty hall on the throne of sovereignty. He
dispensed justice by rewarding the loyal and banishing the
hostile and made the increase of dominion and success a vehicle
for worship and supplication.

[89] The first Jesuit mission, 1578; from *Akbar and the
Jesuits: an account of the Jesuit missions to the court of Akbar* by
Pierre du Jarric SJ.

(Father Pierre du Jarric (1566–1617) based his *Histoire des choses
plus memorables des Indes Orientales . . .* on reports and letters from
Jesuit priests, mostly Portuguese, active at the Mogul Court.)

About the month of March in the year 1578, the good priest,
whose name I have not discovered, reached Pateful [*Fattephur
Sikri*], where the King then held his court, and was received with
much kindness. It was not long before his Majesty told him the
reason why he had sent for him, which was, he said, that he might
clear his mind of certain doubts which prevented him from
deciding whether it was better to follow the law of the Christians
or the law of Mahomet. The priest, accordingly, expounded to
him the main principles of our faith, at the same time opening his
eyes to the worthlessness of the law of Mahomet.

Echebar heard these things with evident gladness; and so
strongly was he moved to abandon his faith that, one evening
while conversing with his Caziques, or Mullas, as the priests of
the Mahometan religion are called, he told them frankly that he
had decided to follow the counsel of the good priest, and pray to
God for light to see the truth, and the path to salvation. At this
discussion, his Soldan of Mecque [*Mecca*], the chief of all his
Mullas or Caziques, was present, who, the moment these words
fell from the King's lips, said, 'Your Majesty follows a good law,
and has no reason to doubt it, or to seek another.' On hearing
this, the King rose to his feet and exclaimed, 'May God help us!

May God help us!' repeating the words as if to imply that he was far from satisfied with the law that he followed, and that he would gladly have knowledge of a better.

A few days later, he asked the same priest to teach him to speak Portuguese; for he had a great desire (or so he said) to know that tongue, that he might the better understand his exposition of the Christian law. This the priest commenced to do with much care and zeal; and the first word that he taught the King was the sweet name of Jesus. The King found such pleasure in this holy word that he repeated it at each step as he walked up and down in his house.

One evening the same priest was disputing with the Mullas in the royal ante-chamber, while the King sat listening in his private apartment. In the course of the dispute, the priest said that the law of Mahomet was a tissue of errors and lies. This so enraged the Mullas that they were on the point of laying violent hands on him when the King entered and restrained them, appeasing their anger by telling them that it was no unusual thing for one engaged in a disputation to hold his own views to be true, and those of his adversaries to be false.

Sometime after these visits and disputes, Echebar, learning that the house in which the Fathers were lodged was inconvenient for them, owing to the din and bustle of the crowded thoroughfare in which it was situated, provided a more suitable residence for them within the precincts of his own palace. He did this partly from a desire to have them near at hand, so that he could visit them more often, or send for them whenever he wished, or had leisure to see them.

In this lodging the Fathers fitted up, as well as they could, a small chapel, in which they held divine service; and here, on several occasions, they were visited by the King. His Majesty entrusted his second son to them that they might teach him Portuguese, and to read and write after the European style, at the same time instructing him in the mysteries of the Christian faith. It may here be mentioned that in the year 1582, when these Fathers were at his court, Echebar had three sons and two daughters. The eldest son, who has since succeeded him on the throne, was then about 17 or 18 years of age. His proper name was Scieco; but he was always known as Sciecogio, the word Gio being added as a title of honour, just as in certain parts of Europe the word Dom is placed before the names of persons of rank or

The Jesuits and the mullahs debate before Akbar I;
from the Akbar-nama c. 1605

distinction. In the language of these people, Gio signifies 'soul'; so that Sciecogio is equivalent to the soul, or the person, of Scieco. The second son, whose name was Pahari, was 13 years of age. It was he who was placed under the Fathers to learn Portuguese and the rudiments of Christianity, to the study of which he showed himself well inclined. He was a lad of considerable promise, being both intelligent and docile. The last of the three was called Dan, which is the same as Daniel.

Eight days later, he again came to the oratory, accompanied this time by his three sons, and some of the chief nobles of his court. For a while he stood apart, looking attentively at the various objects in the chapel, and expressing his admiration of them in the presence of his courtiers. He then removed his shoes from his feet, and ordered his sons and all who were with him to do likewise, this being the custom observed by Moslims when entering their mosques. He showed great reverence for the pictures of our Saviour and the blessed Virgin, and even for those of other saints; and he ordered his painter to make copies of those which the Fathers had placed in their chapel. He also ordered his goldsmith to make for him a casket of gold with a richly carved lid, similar in shape to the copper casket in which the Fathers carried the images of our Saviour and the Virgin. Before leaving, he told the Fathers that their law appealed to him very strongly; but that there were two points in it which he could not comprehend, namely, the Trinity and the Incarnation. If they could explain these two things to his satisfaction, he would, he said, declare himself a Christian, even though it cost him his kingdom.

[90] Akbar moves to Agra; from *Indian Travels of Thévenot and Careri* edited by Surendranath Sen.

The Province of *Agra* hath above forty towns in its dependance, and, as they say, above three thousand four hundred Villages. *Fetipour* is one of the Towns; it was heretofore called *Sicari*, and the Name *Fetipour*, which signifies, *The enjoyment of what one desires*, was given it by *Ecbar*, because of the happy news he received there of the birth of a Son, when he was upon his return from a Warlike expedition. This Town is about six Leagues from *Agra*; it hath been very lovely, and that *Great Mogul* in the beginning of his Reign, having rebuilt the Walls of it, made it the Capital of his Empire. But the Ambition Kings have to make small things great, prompting *Ecbar* to build a Town where there was nothing but a Village, or at most, but a Bourg named *Agra*, the Town of *Fetipour* was not only neglected, but hath been since wholly abandoned; for so soon as *Agra* was become a Town, and that the King had given it his Name, calling it *Ecbarabad*, a place built by *Ecbar*, he went to reside there and forsook *Fetipour*.

Though this Town of *Fetipour* be much decay'd, yet there is still a large Square to be seen in it, adorned with fair Buildings; and the stately entry of *Ecbar's* Palace is still entire, and has adjoyning to it one of the loveliest Mosques in the East, built by a Mahometan a *Calender* by profession, who lies buried there as a Saint. The *Calenders* are Dervishes who go bare-footed. This Mosque is still adorn'd with all its Pillars, and lovely Seelings, and indeed, with all that can beautifie a fair Temple. Near to it there is a great Reservatory which supplies the whole Town with Water, and was the more necessary that all the Springs thereabouts are Salt; and the unwholsome Waters were one of the chief causes that obliged the *Great Mogul* to settle elsewhere.

[91] By fast cart to Fattephur Sikri in 1585; from the *Narrative* of Ralph Fitch in *Early Travels in India* edited by William Foster.

(Ralph Fitch was a member of an embassy to Akbar carrying a letter from Elizabeth I in the interest of trade. After travelling throughout India he made further extensive journeys through Siam to Malacca.)

Agra is a very great citie and populous, built with stone, having faire and large streetes, with a faire river running by it, which falleth into the Gulfe of Bengala. It hath a faire castle and a strong, with a very faire ditch. Here bee many Moores and Gentiles. The king is called Zelabdim Echebar; the people for the most part call him the Great Mogor. From thence we went for Fatepore, which is the place where the king kept his court. The towne is greater then Agra, but the houses and streetes be not so faire. Here dwell many people, both Moores and Gentiles. The king hath in Agra and Fatepore (as they doe credibly report)

1,000 elephants, thirtie thousand horses, 1,400 tame deere, 800 concubines: such store of ounces, tigers, buffles, cocks, and haukes, that is very strange to see. He keepeth a great court, which they call Dericcan. Agra and Fatepore are two very great cities, either of them much greater then London and very populous. Betweene Agra and Fatepore are 12 miles, and all the way is a market of victuals and other things, as full as though a man were still in a towne, and so many people as if a man were in a market. They have many fine cartes, and many of them carved and gilded with gold, with two wheeles, which be drawen with two litle buls about the bignesse of our great dogs in England, and they will runne with any horse, and carie two or three men in one of these cartes; they are covered with silke or very fine cloth, and be used here as our coches be in England. Hither is great resort of marchants from Persia and out of India, and very much marchandise of silke and cloth, and of precious stones, both rubies, diamants, and pearles. The king is apparelled in a muslin tunic made like a shirt tied with strings on the one side, and a little cloth on his head coloured oftentimes with red or yealow. None come into his house but his eunuches which keepe his women. Here in Fatepore we staied all three untill the 28 of September 1585.

[92] Brackish water; from the *Journal 1608–11* of William Finch in *Early Travels in India* edited by William Foster.

Under the court yard is a goodly tanke of excellent water; none other being to be had through the citie, but brackish and fretting, by drinking whereof was caused such mortality that the Acubar, before it was quite finished, left it, and remooved his seat to Agra; so that this goodly citie was short lived, in fifty or sixty yeares space beeing built and ruinate.

The north north-west side of the citie, without the walles, is a goodly lough for 2 or 3 c. in length, abounding with good fish and wilde fowle; all over which groweth the herbe which beareth the hermodactyle, and another bearing a fruit like a goblet, called camolachachery, both very cooling fruits. The herbe which beareth the hermodactyle is a weed abounding in most tankes neare Agra, spreading over all the water; the leafe I observed not, but the fruit is inclosed with a three cornered shell of a hard woodie substance, having at each angle a sharpe picked pricking point and is a little indented on both the flat sides like two posternes. The fruit, being greene, is soft and tender, white, and of a mealish taste, much eaten in India, being exceeding cold in my judgement, for alwayes after it I desired aqua-vitae. It is called by the people Singarra. The other beareth a fruit in maner of a goblet, flat on the toppe and of a soft greenish substance, within which a little eminent stand sixe or eight small fruits like akornes, divided from each other and inclosed with a whitish filme, at the first of a russettish greene, tasting like a nut or akorne; in the middest is a small greene sprigge naught to be eaten.

[93] A tower of tusks and a 'conceited' stable; from *Travels in Europe and Asia (1608–67)* by Peter Mundy.

Under the Cittie is a Lake of 10 or 12 mile long, haveing store of Fish. By it is a curious Tower of a greate highte, to bee ascended within side, haveinge on the outside peeces of white Marble made in forme of Eliphants Teeth built into it and sticking out about three quarters of a yard, and soe much distance betwene one another, haveinge on the Topp a fine Chowtree and a Copulae, supported with pillars, to bee ascended within side with stepps. It is Comonly called the Towre of Eliphants teeth, many thinckinge them to bee reall.

There is also a conceited Stable standinge on the side of the hill Towards the lake, which is made into severall flatts or degrees, like stepps one above another with pillars and arches to support a Coveringe to it. On each of those degrees stood a Ranck of horses; the entrance att one end.

Likewise a Parke or meadowe walled in, wherein were severall beasts. Amonge the rest Nilgaues, a kind of deere as high as a good Colte or Mule with short hornes.

[94] Eighteenth-century polo – 'an amusement similar to Goff'; from *Select Views in India Drawn on the Spot* by William Hodges.

(A pupil of Richard Wilson, excelling in landscapes, William Hodges (1744–97) went as artist with Cook's second expedition to the South Seas. He travelled to India under the patronage of Warren Hastings, and remained for six years. His *Select Views in India* contains a set of magnificent aquatints of scenic interest which inspired a desire to travel in, among others, the great explorer Humboldt.)

The town of Futtypoor was formerly known by the name of Sicri, and received its present appelation from the Mogul Emperor Akbar, who entitled it Futtypoor, i.e. Place of Victory, from a decisive defeat which he gave near it to the Patans in the beginning of his reign. He adorned the spot of engagement with a beautiful mosque, a convent for Dervishes, and a fortified palace, and, on the banks of an extensive lake near the town, he erected pleasure houses, and a spacious enclosure for playing at the Chougaun, an amusement similar to the Scotch exercise of Goff, only with this difference, that the players at Chougaun are mounted on horses, and they use long maces headed with iron. The artificial bank, which formed the lake, has been since broken down, and that part which was covered in water thrown into cultivation – which, however more useful, is certainly less beautiful; but Futtypoor was still more delightful to the Emperor, from the circumstance of it being the residence of the holy Dervish, Shekh Selum Chishtee, whose memory is still highly venerated throughout Hindostan. Akbar had lost several sons in their infancy, and was fearful he should have no male issue. In order to prevent so great an affliction, he besought the prayers of the holy Shekh and sent two of his pregnant wives to lye-in at his hermitage, hoping that their issue would receive benefit from the Shekh's prayers. Two sons were born, and the eldest was named Selum, in compliment to the Shekh, and succeeded his father Akbar by the title of Jehangir. Futtypoor has ever since been a celebrated resort for pregnant ladies, who come to pray at the tomb of the Saint, and whose descendants, living near it, reap great benefit from the oblations of such pilgrims.

[95] Human chess; from *Up the Country* . . . by Emily Eden.

It was lucky we had our halt at Futtehpore-Sickrey. Except Delhi, it is the most interesting place we have seen, and there is more to sketch, and in these hurried journeys I do not think it any sin to sketch on Sunday. There is a tomb of marble here, carved like lace – it would make such a splendid dairy for Windsor Castle, it looks so cool and so royal – and there is a beautiful gateway, the arch of which is ninety feet high; and then there are some remains of the Emperor Akbar, which give a good idea of the magnificent fellow he was. The throne in which he sat to hear petitions stands in the centre of a hall, with a cross of stone balconies, abutting from it, to four open arches. His ministers were placed at each end of that cross, their seats looking out on the courts below, so any grievance that was stated *to* them, or *against* them, they were obliged to announce at the full extent of their voices, else the Emperor could not hear them, and the petitioner below was made certain that his grievance was rightly stated. This throne, &c., is most beautifully carved, as you will see whenever I send my sketch books home. There is also a lovely carved room, all over European devices, supposed to have been built by the directions of a favourite wife, whom he imported from Constantinople. In the centre of the court, a *pucheesee* board (pucheesee is a sort of chess) is laid out in squares of marble, and there is a raised seat on which Akbar sat and played the games; the *pieces* were all female slaves splendidly dressed, and whoever won carried off the sixteen ladies.

[96] An all-round view in 1920; from *Roving East and Roving West* by E.V. Lucas.

(E.V. Lucas (1868–1935) was a frequent contributor to *Punch* and chairman of the publishers Methuen. He visited Lutyens in Delhi in 1920.)

All Shah Jahan's creations – the Taj, the marble mosque, the palaces both here and at Delhi, even the great Jama Masjid at Delhi, have a certain sensuous quality. They are not exactly decadent, but they suggest sweetness rather than strength. The Empire had been won, and Shah Jahan could indulge in luxury and ease. But Akbar had had to fight, and he remained to the end a man of action, and we see his character reflected in his stronghold Fatehpur-Sikri, which one visits from Agra and never forgets. If I were asked to say which place in India most fascinated me and touched the imagination I think I should name this dead city.

Akbar, the son of Babar, is my hero among the Moguls, and this was Akbar's chosen home, until scarcity of water forced him to abandon it for Agra. Akbar, the noblest of the great line of Moguls whose splendour ended in 1707 with the death of Aurungzebe, came to the throne is 1556, only eight years before Shakespeare was born, and died in 1605, and it is interesting to realize how recent were his times, the whole suggestion of Fatehpur-Sikri being one of very remote antiquity. Yet when it was being built so modern a masterpiece as *Hamlet* was being written and played.

The walls of Fatehpur-Sikri are seven miles round and the city rises to the summits of two steep hills. It was on the higher one that Akbar set his palace. Civilization has run a railway through the lower levels; the old high road still climbs the hill under the incredibly lofty walls of the palace. The royal enclosure is divided into all the usual courtyards and apartments, but they are on a grander scale. Also the architecture is more mixed. Here is the swimming bath; here are the cool, dark rooms for the ladies of the harem in the hottest days, with odd corners where Akbar is said to have played hide-and-seek with them; here is the hall where Akbar, who kept an open mind on religion, listened to, and disputed with, dialecticians of varying creeds – himself seated in the middle, and the doctrinaires in four pulpits around him; here is the Mint; here is the house of the Turkish queen, with its elaborate carvings and decorations; here is the girls' school, with a courtyard laid out for human chess, the pieces being slave-girls; here is a noble mosque; here is the vast court where the great father of his people administered justice, or what approximated to it, and received homage. Here are the spreading stables and riding school; here is even the tomb of a favourite elephant.

And here is the marble tomb of the Saint, the Shaikh Salim, whose holiness brought it about that the Emperor became at last the father of a son – none other than Jahangir. The shrine is visited even to this day by childless wives, who tie shreds of their clothing to the lattice-work of a marble window as an earnest of their maternal worthiness.

From every height – and particularly from the Paneh Mahal's roof – one sees immense prospects and realizes what a landmark the stronghold of Fatehpur-Sikri must have been to the dwellers in the plains; but no view is the equal of that which bursts on the astonished eyes at the great north gateway, where all Rajputana is at one's feet. I do not pretend to any exhaustive knowledge of the gates of the world, but I cannot believe that there can be others set as this Gate of Victory is in the walls of a palace, at the head of myriad steps, on the very top of a commanding rock and opening on to thousands of square miles of country. Having seen this amazing landscape one descends the steps to the road, and looking up is astonished and exalted by seeing the gate from below. Nothing so grand has ever come into my ken. The Taj Mahal is unforgettingly beautiful; but this glorious gate in the sky has more at once to exercise and stimulate the imagination and reward the vision.

On the gate are the words: 'Isa (Jesus), on whom be peace, said: "The world is a bridge; pass over it, but build no house on it. The world endures but an hour; spend it in devotion."'

Sikandra

[97] Akbar's tomb; from the *Journal 1608–11* of William Finch in *Early Travels in India* edited by William Foster.

King Acabars sepulchre is 3 c. distance from Agra in the way to Lahor; nothing neere finished as yet, after tenne yeares worke. It is placed in the midst of a faire and large garden inclosed with bricke walls, neere two miles in circuit; is to have foure gates (but one of which is yet in hand), each, if answerable to this foundation, able to receive a great prince with a reasonable traine. Alongst the way side is a spacious moholl for his fathers women (as is said) to remayne and end their dayes in deploring their deceased lord, each enjoying the lands they before had in the Kings time, by the pay or rents of five thousand horse the principall; so that this should be to them a perpetuall nunnery, never to marry againe. In the center of this garden stands the tombe foure square, about three quarters of a mile in compasse. The first inclosure is with a curious rayle, to which you ascend some six steps into a small square garden quartered in curious tankes, planted with variety of sweets; adjoyning to which is the tombe, rounded with this gardenet, being also foure square, all of hewne stone, with faire spacious galleries on each side, having at each corner a small beautifull turret, arched over head and covered with various marble. Betwixt corner and corner are foure other turrets at like distance. Here, within a faire round coffin of gold, lieth the body of this monarch, who sometimes thought the world too little for him. This tombe is much worshipped both by the Moores and Gentiles, holding him for a great saint. The tomb was not finished at my departure, but lay in manner of a coffin, covered with a white sheet interwrought with gold flowers. By his head stands his sword and target and on a small pillow his turbant, and thereby two or three faire gilded bookes. At his feet stand his shooes, and a rich bason and ewre. Every one approaching neere makes his reverence and puts off his shooes, bringing in his hand some sweete smelling flowers to bestrew the carpets or to adorne the tombe.

There are in continuall worke about this and other buildings about it, the moholl and gate, not so few as three thousand. The

Sikandra as drawn by Peter Mundy in the early seventeenth
century; drawing from Peter Mundy's *Travels in Europe and Asia*

stone is brought from a rich quarrey neere Fetipore, which may be cut in length and forme as timber with sawes, and plankes and seelings are made thereof.

[98] 'The designe sett downe'; from *Travels in Europe and Asia (1608–67)* by Peter Mundy.

Kinge Ecbars Tombe is at Shecundra, two miles from Agra, standing in a great Garden with four great gates, whereof one principall excellinge all others that I have seene in India for hight, curious Invention in buildinge, paintinge etts. haveinge two extraordinarie high spires like to those att Constantinople from whence in a longe walke you goe to the monument itselfe whose outward frame resembleth the mauseolo pictured among the 7 wonders, fower square, lesseninge towards the topp, haveinge severall galleries round about, adorned with Copulaes of which the lower galleries conteyne the more, the borders on the outside etts. of redd stone through Cutt with curious workes, theis galleries ascendinge one from another to the Topp, on which is a square litle Court, the pavements chequered with white and a reddish marble, the midle of which is over the midle of the whole, where stands a Tombestone in forme of a herse of one entire peece of marble, curiously wrought and engraven with letters and flowers etts. This hath 4 turretts with Copulaes, att each Corner one; from one to another are galleries alofte and under foote marble, the sides alsoe, which are artificially through Cutt as afore mentioned.

The said Tombestone lyes just over the place where the said kinge is buried. From hence beinge discended, and desirous to enter in, wee were not permitted, by reason the Kinge keepes the key of the doore which is alsoe sealed with his signett. The garden and the other gates were not yett finished. There is mention made of it in Purchas. The designe thereof I have sett downe on thother side as well as I can remember [*see previous page*].

[99] Christian pictures in the seventeenth century; from *Storia do Mogor* by Niccalao Manucci.

Finding himself conqueror of almost the whole of Hindūstān, Akbar followed the example of his father. Although he made little account of his soul, he took care to prepare a resting-place for his body with extreme magnificence. For the site he chose a garden on the road to Dihlī, at three leagues' distance from Āgrah on the west, to which he gave the name of Secandara (Sikandrah) – that is to say, 'Alexandria.'

This mausoleum is a very large dome of great height, made all of marble adorned with many kinds of precious stones, the roof all gilded and enamelled in many pleasing colours. The garden is very large and pleasant, walled in on all sides, with various seats inside. There were drawings of human figures. Over these the king Aurangzeb ordered a coat of whitewash to be applied, so that the drawings might not be seen. He said such things were prohibited by the Mahomedan religion. I obtained entrance to this garden several times to inspect the mausoleum, being anxious to see the above-named figures before Aurangzeb should order them to be covered over.

The figures in the principal gateway of the garden were a crucifix, the Virgin Mary, and Saint Ignatius. I had a great desire to obtain entrance into the great dome I have spoken of, and at last one of the officials at the mausoleum, who was a friend of mine, and also wanted to make use of me, believing I was a physician, took me with him. The condition was that I should make a bow such as he made, with great reverence and punctiliousness, just as if the king were still alive. He opened the door, and I joined with him in making a very low bow in total silence, then barefooted I went round and saw everything. As I have already said, there was a holy crucifix delineated on the wall, on the right hand of the crucifix the image of Our Lady with the infant Jesus in her arms, while on the left was Saint Ignatius, the whole delineated. In the ceiling of the dome were great angels and cherubim and many other painted figures. There were also many censers which were lighted every day. The hall is paved all over with stones of different colours.

Outside the mausoleum, in the garden, were many Molas – that is to say, learned men – reading the Qurān. On the dome outside, on the very highest point, was a ball, and upon it a pyramid, the whole gilt. Most curious of all is the reason for having these paintings; it was only because they were a novelty in those days; it was not on account of religion.

The Mausoleum of Akbar, Sikandra;
from a portfolio made by Delhi draughtsmen, 1816–22

[100] 'Grotesque buildings'; from *Up the country* . . . by
Emily Eden.

We went yesterday to see Secundra, where Akbar is buried, and
his tomb of beautiful white marble is up four stories of grotesque
buildings, well worth seeing, so much so that, as G. had a durbar
to-night and could not go out, F. and I went back alone, and had
rather a rest, in sketching there, for two hours, but it is impossible
to make anything of these elaborate Mogul buildings, they are
all lines and domes, and uncommonly trying to the patience.

Life, Customs and Morals in Delhi and Agra

The Sultán next directed his attention to the means of preventing rebellion, and first he took steps for seizing upon property. He ordered that, wherever there was a village held by proprietary right, in free gift or as a religious endowment, it should by one stroke of the pen be brought back under the exchequer. The people were pressed and amerced, money was exacted from them on every kind of pretence. Many were left without any money, till at length it came to pass that, excepting *maliks* and *amírs*, officials, Multánís, and bankers, no one possessed even a trifle in cash. So rigorous was the confiscation that, beyond a few thousand *tankas*, all the pensions, grants of land, and endowments in the country were appropriated. The people were all so absorbed in obtaining the means of living, that the name of rebellion was never mentioned. Secondly, he provided so carefully for the acquisition of intelligence, that no action of good or bad men was concealed from him. No one could stir without his knowledge, and whatever happened in the houses of nobles, great men, and officials, was communicated to the Sultán by his reporters. Nor were the reports neglected, for explanations of them were demanded. The system of reporting went to such a length, that nobles dared not speak aloud even in the largest palaces, and if they had anything to say they communicated by signs. In their own houses, night and day, dread of the reports of the spies made them tremble. No word or action which could provoke censure or punishment was allowed to transpire. The transactions in the *bázárs*, the buying and selling, and the bargains made, were all reported to the Sultán by his spies, and were kept under control. Thirdly, he prohibited wine-drinking and wine-selling, as also the use of beer and intoxicating drugs. Dicing also was forbidden. Many prohibitions of wine and beer were issued. Vintners and gamblers and beer-sellers were turned out of the city, and the heavy taxes which had been levied from them were abolished. The Sultán directed that all the china and glass vessels of his banqueting room should be broken, and the fragments of them were thrown out before the gate of Badáún, where they formed a heap. Jars and casks of wine were brought out of the royal cellars, and emptied at the Badáún gate in such abundance, that mud and mire was produced as in the rainy season. The Sultán himself entirely gave up wine parties. He directed the *maliks* to mount elephants and to go to the gates of Dehlí, through the streets and wards, *bázárs* and *saráís*, proclaiming the royal command that no one should drink, sell, or have anything to do with wine. Those who had any self-respect immediately gave up drinking; but the shameless, the dissolute, and vile characters used to make and distil wine in the distilleries, and to drink and sell it clandestinely at a great price. They put it into leather bottles, and conveyed it hidden in loads of hay, firewood, and such like. By hundreds of tricks and devices, and by all sorts of collusion, wine was brought into the city. Informers searched diligently, and the city gate-keepers and spies exerted themselves to seize the wine, and apprehend the contrabandists. When seized, the wine was sent to the elephant-stables and given to those animals. The sellers, the importers, and drinkers of wine, were subjected to corporal punishment, and were kept in prison for some days. But their members increased so much that holes for the incarceration of offenders were dug outside the Badáún gate, which is a great thoroughfare. Wine-bibbers and wine-sellers were placed in these holes, and the severity of the confinement was such that many of them died. Many others were taken out half dead, and were long before they recovered their health and strength. The terrors of these holes deterred many from drinking. Those who were unable to give up their habit went out to the fords of the Jumna, and to villages ten or twelve kos distant to procure their liquor. In Ghiyáspur, Indarpat, Kílúgharí, and towns four or five *kos* from Dehlí, wine could not be sold or drunk publicly. Still some desperate men used to keep it, drink it, and even sell it privately. They thus disgraced themselves and got confined in the pits. The prevention of drinking being found to be very difficult, the Sultán gave orders that if the liquor was distilled privately, and drunk privately in people's own houses; if drinking parties were not held, and the liquor not sold, then the informers were not to interfere in any way, and were not to enter the houses or arrest the offenders. After the prohibition of wine and beer in the city, conspiracies diminished, and apprehension of rebellion disappeared.

Fourthly, the Sultán gave commands that noblemen and

great men should not visit each other's houses, or give feasts, or hold meetings. They were forbidden to form alliances without consent from the throne, and they were also prohibited from allowing people to resort to their houses. To such a length was this last prohibition carried that no stranger was admitted into a nobleman's house. Feasting and hospitality fell quite into disuse. Through fear of the spies, the nobles kept themselves quiet; they gave no parties and had little communication with each other. No man of a seditious, rebellious, or evil reputation was allowed to come near them. If they went to the *saráís*, they could not lay their heads together, or sit down cosily and tell their troubles. Their communications were brought down to a mere exchange of signs. This interdict prevented any information of conspiracy and rebellion coming to the Sultán and no disturbance arose.

[102] Relating to yogis, horses and lethal weapons in the early sixteenth century; from *The Book of Duarte Barbosa* . . .

(Duarte Barbosa came to India in 1500 in the service of the Portuguese Government. He spent most of his time in India on the Malabar coast (Cochin) and was celebrated for his knowledge of the language. It seems that only the Yogis interested him in Delhi.)

Still further inland there is a great kingdom named Dely, with many lands, and cities both great and rich, where dwell merchants of importance. The inhabitants thereof are Moors, and the King also is a Moor and a very great Lord. This kingdom was of old in the possession of the Heathen, and there are even yet some who dwell there in great affliction; but many who are of noble birth and men of honour, unwilling to stay under the power of the Moors, go forth (for the most part of them) from that land and assume poor attire, resolving to go through the whole world sojourning in no place whatsoever; and this they continue to do until they die during their pilgrimage.

These men possess nothing of their own, for they have lost what estates they once had; they go naked and barefoot, they wear nothing on their heads, and they hide their nakedness only with bands of Moorish brass, on which hang girdles of many coins which dangle on both sides; these are of the width of four fingers, cylindrical in shape, with many figures carved on them [*both of men and women*]. These they wear so tight that they make their bellies stand out over them. And from the same band a strip of this brass passes from behind between the buttocks, so as to form a cod-piece in front.

To the corners of these bands their waist cloths are attached, when they wish to fasten them with their clasps, and all so tight that it gives them great pain. Besides this they carry heavy iron chains on their necks and waists. Their bodies and face are smeared with ashes. They carry a small horn or trumpet, on which they blow, and whithersoever they come they call out and demand food, more especially at the houses of worship, or those of kings or great Lords. They go about in bands, like the Egyptians with us, nor is it their custom to abide long in one place, but for a few days only. These men are called *Jogues* or *Coamerques*, which is as much as to say 'servants of God.' These heathen are tawny men, well-built and tall, with handsome faces. They never comb their hair but wear it in matted locks. I have ofttimes asked them wherefore they went about thus, to which they replied that they always carried these iron chains as a penance for the great sin they had committed, in that they were unwilling to endure taking arms for the defence of their honour, and had allowed themselves to be overcome by a wicked people like the Moors; and that they went naked as a token of their great loss of honour, because they had submitted to be deprived of their lands and houses in which God had brought them up. And now, they said, they wished for no property, as they had lost their own and they ought rather to have died; and that they smeared themselves with ashes to remind them that of dust and ashes they were made, and to these they must return; all else was falsehood.

Each of them carries with him a small bag of these ashes. The Heathen of the land show them great honour and respect, to whom they give of these ashes, marking them therewith and making streaks on their breasts, foreheads and shoulders; and this custom prevails much among them.

These men eat every kind of food, nor do they observe any other form of idolatry. They touch men of every class and wash not themselves thereafter according to the rule, as do the other Heathen, unless they desire so to do.

There are very good horses in this kingdom of Dely, which are born and bred there. The natives thereof, Moors as well as

Heathen, are good fighting men and good riders. They are armed with weapons of all kinds, are very strong and good archers as well. They have right good spears, swords, steel maces and battleaxes with which they fight, and mostly carry steel disks which they call *Chacaras*, about two fingers in thickness, as sharp as razors at the edge, but blunt inside. They are of the breadth of a small plate, and there is a hole in the middle. Everyone carries as many as ten of them on the left arm; and they take one into the battle. They place it on the finger of the right hand, putting the finger a little round it so as to give it a grasp, and hurl it straight at the enemy. If they hit an arm, leg or neck they cut right through, and thus they cause great injury; and there are men here very skilful at this.

[103] Babur takes a dim view of India; from Babur's *Memoirs* edited by F.G. Talbot.

Hindustan is a country that has few pleasures to recommend it. The people are not handsome. They have no idea of the charms of friendly society, of frankly mixing together, or of familiar intercourse. They have no genius, no comprehension of mind, no politeness of manner, no kindness or fellow-feeling, no ingenuity or mechanical invention in planning or executing their handicraft works, no skill or knowledge in design or architecture; they have no good horses, no good flesh, no grapes or musk-melons, no good fruits, no ice or cold water, no good food or bread in their bazars, no baths or colleges, no candles, no torches, not even a candlestick.

[104] The death of Humayun in 1556 enables the Turkish admiral to depart; from *The Travels and Adventures of the Turkish Admiral Sidi Ali Reis*.

(After his ships were defeated by the Portuguese, Sidi Ali Reis managed to reach India. He spent two unwilling years at Humayun's court before being allowed to walk home.)

As soon as Humayun heard of our arrival, he sent the Khanikhanan and other superior officers with 400 elephants and some thousand men to meet us, and, out of respect and regard for our glorious Padishah, we were accorded a brilliant reception. That same day the Khanikhanan prepared a great banquet in our honour, and as it is the custom in India to give audience in the evening, I was that night introduced with much pomp and ceremony into the Imperial hall. After my presentation I offered the Emperor a small gift, and a chronogram upon the conquest of India, also two Ghazels, all of which pleased the Padishah greatly. Forthwith I begged for permission to continue my journey, but this was not granted. Instead of that I was offered the governorship over the district of Kharcha. I refused, and again begged to be allowed to go, but for only answer I was told that I must at least remain for one year, to which I replied: 'By special command of my glorious Padishah I went by sea to fight the miserable unbelievers. Caught in a terrible hurricane, I was wrecked off the coast of India; but it is now my plain duty to return to render an account to my Padishah, and it is to be hoped that Gujarat will soon be delivered out of the hands of the unbelievers.' Upon this Humayun suggested the sending of an envoy to Constantinople to save my going, but this I could not agree to, for it would give the impression that I had purposely arranged it so. I persisted in my entreaties and he finally consented, adding however: 'We are now close upon the three months of continuous rainy season. The roads are flooded and impassable, remain therefore till the weather improves. Meanwhile calculate Solar and Lunar Eclipses, their degree of latitude and their exact date in the Calendar. Assist our astrologers in studying the course of the sun, and instruct us concerning the points of the Equator. When all this is done, and the weather should improve before the three months are over, then thou shalt go hence.'

All this was said solemnly and decisively. I had no alternative, but must submit to my fate. I took no rest however, but laboured on night and day. At last I had accomplished the astronomical observations, and about the same time Agra fell into the hands of the Padishah. I immediately wrote a chronogram for the occasion which found much favour. One day, during an audience, the conversation turned upon Sultan Mahmud of Baukur, and I suggested that some official contract should be made with him, to which Humayun agreed. The document was drawn up, and the Emperor dipping his fist in saffron pressed it upon the paper, this being the Tughra or Imperial signature.

Thereupon the document was sent to Sultan Mahmud.

The Sultan was much pleased and both he and his Vizier Molla Yari expressed their thanks for my intervention in a private letter, which I showed to His Majesty, who had entrusted me with the transaction.

This incident furnished the material for a Ghazel, with which the Sovereign was so delighted that he called me a second Mir Ali Shir. I modestly declined the epithet, saying that it would be presumption on my part to accept such praise, that, on the contrary, I should consider myself fully rewarded to be allowed to gather up the gleanings after him. Whereupon the Sovereign remarked: 'If for one more year thou perfectest thyself in this kind of poetry thou wilt altogether supplant Mir Ali Shir in the affections of the people of the Djagatai's.' In a word Humayun loaded me with marks of his favour. One day I was talking to Khoshhal, the Imperial archer, and the Sovereign's special confident; a superb youth. He used to take part in the poetical discussions, and provided me with material for two Ghazels which soon became popular all over India and were in everybody's mouth.

In a word, poetical discussions were the order of the day, and I was constantly in the presence of the Emperor. One day he asked me whether Turkey was larger than India, and I said: 'If by Turkey your Majesty means Rum proper, then India is decidedly the larger, but if by Turkey you mean all the lands subject to the ruler of Rum, India is not by a tenth part as large.' 'I mean the entire empire,' replied Humayun. 'Then,' I said, 'it appears to me, your Majesty, that the seven regions over which Alexander the Great had dominion, were identical with the present Empire of the Padishah of Turkey. Perhaps he only owned a portion of each of these regions in the same way as the Padishah of Turkey does.' 'But has the ruler of Turkey possessions in all these regions?' asked Humayun. 'Yes certainly,' I replied, 'the first is Yemen, the second Mecca, the third Egypt, the fourth Aleppo, the fifth Constantinople, the sixth Kaffa and the seventh Ofen and Vienna. In each of these regions the Padishah of Turkey appoints his Beglerbeg and Kadi, who rule and govern in his name.' The Sovereign (Humayun) turning to his nobles said: 'Surely the only man worthy to bear the title of Padishah is the ruler of Turkey, he alone and no one else in all the world.'

When the conversation turned upon the poetical works of Mir

Khosru I quoted some of his best poems, and under their influence I conceived a most telling distich. I turned to the Emperor saying, 'It would be presumption on my part to measure my powers against those of Mir Khosru, but he has inspired me, and I would fain recite my couplet before your Majesty.' 'Let us hear it,' said Humayun, and I recited the following:

'Truly great is only he, who can be content with his daily bread.
For happier is he than all the kings of the earth.'

'By God,' cried the Monarch, 'this is truly sublime!'

It is not so much my object here to make mention of my poetic effusions, but rather to show up Humayun's appreciation of poetry.

On another occasion I called upon Shahin Bey, the keeper of the Imperial Seal, and asked him to use his influence to obtain permission for me to depart. In order not to come empty-handed I brought him two Ghazels, and begged him urgently to intercede for me. Shahin Bey promised to do his best, and one day he actually brought me the glad news that my petition had been granted, but that I was expected to offer my request formally in verse. The rainy season was now at an end, I wrote to the Monarch, enclosing two Ghazels, which had the desired effect, for I received not only permission to leave, but also presents and letters of safe conduct.

All was ready for the start. Humayun had given audience on Friday evening, when, upon leaving his castle of pleasure, the Muezzin announced the Ezan just as he was descending the staircase. It was his wont, wherever he heard the summons, to bow the knee in holy reverence. He did so now, but unfortunately fell down several steps, and received great injuries to his head and arm. Truly the proverb rightly says, 'there is no guarding against fate.'

Everything was confusion in the palace, but for two days they kept the matter secret. It was announced to the outer world that the Sovereign was in good health, and alms were distributed amongst the poor. On the third day, however, that was on the Monday, he died of his wounds. Well may the Koran say, 'We come from God and to Him do we return.' Meanwhile the Khans and Sultans were in the greatest consternation; they did not know how to act. I tried to encourage them and told them how at the death of Sultan Selim the situation was saved by the wisdom of Piri Pasha, who managed to prevent the news of his death from being noised abroad. I suggested that, by taking similar measures, they might keep the Sovereign's death a secret until the Prince should return. This advise was followed. The council of state met as usual, the nobles were summoned, and a public announcement was made that the Emperor intended to visit his country seat, and would go there on horseback. Soon after, however, it was announced that on account of the unfavorable weather, the trip had to be abandoned. On the next day a public audience was announced, but as the astrologers did not prophesy favorably for it, this also had to be given up. All this, however, somewhat alarmed the army, and on the Tuesday it was thought advisable to give them a sight of their Monarch. A man called Molla Bi, who bore a striking resemblance to the late Emperor only somewhat slighter of stature, was arrayed in the imperial robes and placed on a throne specially erected for the purpose in the large entrance hall. His face and eyes were veiled. The Chamberlain Khoshhal Bey stood behind, and the first Secretary in front of him, while many officers and dignataries as well as the people from the riverside, on seeing their Sovereign made joyful obeisance to the sound of festive music. The physicians were handsomely rewarded and the recovery of the Monarch was universally credited.

I took leave of all the grandees, and with the news of the Emperor's recovery I reached Lahore about the middle of the month Rebiul Evvel.

[105] 'Burne they would'; from the *Journal 1608–13* of William Hawkins in *Early Travels in India* edited by William Foster.

The custome of the Indians is to burne their dead, as you have read in other authors, and at their burning many of their wives will burne with them, because they will bee registred in their bookes for famous and most modest and loving wives, who, leaving all worldly affaires, content themselves to live no longer then their husbands. I have seene many proper women brought

before the King, whom (by his commandment) none may burne
without his leave and sight of them; I meane those of Agra. When
any of these commeth, hee doth perswade them with many
promises of gifts and living if they will live, but in my time no
perswasion could prevaile, but burne they would. The King,
seeing that all would not serve, giveth his leave for her to be
carried to the fire, where she burneth herselfe alive with her dead
husband.

[106] The drug scene; from *Travels in Europe and Asia (1608–
67)* by Peter Mundy.

There were also many feild of Poppie of which they make opium
they call aphim, much used for many purposes. The seed thereof
they putt on their bread, I meane of white poppye. Of the huskes
they make a kind of Beveredge called Post, steepeing them in
water a while, and squeezinge and strayninge out the liquor,
they drinck it, which does enebriate. In the like manner they use
a certaine plant called Bang workeinge the same effect, soe that
most commonly they will call a druncken fellowe either Ahimee,
Postee, or Bangguee. A wine drunckard is called Muttwallee.

[107] Paan – what it is; from *Travels in Europe and Asia
(1608–67)* by Peter Mundy.

Wee also sawe some feilds of Paan, which is a kinde of leafe much
used to bee eaten in this Countrie, thus: First they take a kinde of
Nutt called Saparoz [*supārī, areca-nut*], and comonly with us
Bettlenutt, which, broken to peeces, they infold in one of the said
leaves, and soe put it into their mouthes. Then take they of the
said leaves, and puttinge a little slaked lyme on them, they also
put into their mouthes, and after them other, untill their
mouthes are reasonably filled, which they goe champinge,
swalloweing downe the Juice till it be drie; then they spitt it out.
It is accompted a grace to eat it up and downe the Streets and [*is*]
used by great men. There is noe visitt, banquett, etts. without it,
with which they passe away the tyme, as with Tobaccoe in
England; but this is very wholsome, sweete in smell, and stronge
in Taste. To Strangers it is most comonly given att partinge, soe

that when they send for Paan, it is a signe of dispeedinge, or that it is tyme to be gon.

[108] A vegetable matter; from *Observations (1616)* by Thomas Coryat in *Early Travels in India* edited by William Foster.

One day in the yeere, for the solace of the Kings Women, all the Trades-mens Wives enter the Mohal with some-what to sell, in manner of a Faire, where the King is Broker for his Women, and with his gaines that night makes his supper, no man present, (observe that whatsoever is brought in of virill shape, as instance in Reddishes, so great is the jealousie, and so frequent the wickednesse of this people, that they are cut and jagged for feare of converting the same to some unnaturall abuse) by this meanes hee attaines to the sight of all the prettie Wenches of the Towne: at such a kind of Faire he got his beloved Normahal.

[109] The parade of Prince Dara in 1659; from *Travels in the Mogul Empire (1659–67)* by François Bernier.

When the unhappy Prince was brought to the gates of *Dehli*, it became a question with *Aureng-Zebe*, whether, in conducting him to the fortress of *Goüaleor*, he should be made to pass through the capital. It was the opinion of some courtiers that this was by all means to be avoided, because, not only would such an exhibition be derogatory to the royal family, but it might become the signal for revolt, and the rescue of *Dara* might be successfully attempted. Others maintained, on the contrary, that he ought to be seen by the whole city; that it was necessary to strike the people with terror and astonishment, and to impress their minds with an idea of the absolute and irresistible power of *Aureng-Zebe*. It was also advisable, they added, to undeceive the *Omrahs* and the people, who still entertained doubts of *Dara's* captivity, and to extinguish at once the hopes of his secret partisans. *Aureng-Zebe* viewed the matter in the same light; the wretched prisoner was therefore secured on an elephant; his young son, *Sepe-Chekouh*, placed at his side, and behind them, instead of the executioner, was seated *Bhadur-Kan*. This was not one of the majestic elephants of *Pegu* or *Ceylon*, which *Dara* had been in the habit of mounting, pompously caparisoned, the harness gilt, and trappings decorated with figured work; and carrying a beautifully painted howdah, inlaid with gold, and a magnificent canopy to shelter the Prince from the sun: *Dara* was now seen seated on a miserable and worn-out animal, covered with filth; he no longer wore the necklace of large pearls which distinguish the princes of *Hindoustan*, nor the rich turban and embroidered coat; he and his son were now habited in dirty cloth of the coarsest texture, and his sorry turban was wrapt round with a *Kachemire* shawl or scarf, resembling that worn by the meanest of the people.

Such was the appearance of *Dara* when led through the *Bazars* and every quarter of the city. I could not divest myself of the idea that some dreadful execution was about to take place, and felt surprise that government should have the hardihood to commit all these indignities upon a Prince confessedly popular among the lower orders, especially as I saw scarcely any armed force. The people had for some time inveighed bitterly against the unnatural conduct of *Aureng-Zebe*: the imprisonment of his father, of his son *Sultan Mahmoud*, and of his brother *Morad-Bakche*, filled every bosom with horror and disgust. The crowd assembled upon this disgraceful occasion was immense; and everywhere I observed the people weeping, and lamenting the fate of *Dara* in the most touching language. I took my station in one of the most conspicuous parts of the city, in the midst of the largest bazar; was mounted on a good horse, and accompanied by two servants and two intimate friends. From every quarter I heard piercing and distressing shrieks, for the Indian people have a very tender heart; men, women, and children wailing as if some mighty calamity had happened to themselves. *Gion-kan* rode near the wretched *Dara*; and the abusive and indignant cries vociferated as the traitor moved along were absolutely deafening. I observed some *Fakires* and several poor people throw stones at the infamous *Patan*; but not a single movement was made, no one offered to draw his sword, with a view of delivering the beloved and compassionated Prince. When this disgraceful procession had passed through every part of *Dehli*, the poor prisoner was shut up in one of his own gardens.

Aureng-Zebe was immediately made acquainted with the impression which this spectacle produced upon the public mind, the indignation manifested by the populace against the *Patan*, the threats held out to stone the perfidious man, and with the fears entertained of a general insurrection. A second council was consequently convened, and the question discussed, whether it were more expedient to conduct *Dara* to *Goüaleor*, agreeably to the original intention, or to put him to death without further delay. By some it was maintained that there was no reason for proceeding to extremities, and that the Prince might safely be taken to *Goüaleor*, provided he were attended with a strong escort: *Danech-Mend-kan*, although he and *Dara* had long been on bad terms, enforced this opinion with all his powers of argument: but it was ultimately decided that *Dara* should die, and that *Sepe-Chekouh* should be confined in *Goüaleor*. At this meeting *Rauchenara-Begum* betrayed all her enmity against her hapless brother, combating the arguments of *Danech-Mend*, and exciting *Aureng-Zebe* to this foul and unnatural murder. Her efforts were but too successfully seconded by *Kalil-ullah-kan* and *Chah-hest-kan*, both of them old enemies of *Dara*; and by *Takarrub-kan*, a wretched parasite recently raised to the rank of *Omrah*, and formerly a physician. This man rendered himself conspicuous in the council by his violent harangue. '*Dara* ought not to live,' he exclaimed; 'the safety of the State depends upon his immediate execution; and I feel the less reluctant to recommend his being put to death, because he has long since ceased to be a *Musulman*, and become a *Kafer*. If it be sinful to shed the blood of such a person, may the sin be visited upon my own head!' An imprecation which was not allowed to pass unregarded; for divine justice overtook this man in his career of wickedness: he was soon disgraced, declared infamous, and sentenced to a miserable death.

The charge of this atrocious murder was intrusted to a slave of the name of *Nazer*, who had been educated by *Chah-Jehan*, but experienced some ill-treatment from *Dara*. The Prince, apprehensive that poison would be administered to him, was employed with *Sepe-Chekouh* in boiling lentils, when *Nazer* and four other ruffians entered his apartment. 'My dear son,' he cried out, 'these men are come to murder us!' He then seized a small kitchen knife, the only weapon in his possession. One of the murderers having secured *Sepe-Chekouh*, the rest fell upon *Dara*, threw him down, and while three of the assassins held him, *Nazer* decapitated his wretched victim. The head was instantly carried to *Aureng-Zebe*, who commanded that it should be placed in a dish, and that water should be brought. The blood was then washed from the face, and when it could no longer be doubted that it was indeed the head of *Dara*, he shed tears, and said, '*Ai Bed-bakt!* Ah wretched one! let this shocking sight no more offend my eyes, but take away the head, and let it be buried in *Houmayon's* tomb.'

[110] 'The heat in Hindoustan'; from *Travels in the Mogul Empire (1659–67)* by François Bernier.

Without doubt, the cities of *Europe* may boast great beauties; these, however, are of an appropriate character, suited to a cold climate. Thus *Dehli* also may possess beauties adapted to a warm climate. The heat is so intense in *Hindoustan*, that no one, not even the King, wears stockings; the only cover for the feet being *babouches*, or slippers, while the head is protected by a small turban, of the finest and most delicate materials. The other garments are proportionably light. During the summer season, it is scarcely possible to keep the hand on the wall of an apartment, or the head on a pillow. For more than six successive months, everybody lies in the open air without covering – the common people in the streets, the merchants and persons of condition sometimes in their courts or gardens, and sometimes on their terraces, which are first carefully watered.

[111] A sturdy independence in the seventeenth century; from *Storia do Mogor* by Niccalao Manucci.

It is quite true that if the common people here have four rupees, they are quite high and mighty and decline service. It is only when they have nothing to eat that they take service. They have no skill unless it is forced on them by harsh treatment. For the people of India never pay without being forced, and to collect half the total quantity of supplies that they are under obligation to pay the crown it is necessary to tie up the principal husbandmen. It is the peasants' habit to go on refusing payment, asserting that they have no money. The chastisement and the instruments are very severe. From time to time they pay a trifling instalment, and the punishment being renewed again and again, they begin to pay little by little. This habit is much honored among husbandmen – that is, never to pay readily; and to undergo these torments and this disgrace is among them an honour.

[112] How to rid yourself of *Filaria medinensis*; from *Travels in the Mogul Empire (1659–67)* by François Bernier.

I am happy, on leaving, at the idea of not being any longer exposed to the danger of eating the bazaar bread of Dehli which is often badly baked and full of sand and dust. I may hope, too, for better water than that of the capital, the impurities of which exceed my power of description; as it is accessible to all persons and animals, and the receptacle of every kind of filth. Fevers most difficult to cure are engendered by it, and worms are bred in the legs which produce violent inflammation, attended with much danger. If the patient leave Dehli, the worm is generally soon expelled, although there have been instances where it has continued in the system for a year or more. They are commonly of the size and length of a treble string of a violin, and might easily be mistaken for a sinew. In extracting them great caution should be used lest they break; the best way is to draw them out little by little from day to day, gently winding them round a small twig the size of a pin.

[113] Dangers on the road to Agra, 1695; from *Indian Travels of Thévenot and Careri* edited by Surendranath Sen.

The Province of Dehly bounds that of Agra to the North, and at present the *Great Mogul Auran-zeb* keeps his Court in the chief City of it, which is about fourty five Leagues distant from Agra. In *Indostan* it is called *Gehan-abad*, and elsewhere *Dehly*.

The Road betwixt these two Towns is very pleasant; it is that famous Alley or Walk one hundred and fifty Leagues in length, which King *Gehanguir* planted with Trees, and which reaches not only from *Agra* to *Dehly*, but even as far as *Lahors*. Each half League is marked with a kind of Turret: There are threescore and nine or threescore and ten of them betwixt the two Capital

Cities, and besides there are little Serraglio's or Carvanseras, from Stage to Stage for lodging Travellers. However there is nothing worth the observing about these Serraglios, unless in that which is called *Chekiserai*, which is six Leagues from *Agra*. In that place there is the Ancient Temple of an Idol, and it may be reckoned amongst the largest and fairest Pagods of the Indies. It was more frequented than now it is, when the *Gemna* washed the Walls thereof, because of the convenience of Ablutions: But though that River hath fallen off almost half a League from it, yet many Indians still resort thither, who forget not to bring with them Food for the Apes that are kept in an Hospital built for them.

Though the Road I have been speaking of be tolerable, yet it hath many inconveniencies. One may meet with Tygres, Panthers and Lions upon it; and one had best also have a care of Robbers, and above all things not to suffer any body to come near one upon the Road. The cunningest Robbers in the World are in that Countrey. They use a certain Slip with a running-noose, which they can cast with so much slight about a Mans Neck, when they are within reach of him, that they never fail; so that they strangle him in a trice. They have another cunning trick also to catch Travellers with: They send out a handsome Woman upon the Road, who with her Hair deshevelled, seems to be all in Tears, sighing and complaining of some misfortune which she pretends has befallen her: Now as she takes the same way that the Traveller goes, he easily falls into Conversation with her, and finding her beautiful, offers her his assistance, which she accepts; he has no sooner taken her up behind him on Horse-back, but she throws the snare about his Neck and strangles him, or at least stuns him, until the Robbers (who lie hid) come running in to her assistance and compleat what she hath begun. But besides that, there are Men in those quarters so skilful in casting the Snare, that they succeed as well at a distance as near at hand; and if an Ox or any other Beast belonging to a Caravan run away, as sometimes it happens, they fail not to catch it by the Neck.

[114] Interesting information from the late seventeenth century; from *Indian Travels of Thévenot and Careri* edited by Surendranath Sen.

The Painters of *Dehly* are modester than those of *Agra*, and spend not their pains about lascivious Pictures, as they do. They apply themselves to the representing of Histories, and in many places, one may meet with the Battels and Victories of their Princes, indifferently well Painted. Order is observed in them, the Personages have the suitableness that is necessary to them, and the colours are very lovely, but they make Faces ill. They do things in miniature pretty well, and there are some at *Dehly* who Engrave indifferently well also; but seeing they are not much encouraged, they do not apply themselves to their work, with all the exactness they might; and all their care is to do as much work as they can, for present Money to subsist on.

There are People in *Dehly*, vastly rich in Jewels, especially the *Rajas* who preserve their Pretious Stones from Father to Son. When they are to make Presents, they chuse rather to buy, than to give away those which they had from their Ancestors: They daily encrease them, and must be reduced to an extream pinch, before they part with them.

There is in this Town, a certain Metal called *Tutunac*, that looks like Tin, but is much more lovely and fine, and is often taken for Silver; that Metal is brought from *China*.

They much esteem a greyish Stone there, wherewith many Sepulchres are adorned; and they value it the more, that it is like *Theban* Stone, or *Garnet*. I have seen in the Countries of some *Rajas*, and elsewhere, *Mosques* and *Pagods* wholly built of them.

The Indians of Dehly cannot make a Screw as our Locksmiths do; all they do, is to fasten to each of the two pieces that are to enter into one another, some Iron, Copper, or Silver wire, turned Screw-wise, without any other art than of souldering the Wire to the pieces; and in opening them, they turn the Screws from the left hand to the right, contrariwise to ours, which are turned from the right to the left.

They have a very easie remedy in the Country, to keep the Flies from molesting their Horses, when the Grooms are so diligent as to make use of it: For all they have to do, is to make provision of Citrul Flowers, and rub them therewith. But many slight that remedy, because it must be often renewed, seeing the

Curry-comb and Water takes it off. I cannot tell if these Flowers have the same vertue in our Country.

The Women of *Dehly* are handsome, and the Gentiles very chast; insomuch, that if the *Mahometan* Women did not by their wantonness dishonour the rest, the Chastity of the *Indians* might be proposed as an example to all the Women of the *East*. These *Indian* Women are easily delivered of their Children; and sometimes they'll walk about the Streets next day after they have been brought to Bed.

At *Dehly* are all sorts of Beasts that are known. The King hath many, and private Men who are Rich, have some also. They have Hawks there of all kinds; all kinds of Camels, Dromedaries, Mules, Asses, and Elephants. They have also Elks, and Rhinoceroses which are as big as the largest Oxen. The ordinary Oxen there, are less than ours. Buffles they have also, and those of *Bengala* are the dearest, because they are very stout, and are not at all afraid of Lions. Nor do they want Dogs of all sorts, but those which are brought from *Maurenahar*, or *Transoxiane*, are most esteemed for Hunting, though they be small: However the *Indian* Dogs are better for the Hare. They have also Stags, Lions and Leopards.

There is abundance of all sorts of horses there. Besides the Country breed, which the *Moguls* make use of, and which are very good Horses; they have others also from the Country of the *Ulbecks*, *Arabia*, and *Persia*, those of *Arabia* being most esteemed, and the loveliest of all are constantly reserved for the King. They have neither Oats nor Barley given them in the *Indies*; so that Foreign Horses when they are brought thither, can hardly feed. The way they treat them is thus: Every Horse has a Groom, he curries and dresses him an hour before day, and so soon as it is day makes him drink; at seven of the Clock in the Morning, he gives him five or six balls of a composition called *Donna*, made of three Pounds of Flower, the weight of five *Pechas* of Butter, and of four *Pechas* of *Jagre*; these Balls are at first forced down his Throat, and so by degrees he is accustomed to that way of feeding, which in some Months after, he grows very fond of.

An hour after, the Groom gives the Horse Grass, and continues to do so at certain times, every hour of the day after: and about four of the clock, after noon, he gives him three Pound of dried Pease bruised; he mingles Water with them, and sometimes a little Sugar, according to the disposition the Horse is in; and when Night is drawing on, he carefully prepares his Horses litter, which is of dry Dung, laid very thick, which he is very careful to provide. For that end, he gathers all that his Horse hath made, and when that is not sufficient, he buys from others, who are not so much concerned for the convenience of their Horses.

At *Dehly*, as elsewhere, they take care to adorn their Horses. The great Lords have Saddles and Housses Embroadered, and set sometimes with Pretious Stones, proportionably to the charge they intend to be at: But the finest Ornament, though of less cost, is made of six large flying tassels of long white Hair, taken out of the Tails of wild Oxen, that are to be found in some places of the *Indies*. Four of these large tassels fastened before and behind to the Saddle, hang down to the ground, and the other two are upon the Horses head; so that when the Rider spurs on his Horse to a full speed, or if there be any wind, these tassels flying in the Air, seem to be so many wings to the Horse, and yield a most pleasant prospect.

There are several sorts of Elephants at *Dehly*, as well as in the rest of the *Indies*; but those of *Ceilan* are preferred before all others, because they are the stoutest, though they be the least, and the *Indians* say that all other Elephants stand in awe of them. They go commonly in Troops and then they offer violence to no body, but when they straggle from the rest they are dangerous. There are always some of them that have the cunning and inclination to do mischief; and in the Country these are called, Robbers on the Highways, because if they meet a Man alone, they'll kill and eat him.

Strong Elephants can carry forty *Mans*; at fourscore Pound weight the *Man*. Those of the Country of *Golconda, Siam, Cochin*, and *Saumatra*, are indeed, less esteemed than the Elephants of *Ceilan*, but they are much stronger, and surer footed in the Mountains; and that is the reason, why the great Men, (when they are to Travel,) provide themselves of those, rather than the Elephants of *Ceilan*. However it may be said in general, that Elephants, of what Country or kind soever they be, are the surest footed of all Beasts of Carriage, because it is very rare to see them make a trip: But seeing it is chargeable to feed them, and that besides the Flesh they give them to eat, and the Strong-waters they drink, it costs at least half a *Pistol* a day for the Paste of Flower, Sugar and Butter, that must be given to a single one;

there are but few that keep them: Nay, the great Lords themselves entertain no great number of them; and the *Great Mogul* has not above five hundred for the use of his household, in carrying the women in their *Mickdembers* with grates (which are a sort of Cages) and the Baggage; and I have been assured, that he hath not above two hundred for the Wars, of which some are employed in carrying small Field-pieces upon their Carriages.

When an Elephant is in his ordinary disposition, his Governour can make him do what he pleases with his Trunck. That instrument, which many call a hand, hangs between their great Teeth, and is made of Cartilages or Gristles: He'll make them play several tricks with that Trunck; salute his friends, threaten those that displease him, beat whom he thinks fit, and coud make them tear a Man into pieces in a trice, if he had a mind to it. The governour sits on the Elephants Neck, when he makes him do any thing, and with a prick of Iron in the end of a Stick, he commonly makes him Obey him. In a word, an Elephant is a very tractable Creature, provided he be not angry, nor in lust; but when he is so, the Governour himself is in much danger, and stands in need of a great deal of art, to avoid ruin; for then the Elephant turns all things topsy-turvy, and would make strange havock, if they did not stop him, as they commonly do, with fire-works that they throw at him.

Elephant-hunting is variously performed. In some places they make Pit-falls for them, by means whereof they fall into some hole or pit, from whence they are easily got out, when they have once entangled them well. In other places they make use of a tame Female, that is in season for the Male, whom they lead into a narrow place, and tie her there; by her cries she calls the Male to her, and when he is there, they shut him in, by means of some Rails made on purpose, which they raise, to hinder him from getting out; he having the Female in the mean time on his back, with whom he Copulates in that manner, contrary to the custom of all other Beasts. When he hath done, he attempts to be gone, but as he comes, and goes to find a passage out, the Huntsmen, who are either upon a Wall, or in some other high place, throw a great many small and great Ropes, with some Chains, by means whereof, they so pester and entangle his Trunck, and the rest of his Body, that afterwards they draw near him without danger; and so having taken some necessary cautions, they lead him to the company of two other tame Elephants, whom they have purposely brought with them, to shew him an example, or to threaten him if he be unruly.

There are other Snares besides for catching of Elephants and every Country hath its way. The Females go a Year with their young, and commonly they live about a hundred Years. Though these Beasts be of so great bulk and weight, yet they swim perfectly well, and delight to be in the Water: So that they commonly force them into it by Fire-works, when they are in rage, or when they would take them off from Fighting, wherein they have been engaged. This course is taken with the Elephants of the *Great Mogul*, who loves to see those vast moving bulks rush upon one another, with their Trunck, Head, and Teeth. All over the *Indies*, they who have the management of Elephants, never fail to lead them in the Morning to the River, or some other Water. The Beasts go in as deep as they can, and then stoop till the Water be over their Backs, that so their guides may wash them, and make them clean all over, whilst by little and little they raise their bodies up again.

[115] 'A loss of temper'; from *Storia do Mogor* by Niccalao Manucci.

On reaching Dihlī, I heard that only a short time before the king [*Aurungzeb*] had withdrawn the tobacco tax, owing to a horrible event that happened. All the world knows that the tax-contractors who engage for the taxes and duties are most shameless and mannerless. They spare no respectable persons, except those of the highest position and that chiefly when Mahomedans, such persons being, as they know, very easily roused. It happened that a soldier of strict habits wanted to enter the city, having with him his wife in a covered vehicle, as usual among Mahomedans. A tax-gatherer ordered him to halt, and asked if he had any tobacco. The Mahomedans consume a great deal of this article in smoking. This is why the chief tax-farmer paid five thousand rupees a day at this city (Dihlī) only. From this the reader can understand what would be the revenue from tobacco paid to the King of Hindūstān throughout such a great empire.

The soldier replied that he, being a man of serious habits, did not smoke tobacco, neither he nor his wife, who was in the vehicle, and he might trust his word. The tax-collector would not believe him, and wanted to search the cart. To this the soldier would not consent, not wishing his wife to be seen in public, and remonstrated, saying if such an affront were done him, he would repent of it later on. But the tax-collector would not listen to a word, and uncovered the vehicle to make his search. The soldier laid hand on his sword and cut off the man's head, also wounded several attendants. Not content with this even, he killed his wife too, and a daughter she had with her. He was seized and carried off to prison, and complaint was laid before the king. Upon hearing the soldier's defence, the king abolished the tax and released the soldier, having compassion on him for his loss of temper. Among the Mahomedans it is a great dishonour for a family when a wife is compelled to uncover herself. By this event tobacco was no longer so dear, and numerous merchants lost much from this circumstance, whereby the king conferred a benefit on the poor.

[116] The benefits of British rule, 1803; from the *Majma' u-l Akhbar* of Harsukh Rai in *The History of India as told by its own Historians* edited by Sir H.M. Elliot and J. Dowson.

General Lake, according to the orders of the Government, purchased peace from Jaswant Ráo Holkar, at the expense of some treasure and the restoration of the conquered territory to him, which belonged to the Rájpútána states; after this, the General returned from the territory of the Punjáb to Dehlí.

In these days, the end of the year 1220 AH, and the close of the forty-eighth year of Sháh 'Álam Bádsháh's reign (may his dominion and sovereignty be prolonged to eternity!) Maháraja Holkar came from the Panjáb to Rájpútána, and there having raised the standard of triumph and success, established his rule, and is now engaged in exacting contributions from the Rájas and Ráís of that territory. The English retained the districts of Dehlí and Ágra in their own possession. General Lake triumphantly proceeded from the capital to the eastern part of the country, and Mr. Barlow having been appointed to officiate in place of the Governor-General, took the management of the Government affairs into his hands.

In short, all the chiefs and proud rulers of Hindústán, whose

The British Resident riding in a procession of Akbar II,
Delhi, c. 1815 (detail)

heads touched the heavens, and who from their dignity and
pomp claimed equality with Saturn, now having considered
their safety to lie in repentance and obedience, could not raise
their heads from their knees out of respect to this powerful
people, and all the rebellious and turbulent characters who
always scratched the head of pride and vanity with the nails of
tumult and quarrel, put the cap of their obstinacy upon the
ground of submission, and did not place their foot beyond the
bounds of respect to this body of wise men, who, from their great

humanity and liberality, have subdued every one of their enemies. Whoever sought their protection was much honoured, respected, and treated with great kindness, and they fixed an allowance for his maintenance. Notwithstanding that the English are few in number, yet, by their prudent measures and superior wisdom and understanding, they have introduced such management into the countries conquered by them as never was known in the days of any ancient rulers, although they possessed much greater power and more numerous armies.

For the comfort of their subjects and tranquillity of all the people they have established courts in all their cities and towns, so that, in fact, in apprehension of their equity and justice, the wolf and the lion live in the same den with the goat and the deer; and the wagtail and sparrow sit in the same nest with the falcon and hawk. The powerful fly before the weak, and robbers and highwaymen show the way to benighted travellers. All enjoy rest under their protection, and all are comforted by their justice. If a brief account of the rules and regulations which are made by these great people for the administration of justice were given, it would much lengthen this work. The judges, at the time of hearing complaints, look on all, poor and rich, respectable and mean, with an impartial eye, and punish them according to the law, in proportion to the atrocity of their deeds, so that others may take warning from them, and avoid to commit crime. May Almighty God preserve the shadow of their favour and kindness over the heads of all people, as long as the world exists!

[117] Bishop Heber on the Emperor Akbar II in the 1820s; from *Narrative of a Journey through the Upper Provinces of India* . . . by Bishop Reginald Heber.

Acbar Shah has the appearance of a man of seventy-four or seventy-five; he is, however, not much turned of sixty-three, but, in this country, that is a great age. He is said to be a very good-tempered, mild, old man, of moderate talents, but polished and pleasing manners. His favourite wife, the Begum, is a low-born, low-bred, and violent woman, who rules him completely, lays hold on all his money, and has often influenced him to very unwise conduct towards his children, and the British Government. She hates her eldest son, who is, however, a respectable man, of more talents than native princes usually shew, and, happily for himself, has a predilection for those literary pursuits which are almost the only laudable or innocent objects of ambition in his power. He is fond of poetry, and is himself a very tolerable Persian poet. He has taken some pains in the education of his children, and, what in this country is very unusual, even of his daughters. He too, however, though not more than thirty-five, is prematurely old, arising partly from the early excesses into which the wretched follies of an Eastern court usually plunge persons in his situation, – and partly from his own subsequent indulgence in strong liquors. His face is bloated and pimpled, his eyes weak, and his hand tremulous. Yet, for an Eastern prince as I have already observed, his character is good, and his abilities considered as above the common run.

[118] 'O, thou pearly person!'; from *Narrative of a Journey through the Upper Provinces of India* . . . by Bishop Reginald Heber.

At Mr. Elliott's we found his son, and the two Mr. Fishers, come to pass another Sunday with me. I also found two presents awaiting my acceptance; the one from the old Begum consisted of a garland of withered jonquils, intermixed with tinsel, which was, I believe, supposed to pass for pearls; for after putting the said wreath round my neck, the chobdars who brought it hailed me with an acclamation of 'Ue Motee-wala!' 'O, thou pearly person!' I however had, of course, to receive the gift with many thanks, as a favour from the hand of a princess. The other present, from the King, was more useful to a traveller, consisting of a buck, with his best wishes for my journey. The common deer of this neighbourhood are, indeed, by no means good, and may be had for a rupee apiece; but this had had some little feeding bestowed on it, and we found it by no means bad eating in our march.

[119] A Frenchman gets on well with *les Anglais*; from *Letters from India 1829–32* by Victor Jacquemont.

(Victor Jacquemont, distinguished traveller and scientist, visited Delhi and Agra in 1830. He explored the Himalayas and became a friend of Runjit Singh of the Punjab. Two species of plants, Indian and American, were named after him – *Jacquemontia*.)

I am in M. Fraser's enormous house, a sort of Gothic fort which he has built at great expense on the very spot where Timur once pitched his tent at the siege of Delhi. My host is in the Governor-General's camp, for he is accompanying him to the limits of his jurisdiction. I work alone all day, with no noise going on round me except what is made by the workmen packing my collections, with nothing to disturb me, and no tiresome social engagements. In the evening I get on my horse when it is fine, or take a palanquin when it rains, and go down to the city, where I dine like a regular member of the household with the resident, a man with a subtle and well-stocked mind and retiring habits, who talks better than most Englishmen. M. Maddock has been staying with him, and to complete our party of four there is a budding young diplomatist, sparkling with wit, who never misses his chief's dinners, which means that I spend my evenings pleasantly.

The resident at Delhi receives five thousand rupees, or thirty thousand francs a month, as an entertainment allowance. And since he usually has no more than five or six people at his table, and scrupulously insists upon consuming the thirty thousand francs, you can judge whether the dinners I have here are like those I eat on the road. However, I edify this small company by my stoic sobriety. At ten o'clock we say good-night to M. Martin (the resident), and, with Maddock and Bell (the gay and witty assistant I mentioned), retire to the latter's apartments, where, sitting close together round a good fire, we talk till midnight. There is no inducement to go to bed, for the three of us are well able to pass the time pleasantly together. Besides, they do not willingly let me go. When the last words have been said I light an excellent Havana cigar, wrap myself in my Kashmir dressing-gown, mount my horse and, preceded by two runners with torches in their hands, gallop back to Fraser's fortress. My heart was full as I returned to my quarters to-night, for before getting on my horse I had shaken hands with M. Maddock for the last time. He started this morning for his new kingdom of Katmandu, and before leaving Delhi he wrote me a farewell letter which touches me deeply. If instead of going to Bombay and the Ghats I stubbornly pushed on to Nepal, at the other end of the

Himalayas, what support I should find at Katmandu!

In one of your letters you say that, if the English are so nice to me, they must be very different in India from what they are at home. As a matter of fact there is something in that, especially in the case of those living in the northern provinces to the north of Benares. I think and feel in my own fashion, and express this quite simply and spontaneously in language which, I am told, is always correct, sometimes unusual, strange and often pictur-esque. By acting in this way I at once force the English stiffness to relax. I turn all the English with whom I remain for twenty-four hours into good-natured people (*bons gens*) – into French people.

Delhi shall ever be one of my dearest recollections of the East.

[120] Mild Hindoos, swaggering Moslems in the 1830s; from *Excursions in India* by Captain Thomas Skinner.

The Mahometans of the neighbourhood of Delhi are, I think, a fine-looking race of men; but have something so debauched in their appearance and reckless in their manner, that a stranger is not likely to be favourably impressed by them. The contrast between a Mussulman and Hindoo village, which, in travelling, frequently present themselves alternately, is very striking. The mildness of the one party, with the impudent swagger of the other, show that they never can, as indeed they never do, assimilate. Where the same village is inhabited by people of both religions, they occupy opposite portions of it: and the circum-stances may always be known by there being a well at each end of it; for the Hindoos would not draw water from the same fountain as the Mahometans, for all the wealth of this world.

[121] Nauch boys of degraded character in the mid-nineteenth century; from *From New York to Delhi* by Robert B. Minturn.

That evening I dined at Mr. Skinner's, or, as he is called by the natives, Sēkundur Sahib – Sēkundur, being the Hindoostanee pronunciation of Alexander, which is his first name. The party was very large, as nearly all the officers in the garrison were invited. I suppose fifty sat down to table. All the guests sent their own servants, plates, and silver – which is always customary in India where many are invited. As I was not aware of this habit, I was rather at a loss, having come without servant or plates; but my friend, Captain Russell, was kind enough to provide me with all that was necessary, and lent me one of his two Rhitmutgrás.

Mr. Skinner, is a half-caste, almost black in complexion. His father, the celebrated Colonel Skinner, left his property to each of his sons in succession, on the condition that a certain large portion of it should be spent yearly in entertainments. Accordingly, the hospitality of the Skinners became famous in India, and the races, hunts, coursing-matches, dinners, and nach parties, which they gave, were considered one of the chief attractions of Delhi as a Station.

The house where this dinner was given was situated on the square near the Cashmeeree Gate, and opposite the church of St. James. It was built by Colonel Skinner, and was a spacious one-storied mansion, in a compound filled with shrubbery.

Mr. Skinner having a great deal more black blood than white in his veins, conformed in many respects to native usages, and kept a zēnana, where he had several wives and concubines. One of the latter was said to be a sister of his eldest wife. These little peculiarities cut him off from the society of the ladies of the station, but he always found guests enough among the officers to enable him to comply with the hospitable provisions of his father's will.

The dinner was of the best that could be had, and on the most liberal scale, and the usual amount of 'beershurab' and 'simpkin,' as the natives call ale and champagne, were consumed in honouring the old customs of drinking healths and toasting, which still reign in India.

After dinner we retired into a large drawing-room, where the remainder of the evening was spent in witnessing the performances of some nach girls.

The entertainments at Colonel Skinner's were varied by the introduction of some nach boys. They were about seven years old, and although they did not possess the same undulating grace as the girls, their voices were sweeter, and they sang with more spirit, so that they were quite as interesting. They were dressed in clothes similar to those worn by the nach girls, and they danced in the same way. The characters of these boys were, if possible, more degraded than those of the women.

Nautch girls and hookah-smoking – Sir David Ochterlony in
Indian dress; by a Delhi artist c. 1820

During the evening three Moosulmans of high rank, joined the party. The eldest of the three was a thick-set man, of about forty, with a dark skin, and bushy black beard. He wore a very rich dress of blue cloth, embroidered with gold, and a large red turban, worked with gold thread. The other two were younger, and had much lighter complexions, and no beards. They were dressed in white, but wore kummurbunds and turbans of fine Cashmeer shawls. None of the three was armed, and they all took off their shoes before entering the room. Their manners had a high-bred polish, which would have done honour to a nobleman of the court of Versailles, and which is often found in natives of rank. I was particularly interested by the youngest two, who had very pleasing countenances, and regretted that I could not converse with them, since they did not speak English. I afterwards learned that they were near relatives of Shumsh-ood-Deen, who was hung at Delhi for the murder of his patron and friend, Mr. Frazer.

These native gentlemen, as well as my host, and a few of the officers, smoked their hookahs the whole evening. This is undoubtedly the most luxurious form of smoking. The hookah is similar in principle to a Turkish narghilé, but is much larger, and many persons keep servants whose only business is to attend to their hookahs. The smoke of these pipes has a very pleasant smell, the tobacco being perfumed, and the smoke being conducted through rose-water. They were formerly much used, and have this advantage, that it is allowable to smoke them at table in the presence of ladies, or in a drawing-room. Of late years, however, many new English ideas have been introduced, among which is the smoking of cigars.

[122] 'Young bachelor officers'; from the *Journal* of Lady (Emily) Bayley in *The Golden Calm* edited by M.M. Kaye.

Sometimes I had to receive the young bachelor officers who called, and who had very few topics of conversation beyond those of local interest. Some of them called so often that I got to know the sound of the paces of their horses, and my Father and Aunt Mary used to be much amused to find that I always recognized the trot of the horse of a certain Captain Mainwaring, who had a very smart buggy and fancied himself very much. I have often wondered what became of that man. He belonged to the same regiment as Mr Lees. Other frequent callers were James Prinsep, a very pretty young man whose son married Evie Campbell, and a Mr Barford who wore rings outside his kid gloves. These were both assistants under my Father.

Another assistant who came to Delhi in the course of that year was Gore Ouseley, such a jolly, happy-tempered boy, very clever, but he had never learnt to ride, and had therefore to begin this exercise at Delhi. He amused my Father and me by describing his progress in the art of riding by saying that he and his horse took simultaneous movements in contrary directions!

But in general they were very dull, and sometimes embarrassed me by making proposals of marriage, of which of course I informed my Father on his return from office. On one occasion a particularly ugly and impecunious youth had asked the all-important question, and when I told my Father, a quizzical look came upon his face, and fun to his eye, as he said: 'And I suppose you have accepted him?' . . .

In those days there was no English chemist's shop at Delhi, and all the medicines were provided *gratis* by Government for the use of officers and civilians. There were none of the refined little arrangements in which we are accustomed to see medicines administered in England, and I was amazed and disgusted by getting a dose of senna sent me in a black beer bottle, and huge pills sent in a rough wooden box.

[123] 'Family Dinners for a Month' in 1864; from *The Englishwoman in India . . . by a Lady Resident.*

—— 1st——	—— 2nd ——
Clear Soup.	Mulligatawny.
Roast Leg Mutton.	Beefsteak Pie.
Harico.	Cutlets à la Soubise.
Chicken Curry.	Kabob Curry.
Bread and Butter	Pancakes.
Pudding.	

—— 3rd ——

Vegetable Soup.
Boiled Fowls and
Tongue.
Mutton and Cucumber
Stew.
Dry Curry.
Custard Pudding.

—— 4th ——

Pea Soup.
A-la-mode Beef.
Roast Teal.
Prawn Curry.
Sweet Omelette.

—— 5th ——

Oxtail Soup.
Boiled Mutton and
Onion Sauce.
Chicken Cutlets.
Vegetable Curry.
Plum Pudding.

—— 6th ——

White Soup.
Roast Ducks.
Beefsteak.
Ball Curry.
Sago Pudding.

—— 7th ——

Hare Soup.
Roast Kid and Mint
Sauce.
Mutton Pudding.
Sardine Curry.
Mango Fool.

—— 8th ——

Turnip Soup.
Roast Fowls.
Irish Stew.
Toast Curry.
Arrowroot Jelly.

—— 9th ——

Rice Soup.
Game Pie.
Mutton Cutlets.
Salt Fish and Egg
Curry.
Plantain Fritters.

—— 10th ——

Carrot Soup.
Roast Beef.
Minced Mutton.
Cutlet Curry.
Jam Roll Pudding.

—— 11th ——

Mock Turtle Soup.
Mutton rolled and
spiced.
Boiled Chickens.
Mutton Curry.
Blancmange.

—— 12th ——

Gravy Soup.
Boiled Salt Beef.
Stewed Quails.
Fish Curry.
Batter Pudding.

—— 13th ——

Mutton Broth.
Roast Venison.
Maintenon Cutlets.
Sheep's Head Curry.
Cheese Cakes.

———————————————

—— 14th ——

Tomato Soup.
Jugged Hare.
Débris Pudding.
Curry Puffs.
Rice Flummery.

———————————————

—— 15th ——

Giblet Soup.
Roast Goose.
Boiled Mutton Chops.
Brain Curry.
Potato Pudding.

———————————————

—— 16th ——

Palestine Soup.
Breast of Veal and Peas.
Wild Ducks.
Malay Curry.
Thorpe Pudding.

———————————————

—— 17th ——

Jullienne Soup.
Roast Pork.
Chicken Salad.
Egg Curry.
Arrowroot Pudding.

———————————————

—— 18th ——

Oyster Soup.
Braised Leg Mutton.
Pigeons and Peas.
Gravy Curry.
Fair Rosamond
Pudding.

———————————————

—— 19th ——

Partridge Soup.
Spiced Beef.
Fricasseed Fowl.
Vegetable Curry.
George Pudding.

———————————————

—— 20th ——

Potato Soup.
Stewed Ducks and
Turnips.
Beef Persillade.
Kabob Curry.
Rice Pudding.

———————————————

—— 21st ——

Green Pea Soup.
Stewed Shoulder Veal.
Sheep's Tongues.
Dry Curry.
Imitation Apple and
Rice Edge.

———————————————

—— 22nd ——

Cucumber Soup.
Chicken Pie.
Sheep's Head
Chartreuse.
Mutton Curry.
Tipsy Cake.

———————————————

—— 23rd ——

Pot-au-Feu.
Rock Pigeons.
Prawn Curry.
Snowden Pudding.

—— 24th ——

Gravy Soup.
Roast Fore-quarter
Mutton.
Sweetbreads.
Chicken Curry.
Sago Jelly.

—— 25th ——

Mulligatawny.
Fowls à la Carlsfors.
China Chilo.
Crab Curry.
Lemon Suet Pudding.

—— 26th ——

Mock Turtle Soup.
Roast Mutton.
Fowl and Pillau.
Castle Pudding.

—— 27th ——

White Soup.
Roast Fillet of Veal.
Boiled Mutton Chops.
Chicken Curry.
Chocolate Pudding.

—— 28th ——

Clear Soup.
Boiled Ducks.
Rissoles.
Sheep's Head Curry.
Cocoa-nut Pudding.

[124] On being nice to the natives; from *The Diary of a Civilian's Wife in India, 1877–82* by Mrs Robert Moss King.

It is said that a good deal of mischief is being done by the fashionable visitors who now flock to India in the cold season, are delighted and flattered by all the novelty of native hospitality, courtesy, and often servility, and to whom the English officials are of course in no way either novel or interesting, and who then return home and spread the idea that the English in India require snubbing and the trusty natives exalting. It may be so, but these passing visitors are not in a position to be good judges. A visitor can only see things very superficially, he is wholly irresponsible, and he finds it pleasant to pose as a kind of champion, and be lavishly gracious to the natives and studiously cold to his fellow-countrymen. If his life were cast, as theirs is, among these same natives, he would find this enthusiasm and novelty wear off. He would find that a gulf was fixed between him and men who, however long their acquaintance, would never admit him into their home life, would consider their wives and daughters insulted if he so much as alluded to them, would sooner die than eat at his table, and who in their inmost heart would not sorrow if every Christian were driven into the sea.

[125] Blunt being anti-British; from *India under Ripon, a secret diary* by Wilfred Scawen Blunt.

Ikhram Ullah brought us four Mohammedan gentlemen, with whom we conversed about the political position to be taken up by Mohammedans in India, and their opinion seemed to be that there should be more common action with the Hindus. But one of them was of opinion that the Hindus were impracticable, because they would not permit the killing of cows. He and Kadi Huseyn, a Shiah, talked English, but the Sunnis talked none.

Later we went with Robinson, our black host, to see the fort and the great mosque, among the few wonders of the world. The mosque is far and away the finest mosque, the palace far and away the finest palace; and, except Madura, they stand together first in the universe. The palace is full of intense interest, for it was here that the great events of the last three hundred years happened, and in modern times that the last Emperor of Delhi, after the retaking of the city by the English, was tried ignominiously for murder. A dentist whom we met today tells us he happened to go into the hall of audience during the trial, and saw this last of the Mogul kings crouched before the Military Commission, dressed in a piece of sacking and a coarse turban 'like a coolie'. Here, too, the English soldiers slew and destroyed some thousands of innocent men in revenge for the death of about one hundred. The old Loharo chief assures us 26,000 persons were killed by the soldiers or hanged or shot or 'blown up' during the eight months following the capture of the city. The city was deserted, and whole quarters and suburbs razed to the ground. Such are the resources of civilization. The dentist says he saw nineteen men hanging together in one spot, and put the number executed at several thousands. I suppose no Englishman will ever dare write the real history of that year.

We dined with the Nawab, his son, Prince Suliman Jah, and Ikhram Ullah, and had some instructive conversation. The son, Emir-ed-din Feruk Mirza, who is now reigning chief of Loharo, gave me an amusing account of how young princes were brought up by the British Government when it happened to become their guardian. They are taught to ride and play lawn tennis, and the Resident writes that they are enlightened and loyal princes. Then they are placed on the throne, but find it dull, and go to Calcutta where they spend their money. Then they come back and grind their subjects with taxation, and the Resident writes that they are barbarous and unfit to govern. Lastly, the Government intervenes and administers the country for them. He is a very intelligent young man himself, and his father complains of him because he is too old-fashioned. But I expect he knows better than the old man the ins and outs of our modern diplomacy. The old man is a curious type. During the Mutiny, he tells me, he remained in the city because he could not leave it. But he kept up communication with the English, and for this reason he was not hanged, as most people were, or his property entirely confiscated. It is quite evident to me, however, that, while expressing loudly his loyalty, all his sympathies are with the old *régime*. What he did not like about the mutineers was that most of them were Hindus. But Heaven forgive me if he loves the English. Things, too, have changed mostly since then, and it is my firm conviction that in the case of a new mutiny every man, woman, and child, Mohammedan and Hindu, will join it. The Nawab is a bit of a humbug, but I like him all the same. He belongs to a school which is rapidly passing away, the school which allied itself with the English Government from motives of interest, or sometimes out of a sincere admiration for some individual Englishman. All this is gone. The old men's loyalty has become lip service, and the young men hardly conceal their thoughts. Nothing is more striking in India than the absolute want, at the present day, of native enthusiasm for any particular man. Lord Ripon had this till lately, but he is the last who will have had it.

[126] E.M. Forster and his 'sweet Rajah' in 1921; from *The Hill of Devi* by E.M. Forster.

I must relate exciting developments. I am stopping here with the beloved Rajah of Dewas. He, the Rani, his brother, the Dewan, and 65 attendants have come to attend a Chiefs' Conference, and my day in Delhi, which I have now made two, catches them. I heard through the Darlings of his whereabouts, and wired; he replied that I should be met at the station. This however did not happen, but Rashid, with whom I had also been in touch, was there, and after breakfast we hunted the court out in a tonga: two trains arrived the same time and they had met the wrong one. The Rajah had taken a room for me at a Hotel, but on seeing me exclaimed I must be nearer, and here I am in a delightful upper room, while the courtiers seethe below and the Rajah and his brother are having a bath in the verandah. Some time we are to have a meal, but when or of what is uncertain, nor is it certain when the Rajah will leave Delhi, nor whether for Lahore to stop with the Darlings or for Hardwar to bathe in the sacred river there. He was so sweet when I arrived – darted up from behind and put his hands over my eyes. Dewan Sahib was also pleasant, and they have taught the son and heir to scream less at Europeans, and, with an agonised expression, to shake hands. He is such a beautiful child. The Rani, and many handmaidens, sit crouched in a dense mass behind a screen all the time.

I think I must go now. I hope to add more before evening. . . .

No, I needn't go. The Rajah is doing Pujah after his bath, streams of water from which are flowing over the garden. My meal is coming from the Hotel as it is a fast day in honour of Shiva, and the Court are on a diet of potatoes and sweets. I really don't know what happens next – one so seldom does.

It is now an hour since the embassy started to bring food from the Hotel. Dewan Sahib suggests biscuits and sweets to go on with, but these too have foundered. My room has pictures of Krishna on the walls, interspersed with the Archbishop of Canterbury crowning the King and Queen in Westminster Abbey. And now the light refreshments come – saucers of sultanas and monkey nuts, pastry knobs, cardomum, sweets, cold potatoes and Marie biscuits, grouped round a cup of hot spiced milk.

[127] A Proustian in Delhi; from *Jesting Pilate* by Aldous Huxley.

(Aldous Huxley (1894–1968) visited India in 1930.)

How often, while at Delhi, I thought of Proust and wished that he might have known the place and its inhabitants. For the imperial city is no less rich in social comedy than Paris; its soul is as fertile in snobberies, dissimulations, prejudices, hatreds, envies. Indeed, I should say that in certain respects the comedy of Delhi is intrinsically superior to that which Proust found in the Faubourg Saint-Germain and so minutely analysed. The finest comedy (I speak for the moment exclusively as the literary man) is the most serious, the most nearly related to tragedy. The comedy of Delhi and the new India, however exquisitely diverting, is full of tragic implications. The dispute of races, the reciprocal hatred of colours, the subjection of one people to another – these things lie behind its snobberies, conventions, and deceits, are implicit in every ludicrous antic of the comedians. Sometimes, when a thunderstorm is approaching, we may see a house, a green tree, a group of people illuminated by a beam of the doomed sun, and standing out with a kind of unearthly brightness against the black and indigo of the clouds. The decaying relics of feudalism, the Dreyfus case, the tragedies of excessive leisure – these form the stormy background to the Proustian comedy. The clouds against which imperial Delhi appears so brilliantly comical, are far more black, far more huge and menacing.

In India I was the spectator of many incidents that might have come straight out of '*A la Recherche du Temps Perdu*'; trivial incidents, but pregnant with the secret passions and emotions which Proust could always find, when they were there, beneath the most ordinary gestures, the most commonplace and innocuous words. I remember, for example, the behaviour of an Indian guest at a certain hotel, where the European manager made a habit of strolling about the dining-room during meals, superintending the service, chatting with the diners and, when they rose to leave, opening the door to let them out. The Indian, I noticed, never gave the manager a chance of opening the door for him. When he wanted to leave the dining-room, he would wait till the manager's back was turned and then fairly run to the door, turn the handle and slip through, as though the devil were after him. And indeed the devil *was* after him – the devil in the form of a painful suspicion that, if he gave the manager an opportunity of opening the door for him, the fellow might make a humiliating exception to his rule of courtesy and leave it conspicuously shut.

And then there were the Maharajas. The Chamber of Princes – that remarkable assembly, attended every year by a steadily diminishing number of Indian rulers – was holding its sittings while we were at Delhi. For a week Rolls Royces were far more plentiful in the streets than Fords. The hotels pullulated with despots and their viziers. At the Viceroy's evening parties the diamonds were so large that they looked like stage gems; it was impossible to believe that the pearls in the million-pound necklaces were the genuine excrement of oysters. How hugely Proust would have enjoyed the Maharajas! Men with a pride of birth more insensate than that of Charlus; fabulously rich and possessing in actual fact all the despotic power of which the name of Guermantes is only the faint hereditary symbol; having all the idiosyncrasies and eccentricities of Proust's heroes and none of their fear of public opinion; excessive and inordinate as no aristocrat in the modern West could hope to be; carrying into Napoleonic or Neronian actuality the poor potential velleities towards active greatness or vice that are only latent in men who live in and not above society. He would have studied them with a passionate interest, and more especially in their relations – their humiliating and gravely ludicrous relations – with the English. It would have charmed him to watch some Rajput descendant of the Sun going out of his way to be agreeable to the official who, though poor, insignificant, of no breeding, is in reality his master; and the spectacle of a virtuous English matron, doing her duty by making polite conversation to some dark and jewelled Heliogabalus, notorious for the number of his concubines and catamites, would have delighted him no less. How faithfully he would have recorded their words, how completely and with what marvellous intuition he would have divined the secret counterpoint of their thoughts! He would have been deeply interested, too, in that curious unwritten law which decrees that European women shall dance in public with no Indian below the rank of Raja. And it would, I am sure, have amused him to observe the extraordinarily emollient effects upon even the hardest anti-Asiatic sentiments of the possession of wealth and a royal title. The cordiality with which people talk to the dear Maharaja Sahib – and even, occasionally, about him – is delightful. My own too distant and hurried glimpses of the regal comedies of India made me desire to look more lingeringly, more closely, and with a psychological eye acuter than that with which nature has grudgingly endowed me.

I remember so many other pregnant trifles – The pathetic gratitude of a young man in an out-of-the-way place, to whom we had been ordinarily civil, and his reluctance to eat a meal with us, for fear that he should eat it in an un-European fashion and so eternally disgrace himself in our eyes. The extraordinarily hearty, back-slapping manner of certain educated Indians who have not yet learned to take for granted their equality with the ruling Europeans and are for ever anxious loudly to assert it. The dreadfully embarrassing cringing of others. The scathing ferocity of the comments which we overheard, in the gallery of the Legislative Assembly, being made on the Indian speakers by the women-folk of certain Government members. Listening, I was reminded of the sort of things that were said by middle-class people in England about the workmen at the time of the coal strike. People whose superiority is precarious detest with passion all those who threaten it from below.

Nor must I forget – for Proust would have devoted a score of pages to it – the noble Anglo-Indian convention of dressing for dinner. From the Viceroy to the young clerk who, at home, consumes high tea at sunset, every Englishman in India solemnly 'dresses.' It is as though the integrity of the British Empire depended in some directly magical way upon the donning of black jackets and hard-boiled shirts. Solitary men in dak bungalows, on coasting steamers, in little shanties among the tiger-infested woods, obey the mystical imperative and every evening put on the funereal uniform of English prestige. Women robed in the latest French creations from Stratford-atte-Bowe, toy with the tinned fish, while the mosquitoes dine off their bare arms and necks. It is magnificent.

Almost more amazing is that other great convention for the keeping up of European prestige – the convention of eating too much. Five meals a day – two breakfasts, luncheon, afternoon tea and dinner – are standard throughout India. A sixth is often added in the big towns where there are theatres and dances to justify late supper. The Indian who eats at the most two meals a day, sometimes only one – too often none – is compelled to acknowledge his inferiority.

[128] Red lights in the 1950s; from *Delhi: a study in urban sociology* by A. Bopegamage.

A trip by any person to Garsten Bastion Road or popularly known as G.B. Road or Kutab road at night creates suspicion in the minds of Delhi people about him. For they are the asylums where every type of vice has taken refuge. They are the places where culprits, hobos, criminals, prostitutes and all other restless and unsettled individuals live. These are such notorious spots in Delhi that a city daily very rarely brings out an issue without a report pertaining to them.

We do not know how many brothel houses and prostitutes are found in the City of Delhi today. But they are extant. That such a trade thrives is an open secret which every adult man and woman knows about. Not even the police know the total figures. Censuses of different decennial periods give different figures; but we do not know how far they are true. The 1931 Census speaks of 325 persons as 'procurors and prostitutes.' This number must have risen by about four times since then as many a woman, ousted from her legitimate hearth and home, had drifted in the city in search of food and shelter. From a social welfare worker we gathered that there are about 700 prostitutes in the city. Taking into account all the available information and piecing it together we can safely place the total above 1,200.

No visitor to these areas during day-time will know where they live because sunlight drives them to the backyards and backlanes. But occasionally, you may see a 'painted woman' peeping through a window or standing on a balcony or wheezing by in a cycle rickshaw covering her head for they are much more particular about observing purdah in day-time than an ordinary woman.

Enter these areas after seven, you will only see a market place of purchase and sale of human beings. You will see the strange spectacle of people enjoying their leisure, though degrading their own fellow beings in the process.

You need not go in search of them. The Delhi *tongawalla* will take you. He is ready at dusk for that job because he knows that there are many customers going that way. Stand at dusk at the entrance of Chelmsford Avenue in Connaught Place or at the Clock Tower in Subzimandi. The *tongawalla* will come to you and will call you. Get into a *tonga*, wink at him and say 'go'. He will take you to the right place and ask you to alight. As soon as you get down the pimps will fall on you. He will tell you where they are. He will tell the price in a sign language. He will ask you what your desire is; whether you wish to have a woman of a particular community. He will ask you whether you want 'new' because he has it ready to cater to the needs of everyone's taste. He will quote the price. If you agree, the whole business is over in a moment.

But the regular customer who knows the trick of the trade bargains well. When rupees five is quoted as the price he will offer two and after long higgling and haggling the price does drop down to that amount. Prices always vary. The price varies from one street to another. Charges may be less on Kutab Road because the poorer amongst these fallen creatures live there.

We cannot deny that there is clandestine prostitution in Delhi. There are persons who want to do things under cover, who want to lead that kind of life while attempting to escape the stigma associated with it. Clandestine prostitution is mostly confined to the New City. It has no exact location. The places of its practice change. You may meet a clandestine prostitute at the club, at the dine and dance hotel; you may meet her in a taxi and sometimes even on the streets. Or just speak to some taxi-walla he will arrange that one to meet you. You may be able to get her even on the phone. But clandestine prostitution is a costly business in Delhi.

It is said that about hundred years ago, prostitution in Delhi was regarded as a decent profession, for many of the prostitutes catered to the needs of the noblemen. Their sons were sent to them to learn the art of making friends with strangers and also to study the know-how of social life. But today it has turned to be the most degrading profession that a woman in Delhi could follow.

We found from enquiries that there are two kinds of prostitutes in Delhi. There are those who have entered the group of their own free will and those who are forced to follow it, the so-called 'white-slaves' as the term is used in popular discourses. When those who willingly enter the profession fail to meet the demand, 'white-slaves' are brought in. They are brought into these areas on promises of good money, good life. But when they enter the profession, we were told, the life of the 'white-slaves' becomes that of chattels. They are forced to do what their masters or mistresses ask them to. They are scolded, they are beaten and they have to see that enough income is earned for their pimps in order to secure their daily bread.

Prostitution is openly tolerated in Delhi, the Government knows that it exists and so does every adult. There are even laws concerning brothel houses and other connected activities and sometimes we read reports of cases where they are applied. Perhaps it is tolerated in order to provide an outlet for the needs of the unmarried middle-aged man or to the visitor in the city for we were informed by the pimps that visitors from outside form a large part of the customers. No other explanation seems to offer the *raison de etre* for this evil to exist. People do not want evil to thrive, for every year, Ravana and also Kumbha-karna, the symbolic effigies of evil are destroyed and set fire to before everyone on the Ram Lila Day.

No one in the city finds it difficult to locate these areas. They are not far away. They are found in the heart of the city. They can be reached in eight to ten minutes ride from the industrial, commercial and the administrative centres. There is that well-known road where engineering and building construction materials are sold during day time. When the business of the day is over and the shops are closed for the night the 'painted women' and pimps take a stand on the pavements and the back lanes and start their business.

[129] A visit to Mr Chaudhuri; from *Gone Away: an Indian journal* by Dom Moraes.

This morning Delhi is swept by the loose, wild rain that always follows days of heat and thunder. Frogs appear in ditches that have been dry for days; the awnings of the hotel bubble and drip; the trees turn green. 'God in his mercy has sent this' – Vincent Sheean, looking mock-solemnly at the sky – 'It will cool Panditji's brow.' The lassitude of the last few days lifts from me. I occupy myself making and shaking Bloody Maries and Old

Fashioneds in thermos-flasks, Marilyn acting as taster, solemnly waggling her eyebrows in approbation. Wet journalists come into my father's room, but the rain seems to have broken a thread in the air. The talk is no longer of Nehru and Krishna Menon but of the weather.

I want to see Nirad Chaudhuri. Chaudhuri has no telephone. So I ring and ask Khushwant for the address. He seems a bit vague; somewhere near the Kashmiri Gate, he says, but if we go there and ask for Nirad Chaudhuri anyone will direct us: he is a known and beloved figure in the vicinity. Ring Ved, who picks me up in a taxi after lunch.

A long drive to the Kashmiri Gate: meanwhile the sun gropes through the clouds and the afternoon fills slowly with heat. When we reach the Kashmiri Gate stop the taxi and ask a passerby where Nirad Chaudhuri lives. He does not know. Conclude that he is not a local inhabitant and push on. An area of exceedingly tortuous streets all mixed up like grandmother's knitting. Heat-haze after the rain, making the road look as if it were covered with oil, and clouds of flies everywhere. Send the taxi-driver to inquire at various shops, but draw a blank. Get out ourselves. Swarms of children immediately surround us. 'King of the world, give me money. My mother is dead, my father is dead.' We hold out some coins, they are snatched from our hands and all the children begin to fight over them, tearing one another with their nails. Their small bodies are like relief-maps, so far do the bones stick out.

Ask a photographer (Sikh) where Nirad Chaudhuri lives. He pushes his turban forward and scratches his head like a Mummerset man. First time I have ever seen a Sikh do this, and I watch in fascination. Finally takes his hand away from his head, fingernails coated in oil and scurf, and says do we mean a tall youth called Chaudhuri who goes to school? No, we say, but perhaps his father. His father, the Sikh says, is a lentil-seller by the Gate. No, we say again. The Sikh goes back to scratching his head. Then he asks is it an old man called Nirala? No, we say, a middle-aged man called Nirad Chaudhuri, a writer. Ved adds that he is a Bengali. The Sikh snaps his fingers triumphantly. 'Oh, that fellow! The Bengali Babu!' He gives us directions. As we drive off he runs after us shouting that if we ever want our photographs taken his is infinitely the best shop in Delhi.

Reach Chaudhuri's house, tall and wooden in a crooked street off the Kashmiri Gate. Climb three flights of groaning stairs. It is

now very hot and my shirt is damp and heavy with sweat. Ved
has a suit on and is worse off, but refuses to remove his jacket
because he is wearing braces. By the time we reach the top floor
we are both in a vile temper. We emerge into a broad veranda
where a naked figure is asleep on a sheet. Ved bends and shakes it
impatiently. '*Hai mai*, brother, get up and call your master.'
Figure springs up, wraps the sheet round itself to form a waist-
cloth, and says with dignity, 'I am Mr. Chaudhuri.'

Ved and I dumbstruck. Chaudhuri, however, seems to take it
all in his stride. 'Mr. Mehta and Mr. Moraes? I have seen your
pictures in the papers. Please come in.' The main room is
spacious but a little bare, the corners filled with heaped up books.
Chaudhuri disappears for a moment, reappearing in a shirt and
trousers. He is a small frail man with a sharp bespectacled face
and a tiny moustache. We ask him about his new book.

'Oh I am *very* pleased about that. *Very* pleased. It has got some
fine reviews in England. The English will understand such a
book, you see. But here it has got bad reviews of course. Here they
do not understand.'

He gestures frequently, bobbing his head as he makes his
points.

'You will not believe it, the Indians do not want to know me.
No! It is the foreign diplomats who are my friends. I have been to
ten parties in the last fortnight – *all* given by foreign diplomats!
Now will you believe that? Is that not extraordinary? I get on
better with foreigners, you see. I understand foreigners. Now one
of my friends is in the French Embassy. His is the last party I have
been to. How tastefully his house is decorated! How gracious is
the way in which he lives! Every man can be judged by his habits
and surroundings at home.'

Ved and I remain silent. Chaudhuri continues: 'I am now
writing a book about India. That also will be appreciated in
England and attacked here. But I feel that if I write three or four
books, perhaps I may achieve some reputation in England. Is
that so? If you write three or four books do you achieve a
reputation in England?'

I say cautiously that it depends on the books. Chaudhuri is
very eager to know more. 'I want to settle in England, you know.
I was only there for five weeks, in 1955, but I felt as if my whole
life had been a preparation for those five weeks, and after that I
feel myself at a loss till I can return.'

He says: 'How beautiful is Hyde Park! And there is so much

tradition there in England! The eating places are like palaces –
Lyons', the A.B.C.'

I feel at a loss for words. It seems to me a totally new view of
London. If we had met in London I would have thought this a
mad kind of poetry; here, with the Kashmiri Bazaar teeming
below, the whole thing seems grotesque. I relapse into silence,
while Chaudhuri talks to Ved about literature. He thinks *A
Passage to India* Forster's worst novel because, he says, it was
improbable: during British days a person like Aziz would never
have been able to ask Miss Quested and Mrs. Moore to tea or to
picnics. He very gleefully adds that he had pointed this out to
Forster. Forster, he says, had taken his point.

When we leave he says earnestly: 'I am glad to have met you,
but take my advice, and return at once to England. If you stay
here you will perish. They will not understand you here.'

[130] Clubs as 'colour-blenders'; from *Where the Lion Trod*
by Gordon Brooke-Shepherd.

Fortunately, the club can act as a colour blender as well as a
colour barrier; and of this happier variety the supreme example
in India is, I suppose, the Gymkhana in New Delhi. This famous
club was mixed before the war and it is now, if anything, even
more mixed. Independence has, however, affected less its
membership than its administration: the close British control of
old has been replaced by an even closer Indian control today.
Again, it is the gilt letter-boards which bear the best silent
witness to the change. The Roll of Presidents displayed in the
hall begins with Sir Harcourt Butler for 1913–15 and works
down an unbroken procession of Englishmen and a fairly
constant parade of knighthoods until the Rt. Hon. Sir Patrick
Spens who, in 1945–47, saw out the British Raj. Then the Indian
dynasty takes over, beginning, as a sort of transitional shock-
absorber, with the resplendent figure of Sir Usha Nath Sen, Kt.,
CBE.

Yet the life of the club itself in no way reflects this climacteric
in gilt. Superficially, at any rate, the Gymkhana has been
preserved intact by its new masters as carefully as any Protected
Monument. The little rubber ball still slaps despairingly round
the Willingdon Squash Courts; twenty or more superb grass

tennis courts are still in play whenever the shade temperature drops below the nineties; and tea is still served on the lawn in that magic half-hour between the last game and the swift, early Indian sunset. The overall impression is of complete social harmony between the 80 per cent Indian members and the remaining 20 per cent which is made up by the different contingents of the foreign colony. The British are still the largest and the most respected of these foreign contingents; but they are no more than that, and make no claim to be.

Nor did the new regime hesitate to lend a personal hand in keeping the old customs alive. Christmas and New Year, I was assured, were celebrated with all the plum-pudding ritual and plum-pudding jollity of the Raj. Hindu, Moslem, Sikh, Parsee and European members alike all chimed in to sing 'Good King Wenceslas' in clubrooms decorated with Christmas trees, tinsel and paper streamers. And on New Year's Eve, this same band of predominantly Asian minstrels join hands to render 'Auld Lang Syne' – a sight I would have gone a long way to see.

They tell me that, for a decade or two after the departure of the last of the Moghuls from Old Delhi, the Friday processions from the Red Fort to the Jama Masjid were still kept up, almost as though the ingrained habit of a conqueror's ceremonial had gone on moving with a residual momentum of its own. Perhaps this annual chorus of 'Auld Lang Syne' in the Gymkhana Club of New Delhi is a similar trick of social ballistics, performed in the temple of another conqueror who passed over the Ganges plain. My own feeling is that Indian tributes like this to the British way of life, whether they survive in themselves for ten years or a hundred, point to something more lasting. There is absorption here as well as imitation.

Indeed, only on one occasion in dozens of visits did I hear anything resembling a sigh of reproach arising from their midst. I was sitting, one hot spring day, next to a senior British member – a survivor from the old Gymkhana Club – on the stone-flagged terrace by the swimming-pool (Willingdon again). He was about to taste his tankard of beer, and had indeed already opened his mouth to clear a path through the froth, when his chair was pushed violently from behind, and the whole contents were spilt on his lap. The culprit was a 12-year-old son of an Indian Army member who was chasing four yelling friends between the tables on their way to the diving-board.

The chatter all round of Hindi and Hindi English made it difficult to catch the apology. At all events, a few seconds later, insult was added to injury when the five rowdy playmates leapt feet first together into the pool, sending up such a splash that more drops appeared beside the beer stain on the senior British member's white trousers. Unhappily, it was already past tea-time and the water, though fresh and clean that morning, already wore a pronounced five o'clock shadow which would surely take some removing.

I had expected the victim to explode, for he was a fiery individual with a shrunken hawk-nosed face, like some head-hunter's trophy of a 'pukka Sahib'. But all he said, as he dabbed away with his handkerchief, was: 'Silly of me to suggest a drink here; but it used to be such a quiet spot in the old days.'

There was wistfulness, but not much else, in his voice. It was as though all the anger had been drained away long ago in that social levelling process which the ravaged trousers symbolized. In any case, such indignation was rarely justified, for, as I have said, both the provocation and the nostalgia of this particular incident were quite exceptional.

It is perhaps more difficult to maintain the old atmosphere indoors than outdoors; but no effort is spared. The bar manages to attract its customers, even on Delhi's twice-weekly 'dry days', when Indian Puisne Judges can be seen standing rounds of fruit juice to Iron Curtain diplomats and American Point Four advisers. The bridge fours continue their 'post-mortems' in the card-rooms and the games of snooker click away on the billiard tables. Even the club notices do their best to keep pace. The old board devoted exclusively to 'Stabling and Kennels' was still up, for example, though the most horsy items it could offer now were 'six lovely baby bunnies for sale' and 'home needed for two house-trained Siamese kittens'.

Select Bibliography

ABU-L FAZL, *The Akbarnama*, transl. by H. Beveridge, Calcutta, 1912.

ARCHER, MAJOR, *Tours in Upper India*, London, 1833.

BABUR, *Memoirs*, ed. by F.G. Talbot, London, 1909.

BARBOSA, DUARTE, *The Book of Duarte Barbosa: an account of the countries bordering on the Indian ocean and their inhabitants*, transl. by M.L. Dames for the Hakluyt Society, London, 1918.

BAYLEY, LADY (EMILY), *Journal* in *The Golden Calm*, ed. by M.M. Kaye, Exeter, 1980.

BENCE-JONES, MARK, *Palaces of the Raj: magnificence and miseries of the Lords Sahib*, London, 1973.

BERNIER, FRANÇOIS, *Travels in the Mogul Empire (1659–67)*, transl. by A. Constable, London, 1891.

BLUNT, WILFRED SCAWEN, *India under Ripon, a secret diary*, London, 1909.

BOPEGAMAGE, A., *Delhi: a study in urban sociology*, Bombay, 1957.

BROOKE-SHEPHERD, GORDON, *Where the Lion Trod*, London, 1960.

BYRON, ROBERT, Article on New Delhi in *Architectural Review*, January 1931.

CAINE, W.S., *Picturesque India*, London, 1890.

CHUNDER, BHOLANAUTH, *The Travels of a Hindoo to Various Parts of Bengal and Upper India*, London, 1869.

COLLINS, LARRY, and LAPIERRE, DOMINIQUE, *Freedom at Midnight*, London, 1975.

CORYAT, THOMAS, *Observations (1616)* in *Early Travels in India*, ed. by William Foster, London, 1921.

CROFT-COOKE, RUPERT, *The Gorgeous East*, London, 1969.

EDEN, THE HON. EMILY, *Up the Country: letters written to her sister from the upper provinces of India*, London, 1866.

EDWARDES, MICHAEL, *Red Year*, London, 1973.

ELLIOTT, SIR H.M., and DOWSON, J. (eds), *The History of India as told by its own Historians*, 8 vols, London, 1877.

The Englishwoman in India: containing information for the use of ladies proceeding to, or residing in, the East Indies, on the subjects of their outfit, furniture, housekeeping, the rearing of children, duties and wages of servants, management of the stables, and arrangements for travelling, to which are added receipts for Indian cookery, by a Lady Resident, London, 1864.

FINCH, WILLIAM, *Journal 1608–11* in *Early Travels in India*, ed. by William Foster, London, 1921.

FITCH, RALPH, *Narrative* in *Early Travels in India*, ed. by William Foster, London, 1921.

FORSTER, E.M., *The Hill of Devi*, London, 1951.

GUL-BADAN BEGUM, *Hamayun-nama*, ed. by A. Beveridge for the Hakluyt Society, London, 1902.

HAWKINS, WILLIAM, *Journal 1608–13* in *Early Travels in India*, ed. by William Foster, London, 1921.

HEBER, BISHOP REGINALD, *Narrative of a Journey through the Upper Provinces of India from Calcutta to Bombay, 1824–5*, London, 1828.

HODGES, WILLIAM, *Select Views in India Drawn on the Spot*, London, 1786.

HUXLEY, ALDOUS, *Jesting Pilate*, London, 1932.

IBN BATUTA, *Selections of the Travels of Ibn Batuta*, transl. and ed. by H.A.R. Gibb, London, 1929.

IRVING, ROBERT GRANT, *Indian Summer*, New York, 1981.

JACQUEMONT, VICTOR, *Letters from India 1829–32*, transl. by C.A. Phillips, London, 1936.

JARRIC, PIERRE DU, SJ, *Akbar and the Jesuits: an account of the Jesuit missions to the court of Akbar*, transl. by C.H. Payne, London, 1926.

JEEWAN LAL, MUNSHI, Narrative from *Two Native Narratives of the Mutiny*, transl. by C.T. Metcalfe, London, 1898.

KEENE, H.G., *The Turks in India*, London, 1879.

KING, MRS ROBERT MOSS, *The Diary of a Civilian's Wife in India 1877–82*, London, 1884.

KÖNIGSMARCK, COUNT HANS VON, *A German Staff Officer in India*, transl. by P.H. Oakley Williams, London, 1910.

LUCAS, E.V., *Roving East and Roving West*, London, 1921.

MANUCCI, NICCALAO, *Storia do Mogor*, transl. by William Irvine, London, 1907.

METCALFE, SIR THOMAS, *Reminiscences of Imperial Delhie* in *The Golden Calm*, ed. by M.M. Kaye, Exeter, 1980.

MINTURN, ROBERT B., *From New York to Delhi*, London, 1858.

MORAES, DOM, *Gone Away: an Indian journal*, London, 1960.

MUNDY, PETER, *Travels in Europe and Asia (1608–67)*, ed. by R.C. Temple for the Hakluyt Society, London, 1919.

PRINSEP, VALENTINE, *Imperial India: an artist's journals*, London, 1879.

ROE, SIR THOMAS, *The Embassy of Sir Thomas Roe to India*, ed. by William Foster for the Hakluyt Society, London, 1899.

RONALDSHAY, THE EARL OF, *The Life of Lord Curzon*, London, 1928.

ROOSEVELT, ELEANOR, *India and the Awakening East*, London, 1954.

RUSHDIE, SALMAN, *Shame*, London, 1985.

RUSSELL, SIR WILLIAM HOWARD, *The Prince of Wales' tour: A diary in India*, London, 1877.

SARKAR, SIR JADUNATH, *Fall of the Mughal Empire*, Calcutta, 1932–50.

SHOEMAKER, MICHAEL MYERS, *Indian Pages and Pictures*, New York, 1912.

SIDI ALI REIS, *The Travels and Adventures of the Turkish Admiral Sidi Ali Reis*, transl. by A. Vambéry, London, 1899.

SKINNER, CAPTAIN THOMAS, *Excursions in India*, London, 1832.

SLEEMAN, MAJOR-GENERAL W.H., *Rambles and Recollections of an Indian Official*, London, 1883.

TAYLOR, BAYARD, *A Visit to India, China and Japan in the year 1853*, New York, 1893.

THÉVENOT, M. DE, and CARERI, J., *Indian Travels of Thévenot and Careri*, ed. by Surendranath Sen, New Delhi, 1948.

TWINING, THOMAS, *Travels in India a Hundred Years Ago*, ed. by William Twining, London, 1893.

WHITE, COLONEL S. DEWÉ, *Indian Reminiscences*, London, 1880.

Recommended further reading

ARCHER, MILDRED, *Early views of India*, London, 1980.

BENCE-JONES, MARK, *The Viceroys of India*, London, 1982.

DODWELL, H.H. (ed.), *The Cambridge Shorter History of India*, Cambridge, 1934.

EDWARDS, MICHAEL, *King of the World*, London, 1970.

FERGUSSON, JAMES, *History of Indian and Eastern Architecture*, London, 1876.

GASCOIGNE, BAMBER, *The Great Moghuls*, London, 1979.

HANSEN, WALDEMAR, *The Peacock Throne*, London, 1973.

HIBBERT, CHRISTOPHER, *The Great Mutiny: India, 1857*, London, 1978.

MACLAGHLAN, SIR EDWARD, *The Jesuits and the Great Mogul*, London, 1932.

MASON, PHILIP, *The Men Who Ruled India*, London, 1985.

RUSHBROOK WILLIAMS, L.F. (ed.), *A Handbook for Travellers in India, Pakistan, Nepal, Bangladesh and Sri Lanka*, (Murray's Guide) 22nd ed., London, 1978.

Index

Numbers in *italics* refer to illustrations

GENERAL INDEX